Webelos
Handbook

BOY SCOUTS OF AMERICA®

33452
ISBN 978-0-8395-3452-5
©2003 Boy Scouts of America
2010 Printing

Contents

Webelos Scout Parent Guide 1

Welcome to Your Webelos Scout Den! 23

Rank Advancement and Special Awards 39

Activity Badges 81

Physical Skills Activity Badge Group

Aquanaut   83

Athlete   123

Fitness   245

Sportsman   455

Mental Skills Activity Badge Group

Artist   101

Scholar   391

Showman   429

Traveler   461

Community Activity Badge Group

Citizen   143

Communicator   165

Family Member   227

Readyman   365

Technology Activity Badge Group

Craftsman   197

Engineer   211

Handyman   299

Scientist   401

Outdoor Activity Badge Group

Forester   259

Geologist   279

Naturalist   317

Outdoorsman   343

Index and Credits 475

Webelos Scout Parent Guide

Parents, Guardians, or Other Adult Family Members:

This is your part of the *Webelos Handbook*. It tells what this part of Cub Scouting for older boys is all about, how it operates, and how you can help your son as he joins the exciting, challenging Webelos Scout den.

Note: In the front of this book there is a tear-out section for you on youth protection. Please do tear it out (that makes the book easier to handle), read it carefully, and keep it at hand for easy reference.

Welcome to the Webelos Den

The Webelos den will open a new world of adventure for your son: a way to learn new skills, to enjoy lots of outdoor activities, and most of all, to have fun.

This guide will give you a head start on understanding how the program works, and you'll find out how you can help your son and his Webelos den.

After you've read this guide, be sure to sign your name beside Webelos badge requirement 1 on page 49 (under "Approved by"). This will help him earn the Webelos badge.

What Is a Webelos Scout?

Your son has joined the part of the Cub Scouting program of the Boy Scouts of America that is for fourth- and fifth-grade boys. Webelos Scouts are older than boys in the Tiger Cub, Wolf Cub Scout, and Bear Cub Scout levels of Cub Scouting.

If a boy has completed third grade, or if he has not completed third grade but is 10 years old, he's the right age for this den.

Most Webelos Scouts are in this program for about 18 months. This is a transitional program that shifts the emphasis from the home-centered activities of Tiger Cub and Wolf and Bear Cub Scouts to group-centered activities. This is preparation for his later participation in the great adventure of Boy Scouting.

The program will provide your boy with a variety of new experiences that will help him assume responsibilities and gain maturity, knowledge, and skills.

After your son's Webelos Scout experience, and after he has completed the fifth grade and is at least 10 years old, or is age 11, or has earned the Arrow of Light Award and is at least 10 years old, he'll be ready for more independence and adventure in a Boy Scout troop.

The Webelos Den Can Help You

As a parent or guardian, you want the best for your son. You want a close relationship with him, and you want to help him grow physically, mentally, and morally.

This part of Cub Scouting is designed to assist you. The program is geared to your son's developing abilities and changing interests. You'll find yourself growing closer to him as you encourage him in his advancement and when you take a turn assisting with Webelos den activities.

Join him in this adventure!

Advancement

Much of your son's progress will take place through activities centered around his *advancement*. He'll advance by earning activity badges and other awards.

The name *Webelos* comes from "*WE*'ll *BE* *LO*yal *S*couts."

Pronounce it WEE-buh-lows.

Each of the 20 activity badges focuses on a different subject in the areas of physical skills, mental skills, community, technology, and the outdoors. Athlete, Scholar, Citizen, Craftsman, Sportsman—these are just a few of the activity badges. The entire den works on one activity badge each month, mostly in their meetings.

Your son may learn the backstroke for the Aquanaut activity badge, practice first aid skills for the Readyman activity badge, or learn about the minerals that make up the earth's crust for the Geologist activity badge. Each activity badge presents an array of hands-on activities and fascinating information that will enrich his life.

He will also earn the Webelos badge, which has its own set of requirements. Later, he'll be eligible to work on Cub Scouting's highest award, the Arrow of Light.

Your son will keep track of his activity badges on a chart (see pages 75–78 of this book).

If Your Son Is New in Scouting

If your son joined Cub Scouting as a Webelos Scout, he must earn the Bobcat badge before receiving any other award or rank. The Bobcat badge requirements are on page 42.

He will need your help to fully understand the Cub Scout Promise, Law of the Pack, and Character Connections. When he has completed the Bobcat requirements to your satisfaction, he'll receive his Bobcat badge at a pack meeting.

Then he'll be ready to start on his adventures in Webelos Scouting.

Purposes of Cub Scouting

While the Webelos den's activities are tailored to your son's age group, its main purposes are the same as those for Cub Scouting at younger levels:

1. Character Development
2. Spiritual Growth
3. Good Citizenship
4. Sportsmanship and Fitness
5. Family Understanding
6. Respectful Relationships
7. Personal Achievement
8. Friendly Service
9. Fun and Adventure
10. Preparation for Boy Scouts

Character Connections®

Cub Scouting's Character Connections program helps your son *know*, *commit*, and *practice* Cub Scouting's 12 core values while enjoying fun and adventure in his Webelos den. This symbol identifies Character Connections throughout this book and in other Cub Scouting materials.

Character Development

Since its origin, the Scouting progam has been an educational experience concerned with values. In 1910, the first activities for Scouts were designed to build character, physical fitness, practical skills, and service. These elements were part of the original Cub Scout program and continue to be part of Cub Scouting today.

Character development should extend into every aspect of a boy's life. Character development should also extend into every aspect of Cub Scouting. Cub Scout leaders should strive to use Cub Scouting's **12 core values** throughout all elements of the program—service projects, ceremonies, games, skits, songs, crafts, and all the other activities enjoyed at den and pack meetings.

Cub Scouting's 12 Core Values

1. **Citizenship:** Contributing service and showing responsibility to local, state, and national communities.

2. **Compassion:** Being kind and considerate, and showing concern for the well-being of others.

3. **Cooperation:** Being helpful and working together with others toward a common goal.

4. **Courage:** Being brave and doing what is right regardless of our fears, the difficulties, or the consequences.

5. **Faith:** Having inner strength and confidence based on our trust in God.

6. **Health and Fitness:** Being personally committed to keeping our minds and bodies clean and fit.

7. **Honesty:** Telling the truth and being worthy of trust.

8. **Perseverance:** Sticking with something and not giving up, even if it is difficult.

9. **Positive Attitude:** Being cheerful and setting our minds to look for and find the best in all situations.

10. **Resourcefulness:** Using human and other resources to their fullest.

11. **Respect:** Showing regard for the worth of something or someone.

12. **Responsibility:** Fulfilling our duty to God, country, other people, and ourselves.

Where the Webelos Den Fits In

If you're new to Cub Scouting, this will help you understand how it's set up. Your son belongs to a small group called a Webelos *den.* The den is part of a larger Cub Scout *pack* that includes younger boys in the Tiger Cub and Wolf and Bear Cub Scout dens.

The pack is operated by a community organization, such as a school, a church or other religious institution, a service club, or other group interested in helping youth. It's called the *chartered organization* because it holds a charter from the BSA local council that allows it to use the Scouting program.

In addition to their den meetings, Webelos Scouts take part in monthly pack meetings led by an adult volunteer called the *Cubmaster.* Parents and other adult family members can serve on the *pack committee*, which plans pack activities.

Cub Scout Pack Structure

The Webelos Scout Experience

If your son has been in Cub Scouting before, he already knows a little about the Webelos Scout den from his earlier experiences. He may be surprised, though, to see how different it is. You'll find that your part in his experience is different, too.

What's ahead for him now? Well, he's growing up. He's probably taller and more mature than the younger boys in Cub Scouting. He wants more grown-up activities, more responsibility, more independence.

You'll still be involved in his Cub Scouting activities, but it will be different from your role when he was a Tiger Cub, Wolf Cub Scout, or Bear Cub Scout. In the Webelos den, the emphasis is on having fewer Cub Scouting activities to do at home and more to do with the den. A notable exception is in duty to God. This very important part of Cub Scouting must come primarily from within the context of your family and your religious organization. Your synagogue, church, mosque, or other faith-based organization may provide support in many ways. As a parent or guardian, your influence on your son's spiritual growth is key. See "Your Role in Your Son's Spiritual Development" on page 16.

The program is different in many ways from the experience of Cub Scouting for younger boys:

- Webelos Scouts don't do achievements and electives as other boys in Cub Scouting do. Webelos Scouts work on *activity badges.*

- The Webelos den uses activity badges as their monthly program themes.

- When a Tiger Cub, Wolf Cub Scout, or Bear Cub Scout completes requirements, a parent or guardian signs his book. When a Webelos Scout completes requirements, he takes his book to the Webelos den leader or an adult designated as the activity badge counselor (often this is the parent or guardian of a Webelos Scout). For projects that are done at home or with the family and are not easily transportable, the parent or guardian still may be asked to approve the Webelos Scout's completion of an activity badge requirement.

- Webelos Scouts are encouraged to have several parent/son overnight camping trips during the year, as well as other activities that prepare them for becoming Boy Scouts.
- Webelos Scouts have some distinctive choices in their uniform. (You'll find "Webelos Uniform and Insignia" starting on page 20.)

Webelos Scouts are still in Cub Scouting. They take part in Cub Scout pack meetings, events, and outings. But the Webelos den also makes its own plans and enjoys many activities that are not age-appropriate for younger boys.

Protecting Your Children Against Drugs and Child Abuse

Every day, more than 3,000 teenagers start smoking. An American is killed in an alcohol-related accident every 22 minutes. Drinking and driving is the number one killer of teenagers. A variety of illegal, life-ruining drugs is widely available to teens and even younger children. And many children are victims of verbal, physical, or sexual abuse or neglect.

Scouting leaders share your concern about the way young people will react if approached by drug dealers or by friends who have drugs to share. And we all want children and teens to know how to *recognize*, *resist*, and *report* abuse.

Although the reporting of child abuse incidents to authorities has increased significantly in recent years, this isn't true of drug use. Many children try to keep their drug problems a secret, fearing what might happen if the truth comes out.

Drug abuse and child abuse can be devastating to children and families. Explain to your children that their bodies belong to them alone. Tell them to say "NO" to anyone who offers them drugs, including alcohol and tobacco, and to anyone who touches them in an inappropriate manner.

It's important for you to know what's going on in your children's lives, to let them know they can talk about anything with you, to assure them you'll listen with understanding and love. The Boy Scouts of America urges you to take part in your children's activities. Become acquainted with their friends, their friends' families, and their Scouting leaders.

In the Webelos Den

How the Webelos Den Works

The Webelos den has three leaders. They'll need your help if the den is to be successful.

- The *Webelos den leader* is an adult who plans and directs the den activities. Appointed by the pack committee, the Webelos den leader must be at least 21 years old. There also should be an assistant Webelos den leader.

- The *Webelos den chief* is a Boy Scout, a Varsity Scout, or a Venturer who was a Boy Scout. The den chief is trained to help the Webelos den leader, especially in leading games and teaching skills.

- The *Webelos denner* is a Webelos Scout elected by the other boys to help the den leader and den chief.

The den meets each week at the home of the Webelos den leader or at a central meeting place, such as the chartered organization's building. The Webelos den leader, Webelos Scouts, and Webelos Scouts' adult family members set the time and place.

Activity Badge Fun

Each month, the projects and many of the activities at den meetings are centered around one of the 20 activity badges Webelos Scouts may earn. If you have skills or knowledge in any of the activity badge areas, the den leader may ask you to help.

Family members often help the den at its meetings. When your son joins the Webelos den, you may be asked to fill out a questionnaire to indicate your skills and interests that relate to the activity badge areas, the Webelos badge, and the Arrow of Light Award requirements. Your Webelos den leader might ask you to help when the boys are scheduled to work in an area you've noted.

An engineer, for example, could be involved with the Engineer activity badge. The requirements are challenging for a boy but simple for an engineer. He or she could explain what an engineer does and guide the boys in building a catapult, if the den chooses that project.

If you're skilled with tools and know about home repairs and car and bicycle care, you could help with Handyman activity badge projects. Take a look at the activity badge requirements in this book—Sportsman, Scientist, Communicator, Showman, and the rest—and see where you might fit in. Sharing what you know with your son and his friends will be a great experience. (In addition to the activity badge areas, family members will have other opportunities to help at meetings and events.)

The Webelos den leader (or another adult the leader designates) signs or initials each requirement your son completes. After completing the necessary requirements for one activity badge, he'll receive his badge (a small metal emblem to attach to his cap or Webelos colors) during a pack meeting ceremony.

Encourage and help your son earn as many of the 20 activity badges as possible, plus the Webelos badge and the Arrow of Light Award.

Requirements for all badges and awards are in this *Webelos Handbook.*

The Webelos Den at Pack Meetings

The role of the Webelos den in pack meetings differs from that of the younger Cub Scouts. The Webelos den may present an exhibit of projects or a demonstration of skills they've learned in exploring their activity badge for the month. Or they could come up with a skit or stunt that ties their activity badge to the younger Cub Scouts' theme for the month.

The Webelos Scouts are old enough to handle certain responsibilities at pack meetings. They may be asked to set up chairs, usher people to their seats, and direct them to the den exhibits.

During the pack meeting recognition ceremony, your son will receive any badges he has earned. Be sure to attend so you can pin on his newest badge. He'll be proud of his accomplishment and proud to have you doing the honors.

When he has completed the fifth grade and is at least 10 years old, or is age 11, or has earned the Arrow of Light Award and is at least 10 years old, he'll be ready to continue along the Scouting trail that leads to a Boy Scout troop. This will be a highlight of his young life, and you'll want to share the ceremony with him. His graduation will take place at a pack meeting—his last.

Fun and Responsibility for You and Your Webelos Scout

This program offers much to you and your son: challenging new experiences, ways to grow more knowledgeable and skilled, and ways to have fun. At the same time, it presents responsibilities for both of you.

The program asks four things of you as a parent or guardian:

- **Most important, provide a home for your son** where he finds love and security.

- **Help your son.** Much of his work in activity badge areas and for the Webelos badge and Arrow of Light Award will be done in the den, but he'll do some requirements at home; particularly those relating to Character Connections. Be prepared to help.

- **Take an interest in his Webelos activities.** He needs to know that you approve of what he's doing, you're interested in what he's learning, you want to help him, and you're proud of his accomplishments.

- **Pursue leadership in the den and pack.** Some parents and guardians of Webelos Scouts may be asked to serve as den leader, assistant Webelos den leader, Cubmaster, assistant Cubmaster, or pack committee member. If you are asked, please serve if you can. Your son will be proud of you.

The opportunity to work with your son at this age is a precious one. Keep in mind the Cub Scout motto, "Do Your Best." If you and your son strive for your best while he is a Webelos Scout, you'll have a great, productive time together.

Advancement: You Can Help

Your Part at Home

When your son has some of his activity badge work to do at home, he may ask you for help. Your assistance and encouragement will mean a lot to him.

For the Outdoorsman activity badge, for example, he can choose from requirements that include cookouts and family and den camping trips. It's natural for you to be the one to okay his work on such projects. For the Family Member and Fitness activity badges, you'll approve almost all of the requirements. Whenever he asks you to oversee his work and sign the requirement, make sure he does his best.

Webelos Badge and Arrow of Light Award

Your son will practice his skills and study for the Webelos badge and Arrow of Light Award at den meetings. But if he wants to continue practicing and studying at home, encourage and help him.

For details on all the activity badges and other awards, see this *Webelos Handbook.*

Your Role in Your Son's Spiritual Development

A main focus of the Webelos Scout program is to prepare boys for Boy Scouting by moving from more home-based activities of Cub Scouting to more den-based activities. However, as said earlier in this guide, a notable exception to that is in your son's spiritual development and his relationship to God.

The Boy Scouts of America has always held steadfastly to the principle that a Scout has a duty to God, but the organization also has always been completely non-sectarian. BSA does not promote any specific religion. We do encourage youth members and their families to be active in their own faith, in keeping with the BSA Declaration of Religious Principle.

From the non-sectarian nature of BSA, it naturally follows that the leadership for your son's spiritual development, both within and outside Cub Scouting, must come primarily from you. Your son will look to you as his example of how to learn and perform his duty to God. The Webelos Scout program provides support through faith-related requirements for rank advancement and activity badges and by awarding religious emblems he earns with your support and that of your religious or faith-based organization.

On a national level, BSA works closely with P.R.A.Y., a nationwide non-profit organization that coordinates many organized faiths' religious emblem curricula and standards in youth organizations. (P.R.A.Y. stands for Program for Religious Activity with Youth.) A visit to their Web site at http://www.praypub. org can help if you have questions about what religious emblem your son can earn or if you need more information about it.

Your local council of churches or your BSA local council service center should be able to help, as well. Many local councils and districts offer organized opportunities for Scouts of all ages to earn their religious emblems while meeting and sharing fellowship with other Scouts of their faith.

Cub Scout Motto:

Do Your Best

The Den's Outdoor Program

Webelos Scouts take part in more outdoor activities than younger Cub Scouts. Your son will get a taste of the outdoor life of a Boy Scout and learn some of the skills he needs for it.

Cub Scouting's Leave No Trace Awareness Award

Your Webelos Scout can earn Cub Scouting's Leave No Trace Awareness Award with your help. See pages 72–73 for the Leave No Trace Awareness Award guidelines and requirements.

Hiking

The boys will go on occasional nature hikes with the Webelos den leader and some other adults, parents, and guardians. Whether or not you go along, ensure a good experience for your son by helping him prepare. He'll need good socks, comfortable walking shoes, proper clothing, and food to take on the trail.

Webelos Overnight Campouts

The policy of the Boy Scouts of America is to encourage several overnight camping trips and other challenging outdoor activities for Webelos Scouts. You'll always have a major part in Webelos den overnight campouts. Don't worry if you're not an experienced camper. The Webelos den leader and other adults will help you, and you and your son will have fun learning about camping together.

These campouts are for boys AND their adult partners. Without the adults, there can be no trips.

The cooperation of adults is essential. The Webelos den leader cannot be expected to take full responsibility for the health and safety of six or eight boys at an overnight campout. In most cases, the Webelos Scout will be under the supervision of a parent or guardian. In all cases, each Webelos Scout is to be responsible to a specific adult. Boy Scouts of America health and safety and Youth Protection guidelines apply. If you or another adult family member can't attend, find a responsible adult to go with your son.

Planning Overnight Campouts

You'll have a hand in planning the details of each Webelos den overnight campout at a meeting of all participating adults. If you have special outdoor skills, the Webelos den leader may plan an activity in which you can instruct the Webelos Scouts.

Here are some of the topics for the meeting:

Where you're going. The site may be decided before the meeting. It won't be a rugged, pioneering type of camp. Your son won't experience that kind of camping until he's a Boy Scout.

Webelos den overnight campouts should take place in warm weather, at sites reasonably close to home. The events may be held at suitable public campgrounds, local council camps, or privately owned facilities. A location with a tested water supply, toilets, cooking facilities, and an area for indoor activity would be appropriate. Usually tents are used. Tent camping provides an element of adventure. Each adult and boy team brings the tent and other equipment they'll use. Equipment can be borrowed from a Boy Scout troop or rented. Any nearby cabins or shelters should serve only as emergency protection and a base for toilet facilities, water, etc.

How you'll get there. At the meeting, you and the other adults will make plans to share transportation to the campsite.

Who will cook. You and your son will cook for yourselves, so bring food and cooking equipment from home. Plan simple menus together. (This *Webelos Handbook* has some suggestions.)

Cooking can be done on wood or charcoal fires in established grills or fire pits provided by the camp or in charcoal grills provided at the camp or brought from home. Adults who own propane and liquid fuel stoves or lanterns may use them, if allowed by local camping property authorities, but **under no circumstances should boys be permitted to handle liquid fuels or stoves or lanterns fired by such fuel.** Such equipment should be considered personal gear, and adult owners must assume full personal responsibility for these items and for fuel.

Water supply. Be sure the water supply at the camp is safe. If it has not been tested, bring water from home for drinking and cooking. Water will also be needed for cleanup and for fire protection.

Webelos Uniform and Insignia

The Basic Uniform

The basic Webelos uniform is either the blue uniform your son may have worn as a Cub Scout or the tan shirt and olive green trousers he'll wear as a Boy Scout. The choice is yours and your son's, and it may be made at any time. If your son has been a Cub Scout, he might wear his blue uniform until he outgrows it and then switch to the tan and olive green uniform.

The following are worn with either uniform:

- **Webelos cap:** Olive green cap with a plaid front panel and the Webelos emblem centered above the bill. The Webelos Scout insignia (light blue and gold fleur-de-lis embroidered on dark blue background with gold border) is centered above the bill.

- **Neckerchief:** Gold, green, and red plaid, with the Webelos insignia centered 1 inch from the point. The neckerchief slide may be the official Webelos slide or a homemade one.

- **Belt.** The navy blue Cub Scout belt; a Webelos belt buckle is available.

See pages 29–31 for information on how the uniform and insignia are worn.

Obtaining a Uniform

The uniform and uniform accessories may be purchased at stores that are distributors for the Boy Scouts of America. Your Webelos den leader or Cubmaster will know the location of the nearest one.

Suggest that your son earn his uniform by working for it. You might arrange to pay him for special chores around the house. Or he might work around the neighborhood—shoveling snow, running errands, taking care of pets while their owners are away, etc.

Some Cub Scout packs maintain a uniform "bank" with "experienced" uniforms for new members.

Who Contributes to Scouting?

Many people in your community make Scouting programs possible by contributing their financial support, their skills, and their time. Some of these people are:

- **The boy and his parent or guardian.** It's a good idea for your son to pay part of his own way with money he has earned and saved. This might include paying for his annual membership fee, weekly den dues, or *Boys' Life* subscription (through the pack budget plan). You may help him buy his *Webelos Handbook* and uniform. Many parents and guardians also help local Scouting by contributing to the United Way and by participating in Friends of Scouting (FOS) (see below).

- **The chartered organization.** The chartered organization contributes by providing pack leadership and a meeting place.

- **The pack.** The pack maintains itself through its budget plan and its own money-earning projects. The adult leaders who volunteer their time, ideas, and effort contribute by making the program happen for boys.

- **The community.** People in the community support the local council and its services financially by participating in United Way and Friends of Scouting and through bequests and other contributions.

Friends of Scouting

Cub Scouting in your area is administered by an organization called the local council. (It's listed in the telephone book under "Boy Scouts of America.")

The local council provides services to Cub Scout packs, Boy Scout troops, Varsity Scout teams, and Venturing crews. It operates camping facilities, conducts training for leaders, plans and runs councilwide events for all members, and works continually to introduce more young people to Scouting. Most councils receive some support from United Way; however, the majority of council funding comes from other sources, including individual contributions through Friends of Scouting, camping and activities revenue, product sales, and other methods.

Each year, usually in the spring, the local council conducts a special funding campaign called Friends of Scouting (FOS). Parents, guardians, Scouters (volunteers and professionals in Scouting), former members, and other friends of Scouting are invited to contribute. A member of your pack committee will be assigned to ask the pack's families to give to FOS. By donating to FOS, you'll help ensure good Scouting for your Webelos Scout.

Together on the Webelos Trail

Your son sees Webelos Scouting as a chance to have fun, go camping, and make new friends. He also sees it as a step on the way to outdoor adventures in Boy Scouting.

But Webelos Scouting is more than that. For you, it's a new way to grow closer to your son, share his excitement about his expanding physical and mental skills, and create a warm and open relationship with him.

Join him on the Webelos trail. You'll be glad you did.

Webelos badge requirement 1 asks your son to have you read this parent guide. Please sign your name beside that requirement on page 49, under "Approved by."

Welcome to Your Webelos Scout Den!

This book tells you all about the great new adventures you and your friends in the Webelos den can choose.

If you've been a Tiger Cub or a Wolf or Bear Cub Scout, you probably know Webelos Scouts in your pack, and you've seen their plaid neckerchiefs and the colorful activity badges they've earned. Now you're a Webelos Scout—one of the older boys in the pack—and ready for challenging activities and outdoor fun.

If You Are New to Cub Scouting and the Pack

The Webelos den is part of Cub Scouting. It's for the older boys in the pack, and it will prepare you for being a Boy Scout. Here's what to do if you've just joined:

First, register. Ask your Webelos den leader for an application to join the pack. (All dens belong to a Cub Scout pack.) Fill out the application and have your parent or guardian sign it. Give it to your Webelos den leader along with your registration fee.

Second, earn your Bobcat badge. The Bobcat badge is earned after the Tiger Cub rank and before all other ranks. If a boy joins Cub Scouting as a Webelos Scout, he must earn the Bobcat badge before receiving any other award or rank. It won't take long, and you'll learn the Cub Scout Promise, the Law of the Pack, and other things all members of Cub Scouting know. The requirements are explained on page 42. When you complete each requirement, have your parent or guardian initial it.

Fun and Adventure
in the Webelos Den

Get set for fun and adventure!

As a Webelos Scout, you'll learn a lot of new skills. You'll go camping with your den, along with your parent, guardian, or an adult relative or friend.

Everything in the Webelos Scout program is more challenging than the activities younger boys in the pack do.

You'll earn special badges that only Webelos Scouts can wear. At the same time, you'll be getting ready to become a Boy Scout.

Your Webelos Den Meeting

Your Webelos den will meet each week. This is where you'll learn new skills. Go to all the meetings so you won't miss any of the fun, excitement, new information, and badge work.

Den meetings often include games, sports, and making things. Sometimes the den will go on special outings, like a nature hike or an overnight campout.

Your Webelos Den Leader

Your Webelos den leader understands boys your age and also knows about Boy Scouting and can help you get ready for it.

Your Webelos den leader can teach you the right way to build a fire, cook a meal, pitch a tent, and many other skills that are fun.

Webelos den leaders know the importance of the Cub Scout motto, "Do Your Best." They'll help you do your best in improving your skills and learning new ones.

They know the importance of ideals. They believe in God and the greatness of the United States of America. They believe in you and your future. That's why they take the time to lead your Webelos den.

The Webelos Den Chief

Webelos den chiefs are Boy Scouts, Varsity Scouts, or Venturers who were Boy Scouts. They help the Webelos den leader by leading games and teaching you many skills you'll need to know when you move into a Boy Scout troop.

The Webelos Denner

The Webelos denner is a Webelos Scout who has been selected by the Webelos den for a short term of office, usually three to six months. The denner helps the den leader and den chief at meetings and outdoor events. If you're elected denner, do your best.

The Pack Meeting

Your Webelos den plays an important part in the monthly pack meeting. You and your den might demonstrate the new skills you've learned in the past month or exhibit projects you've completed for an activity badge. Because your age group is ready for more responsibility, the Cubmaster (the adult leader of the pack) may ask your den to help set up chairs before the meeting or show adults to their seats.

Each pack meeting includes a special ceremony for Webelos Scouts who have earned badges during the month. Your Webelos den leader will present your badges to you.

Your New Webelos Uniform and Insignia

As a Webelos Scout, you may choose between two uniforms. One is the blue uniform you wore as a Cub Scout. The other is the uniform you can take with you into Boy Scouting—the tan Boy Scout shirt and olive green trousers. You and your family choose which uniform you'll wear.

You'll have three special uniform parts to show you're a Webelos Scout: an olive green cap with a plaid front panel and the Webelos emblem, a plaid Webelos neckerchief, and a Webelos neckerchief slide. The navy blue Cub Scout belt may be worn with both uniforms; a Webelos belt buckle is available. The official Boy Scout olive web belt may be worn with the tan/olive uniform; however, Academics and Sports belt loops fit only on the blue belt.

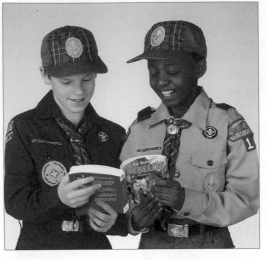

You'll be proud to wear your uniform at all Webelos den meetings, pack meetings, and special events. It shows you're one of the older boys in the pack, on the trail to Boy Scouting.

How to Put on the Neckerchief

You may wear your neckerchief either over or under the collar, but all members in your pack wear it the same way. If it is worn over the collar, turn the collar under.

Roll the long edge over several times, until the neckerchief is about 6 inches long from the rolled part to the tip. Place the neckerchief around your neck and pull the neckerchief slide up snugly. Tie the loose ends or leave them loose, according to the rule of your pack.

The neckerchief should lie smoothly on the back of your shirt. It should measure about 6 inches from the top of the fold down to the tip.

Earning Your Uniform

You can help earn the money to buy your uniform. Consider asking about extra chores at home or in your neighborhood: washing windows, weeding gardens, caring for pets while their owners are away, raking leaves, running errands, shoveling snow.

You may know other ways to earn money for your uniform. Talk over your ideas with your family and your Webelos den leader.

Placement of Awards

Activity badges are small metal emblems. You earn one each time you complete the requirements for one of the 20 activity badges. They are pinned onto the plaid front panel of the Webelos cap. The shield inside the cap should be folded down when attaching awards and then folded up to cover the backs of the pins.

Another way to wear the activity badges is to pin them to the Webelos colors, which are optional. The colors are three ribbons—one gold, one green, one red—fastened together at the top by a pin with the word Webelos on it. The colors are pinned to the right shirt sleeve just below the U.S. flag. (The colors will cover the den emblem and Quality Unit insignia.)

The two rank advancements for Webelos Scouts, the Webelos badge and the Arrow of Light Award, the highest award a boy can earn in Cub Scouting, are cloth patches. They are sewn onto the uniform shirt. There are two different Webelos rank badges. The one to be awarded depends on personal preference.

1. A tan oval-shaped cloth badge with an embroidered Webelos symbol. This badge is worn on the tan uniform shirt. When a boy wears the oval-shaped Webelos badge on his uniform, he does not include Arrow Points or Tiger Cub, Bobcat, Wolf, or Bear rank badges.

2. A diamond-shaped cloth badge with a gold and light blue embroidered Webelos symbol. Worn on the left pocket of the blue or tan uniform shirt with the other badges. Webelos Scouts who did not earn the Tiger Cub badge may wear the

diamond-shaped Webelos badge in the same place the Tiger Cub badge would otherwise be worn.

The Arrow of Light Award, a gold arrow embroidered on a tan background with a blue border, is worn centered below the left pocket. This is the highest award in Cub Scouting and the only Cub Scout badge that may be worn on the Boy Scout uniform.

The compass points emblem is a blue, red, and gold embroidered emblem awarded for earning activity badges beyond those required for the Webelos badge. It is attached to the button of the right pocket. Three metal compass "points" are attached to the emblem when they are earned.

Boys who earned belt loops previously in the Cub Scout Academics and Sports program may continue to wear them. Webelos Scouts may also earn and wear the belt loops. These awards are square metal emblems that slide onto the navy blue belt.

Webelos Scout Insignia

The diagrams on page 34 show you where to place insignia on the sleeves and pockets of the uniform.

Webelos Scouts wear the Tiger Cub, Bobcat, Wolf, and Bear badges, if they have earned them, as shown on page 34. The Arrow of Light Award is centered below the left pocket.

Below the left pocket, you may wear all the Arrow Points you earned as a Cub Scout. Or you may wear two or three on your shirt and place the others on a vest or display them in your room at home. See placement on page 34.

Temporary insignia must be centered on the right pocket. The compass points emblem is fastened to the button under the right pocket flap and then the flap is rebuttoned.

The Webelos denner and assistant denner wear their shoulder cords suspended from the left shoulder of the blue uniform or they wear it, without the tab, under the left epaulet on the tan/olive uniform. The cord is removed when the term of office ends.

CUB SCOUT
OR WEBELOS SCOUT
RIGHT SLEEVE

WEBELOS SCOUT
RIGHT SLEEVE

LEFT SLEEVE

WEBELOS SCOUT
LEFT POCKET OPTIONS

WEBELOS SCOUT
LEFT POCKET
(BLUE OR TAN SHIRT)

WEBELOS SCOUT
LEFT POCKET
(BLUE OR TAN SHIRT)

WEBELOS SCOUT
LEFT POCKET
(TAN SHIRT)

Invite Your Friends

If you have friends your age who are not Webelos Scouts, why not ask them to join your Webelos den? Invite them to a den meeting and introduce them to your Webelos den leader and the other Webelos Scouts. Help them join in games and activities.

The Webelos Advancement Trail

Advancement as a Webelos Scout means growing in knowledge and skills, and you do this through all the experiences that lead to earning activity badges and other awards. This moves you upward along the trail to Cub Scouting's highest award, the Arrow of Light Award. By that time you'll be close to joining a Boy Scout troop.

The requirements for each badge and award are in this book, along with detailed information you'll need for each subject.

You'll do much of your badge work with your den and some of it at home. Read on to learn about these experiences and awards.

Activity Badges

While you are a Webelos Scout, you can work on any or all of the 20 Webelos Scout activity badges! You earn them by completing the requirements with your den or at home (with your Webelos den leader's approval). During den meetings one month, you might concentrate on swimming, and the next month you could be conducting scientific experiments.

Activity badges are colorful metal emblems you pin on the front of your Webelos cap. Or you can pin them to the Webelos colors, which are the gold, green, and red ribbons you may decide to wear on your right sleeve.

Webelos Badge

As soon as you start earning activity badges, you can look forward to earning the Webelos badge. The Webelos rank is the fifth rank in Cub Scouting (coming after Tiger Cub, Bobcat, Wolf, and Bear). As you earn it, you'll learn a lot about Boy Scouting.

As part of your Webelos badge work, you need to earn activity badges, each one from a *different* activity badge group. Two of the badges must be Fitness, from the Physical Skills Group, and Citizen, from the Community Group. The other activity badge may be from the Mental Skills, Technology, or Outdoor Group. (You'll find all the activity badges listed in their groups on page 74.)

There are two Webelos badge options: diamond-shaped and oval. Whichever you choose, you wear the Webelos badge on your left shirt pocket.

Compass Points Emblem

The compass points emblem is awarded after you have earned the Webelos badge and four additional activity badges, for a total of seven. After you receive the emblem, you'll add a metal "compass point" to it for each additional four activity badges you earn. The emblem hangs from the button on your right shirt pocket.

Arrow of Light Award

The Arrow of Light Award is the highest rank in Cub Scouting. Set your sights on it now.

It's more challenging to earn than the Webelos badge, but you can do it! First you'll need the Webelos badge. You need a total of eight activity badges, including Citizen, Readyman, Fitness, and Outdoorsman. (You'll already have three activity badges, including Fitness and Citizen, from earning your Webelos badge.) The total must include at least one activity badge from each of the five activity badge groups.

You'll wear your Arrow of Light Award below the left pocket, as it is worn on the Boy Scout uniform.

By the time you've earned the Arrow of Light Award, you'll have gained knowledge and skills in a lot of subjects, and you'll know a lot about Boy Scouting. You'll be ready to graduate into a Boy Scout troop!

What Happens Now?

In the pages that follow, you'll find the details on each activity badge. The requirements for the Webelos badge, compass points emblem, and Arrow of Light Award are on pages 49–51, 61, and 63–64.

Other awards are explained there, too: religious emblems, the Cub Scout World Conservation Award, the Leave No Trace Award, and the Cub Scout Academics and Sports program.

Rank Advancement and Special Awards

Earning the Bobcat Badge

Welcome to the Webelos den and the Cub Scout pack! It's great to have you with us!

If you haven't earned it before, you should start earning the Bobcat badge right away. The requirements are listed on page 42. You'll learn what you need to know for the Bobcat badge by reading the following pages.

When you're ready, show your parent or guardian what you know about each requirement. Then ask him or her to sign on each line on page 42. When you've done all eight, show that page to your Webelos den leader, and you will be presented your Bobcat badge at a pack meeting.

Bobcat Badge Requirements

Approved by

1. Learn and say the Cub Scout Promise and complete the Honesty Character Connection.

   a. **Know:** Discuss these questions with your family: What is a promise? What does it mean to "keep your word?" What does honesty mean? What does it mean to "do your best?" _____

   b. **Commit:** Discuss these questions with your family. Why is a promise important? Why is it important for people to trust you when you give your word? When might it be difficult to keep your word? List examples. _____

   c. **Practice:** Discuss with family members why it is important to be trustworthy and honest and how you can do your best to be honest when you are doing the activities in Cub Scouting. _____

2. Say the Law of the Pack. Tell what it means. _____

3. Tell what *Webelos* means. _____

4. Make the Cub Scout sign. Tell what it means. _____

5. Show the Cub Scout handshake. Tell what it means. _____

6. Say the Cub Scout motto. _____

7. Give the Cub Scout salute. Tell what it means. _____

8. With your parent or guardian, complete the Bobcat Requirements section of "How to Protect Your Children from Child Abuse: A Parent's Guide." (The guide is a pull-out section that came in the front of this book.) _____

The Cub Scout Promise

I, [say your name], promise

To do my best

To do my duty to God

And my country,

To help other people, and

To obey the Law of the Pack.

What the Cub Scout Promise Means

I Promise

When you promise to do something, you mean you will do it. Even if it is difficult, a Webelos Scout keeps his promise, because it's the right thing to do. He wants people to know he can be trusted.

To Do My Best

When you say, "I will do my best," you mean, "I will try as hard as I can." One boy's best can be different from another boy's best. Webelos leaders don't expect you to be perfect, but they want you to do your best.

To Do My Duty

When you do your duty, you do your share. You do what you ought to do.

Your duty to God is done with God's help. That means you practice your religion at home, in your church or synagogue or other religious group, and in everything you do.

Your duty to your country means being a good American. You obey the laws. You're a good citizen, and you help your community in any way you can.

To Help Other People

This means thinking about other people and their needs. Sometimes this isn't easy, but a Webelos Scout will help others when he can.

Character Connections®— Honesty

Honesty means telling the truth and being a person worthy of trust.

The Law of the Pack

The Cub Scout follows Akela.

The Cub Scout helps the pack go.

The pack helps the Cub Scout grow.

The Cub Scout gives goodwill.

What the Law of the Pack Means

The Cub Scout follows Akela.

Who is Akela? (Say Ah-KAY-la.)

Akela is the Webelos Scout name for a good leader. Some of the people you may call Akela are your father or mother, your teacher, your den chief, your Webelos den leader, your Cubmaster, or anybody who is a good leader.

Before you can be a good leader, you must learn to be a good follower. That's why the first part of the Law of the Pack asks you to follow. Always be sure you choose good leaders to follow. Follow Akela.

The Cub Scout helps the pack go.

When you become a Webelos Scout, you're a member of a Webelos den and a Cub Scout pack. You'll help the pack GO by doing whatever you can to help the pack run smoothly. By doing your part, you'll help everyone in your den and pack get the most out of all their activities.

Help the pack GO by attending all meetings and following the leaders. Your pack will be better in every way because you're in it.

The pack helps the Cub Scout grow.

You'll "grow" in skills and knowledge while you're a Webelos Scout. That's what all the pack leaders want for you, so they plan den and pack activities to help all the Cub Scouts grow.

In your den meetings, while you're having fun earning activity badges, you'll learn new skills and new ways of doing things. Earning the Arrow of Light Award, the highest award in Cub Scouting, will help you prepare for Boy Scouting. That's how the pack helps you "grow."

The Cub Scout gives goodwill.

Goodwill means cheerfulness and kindness. You give goodwill by having a cheerful attitude, by being kind in what you say and do, and by looking for ways to help other people.

Smile and *help*—those are two Webelos Scout words to remember.

The Meaning of *Webelos*

The word *Webelos* (say WEE-buh-lows) has a special meaning. Webelos is made up of the first letters of these words: "*WE*'ll *BE LO*yal *S*couts." Loyal means you'll keep your Cub Scout Promise.

The Cub Scout Sign

Make the sign with your right hand, holding your arm straight up. The two extended fingers stand for two points of the Cub Scout Promise—*help* and *obey*. Give the sign whenever you repeat the Cub Scout Promise or the Law of the Pack.

The Cub Scout Handshake

When you shake hands with another Webelos Scout, a Tiger Cub, or a Wolf or Bear Cub Scout, hold out your right hand as you do for an ordinary handshake. But keep your elbow straight and place your first two fingers along the inside of the other Cub Scout's wrist. This means both of you will *help* others and *obey* the Law of the Pack.

The Cub Scout Motto

"Do Your Best"—That's the Cub Scout motto. Do your best when you're helping your family at home, learning in school, or working on a project for a Webelos activity badge. Even when something seems difficult, you'll feel good if you've done your best.

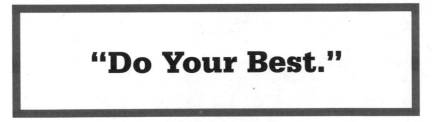

"Do Your Best."

The Cub Scout Salute

Salute with your right hand. Hold your fingers as you do for the sign but with the first two fingers close together. Touch the tips of those fingers to your cap's bill. If you aren't wearing a cap, touch your forehead above your right eyebrow. Salute the U.S. flag during ceremonies.

Sometimes you may also salute your leaders or other Webelos Scouts to show goodwill and courtesy.

Preventing Child Abuse

Your parent or guardian has a booklet that came with your *Webelos Handbook*. It's called "How to Protect Your Children from Child Abuse." Talk with your parent or guardian about the questions and answers in the section called "What If ... ."

Ready for Webelos Adventures

When you complete all the Bobcat requirements and your parent or guardian signs each line on page 42, you'll be ready for Webelos Scout den fun.

Earning the Webelos Badge

The Webelos rank is the fifth rank in Cub Scouting (coming after Tiger Cub, Bobcat, Wolf, and Bear). You can start working on it as soon as you join the Webelos den and have earned the Bobcat badge. To earn the Webelos badge, you must be active in your den at least three months and complete the requirements. The requirements are listed on the following pages.

You'll be proud to reach Webelos rank and receive your badge at a pack meeting.

Webelos Badge Requirements

Approved by

Do these:

1. Have an adult member of your family read the Webelos Scout Parent Guide (pages 1–22) and sign here.

2. Be an active member of your Webelos den for three months. (*Active* means having good attendance, paying your den dues, and working on den projects.)

3. Know and explain the meaning of the Webelos badge.

4. Point out the three special parts of the Webelos Scout uniform. Tell when to wear the uniform and when not to wear it.

5. Earn the Fitness and Citizen activity badges and one other activity badge from a different activity group.

6. Plan and lead a flag ceremony in your den that includes the U.S. flag.

7. Show that you know and understand the requirements to be a Boy Scout:

   a. Demonstrate the Scout salute, Scout sign, and Scout handshake. Explain when you would use them.

   b. Explain the Scout Oath, Scout Law, Scout motto, and Scout slogan.

   c. Explain and agree to follow the Outdoor Code.

8. Faith

After completing the rest of requirement 8,
do these (a, b, and c):

a. **Know:** Tell what you have learned about
faith.
_____ DWM _____

b. **Commit:** Tell how these faith experiences help you live your duty to God.
Name one faith practice that you will
continue to do in the future.
_____ DWM _____

c. **Practice:** After doing these requirements, tell what you have learned about
your beliefs.
_____ DWM _____

And do one of these (**d OR e**):

d. Earn the religious emblem of your faith.*
_____

e. **Do two of these:**

• Attend the mosque, church, synagogue,
temple, or other religious organization
of your choice; talk with your religious
leader about your beliefs. Tell your family and your Webelos den leader what
you learned
_____

⊙ Discuss with your family and your Webelos den leader how your religious beliefs
fit in with the Scout Oath and Scout Law
and what character-building traits your
religious beliefs have in common with
the Scout Oath and Scout Law.
_____

• With your religious leader, discuss and
make a plan to do two things you think
will help you draw nearer to God. Do
these things for a month.

(1) _____ _____

(2) _____ _____

- For at least a month, pray or meditate reverently each day as taught by your family and by your church, temple, mosque, synagogue, or religious group. _____

- Under the direction of your religious leader, do an act of service for someone else. Talk about your service with your family and your Webelos den leader. Tell them how it made you feel. _____

- ⊙ List at least two ways you believe you have lived according to your religious beliefs. _____

_____

* If you earned your faith's religious emblem earlier in Cub Scouting and your faith does not have a Webelos religious emblem, you must complete requirement 8e.

Completion of requirement 8e does not qualify a youth to receive the religious emblem of his faith.

Webelos Scout religious emblems are listed on pages 68–69.

The Meaning of the Webelos Badge

The Webelos badge has a Webelos emblem on it, which contains a blue *W*, the diamond-shaped badge also has the word *Webelos* and a small Scout badge at the bottom. Whichever option you choose, your Webelos badge shows that you are on the Webelos trail that leads from Cub Scouting to Boy Scouting.

Your Uniform

Webelos Scouts may wear either the blue uniform they wore as Cub Scouts or the tan shirt and olive green trousers they will wear as Boy Scouts. You and your family decide which one you will wear.

With either basic uniform, Webelos Scouts wear the Webelos cap, Webelos neckerchief, Webelos neckerchief slide, and the navy blue Cub Scout belt; a Webelos belt buckle is available.

When to Wear the Uniform

Wear your uniform
- To all den meetings and pack meetings
- On campouts and other den activities
- At den service projects
- During Scouting's Anniversary Week in February

The Webelos uniform may *not* be worn
- When you are involved in any distinctly political activity
- When you are appearing on the stage professionally
- When you are participating in demonstrations not authorized by the Boy Scouts of America

Planning and Leading a Flag Ceremony

For Webelos badge requirement 6, you must plan and lead a den flag ceremony using the U.S. flag. Here are some ideas:

- Have the Webelos Scouts give the Cub Scout salute and repeat the Pledge of Allegiance to the flag.
- Parade the U.S. flag and the den flag past the line of Webelos Scouts, who stand at attention and salute.
- Plan a ceremony on the history of the U.S. flag. Each boy in the den can make and color a different paper flag to show how our present flag developed out of earlier flags.
- Have the Webelos Scouts march past the U.S. flag, giving the proper salute.

Understanding the Requirements for Joining Boy Scouting

Working on the Webelos badge helps you find out about values important to Boy Scouts and things they know, including the Scout Oath and Law. By practicing the Scout salute, Scout sign, and Scout handshake now for requirement 7, you'll already know them when you become a Boy Scout.

Scout Oath

On my honor I will do my best to do my duty to God and my country and to obey the Scout Law; to help other people at all times; to keep myself physically strong, mentally awake, and morally straight.

The Meaning of the Scout Oath

When you say "On my honor," that's like saying "I promise." It also means you are the kind of person who always tries to do what is right and you can be trusted to keep this promise. No one can take your honor from you, but you can throw it away by breaking your promise and doing what you know is wrong.

Notice that the Scout Oath has three basic parts. Let's look at what they mean.

TO DO MY DUTY TO GOD AND MY COUNTRY AND TO OBEY THE SCOUT LAW

Your family and religious leaders teach you to know and serve God. By following these teachings, you do your duty to God.

Men and women of the past worked to make America great, and many gave their lives for their country. By being a good family member and a good citizen, by working for your country's good and obeying its laws, you do your duty to your country.

Obeying the Scout Law means living by its 12 points. The Scout Law is explained below.

TO HELP OTHER PEOPLE AT ALL TIMES

Many people need help. A cheery smile and a helping hand make life easier for others. By doing a Good Turn daily and helping when you're needed, you prove yourself a Scout and do your part to make this a better world.

TO KEEP MYSELF PHYSICALLY STRONG, MENTALLY AWAKE, AND MORALLY STRAIGHT

Keeping yourself physically strong means taking good care of your body. Eat the right foods and build your strength.

Staying mentally awake means learn all you can, be curious, and ask questions. Being **morally straight** means to live your life with honesty, to be clean in your speech and actions, and to be a person of strong character.

Scout Law

A Scout is trustworthy, loyal, helpful, friendly, courteous, kind, obedient, cheerful, thrifty, brave, clean, and reverent.

The Meaning of the Scout Law

The Scout Law has 12 points. Each is a goal for every Scout. He does his best to live up to the Law. It is not always easy to do, but a Scout always tries.

A Scout is TRUSTWORTHY.

A Scout tells the truth. He is honest, and he keeps his promises. People can depend on him.

A Scout is LOYAL.

A Scout is true to his family, friends, Scout leaders, school, and nation.

A Scout is HELPFUL.

A Scout cares about other people. He willingly volunteers to help others without expecting payment or reward.

A Scout is FRIENDLY.

A Scout is a friend to all. He is a brother to other Scouts. He offers his friendship to people of all races and nations, and respects them even if their beliefs and customs are different from his own.

A Scout is COURTEOUS.

A Scout is polite to everyone regardless of age or position. He knows that using good manners makes it easier for people to get along.

A Scout is KIND.

A Scout knows there is strength in being gentle. He treats others as he wants to be treated. Without good reason, he does not harm or kill any living thing.

A Scout is OBEDIENT.

A Scout follows the rules of his family, school, and troop. He obeys the laws of his community and country. If he thinks these rules and laws are unfair, he tries to have them changed in an orderly manner rather than disobeying them.

A Scout is CHEERFUL.

A Scout looks for the bright side of life. He cheerfully does tasks that come his way. He tries to make others happy.

A Scout is THRIFTY.

A Scout works to pay his way and to help others. He saves for the future. He protects and conserves natural resources. He carefully uses time and property.

A Scout is BRAVE.

A Scout can face danger although he is afraid. He has the courage to stand for what he thinks is right even if others laugh at him or threaten him.

A Scout is CLEAN.

A Scout keeps his body and mind fit. He chooses the company of those who live by high standards. He helps keep his home and community clean.

A Scout is REVERENT.

A Scout is reverent toward God. He is faithful in his religious duties. He respects the beliefs of others.

Scout Motto

Be Prepared

The Scout motto is "Be Prepared." Someone once asked Robert Baden-Powell, the founder of Scouting, "Be prepared for what?" Baden-Powell replied, "Why, for any old thing." That's the idea. The Scout motto means you are always ready to do your duty and to face danger, if necessary, to help others.

Scout Slogan

Do a Good Turn daily.

The Scout slogan is "Do a Good Turn daily." This doesn't mean you're supposed to do one Good Turn during the day and then stop. It means you do at least one Good Turn a day. It means looking for chances to help and then helping quietly, without boasting about it.

Always remember that a Good Turn is an *extra* act of kindness—something you go out of your way to do.

Demonstrate the Scout Sign, Salute, and Handshake

Scout Sign

The Scout sign shows you are a Scout. Give it each time you recite the Scout Oath and Law. When a Scout or Scouter raises the Scout sign, all Scouts should make the sign, too, and come to silent attention.

To give the Scout sign, cover the nail of the little finger of your right hand with your right thumb, then raise your right arm bent in a 90-degree angle, and hold the three middle fingers of your hand upward. Those fingers stand for the three parts of the Scout Oath. Your thumb and little finger touch to represent the bond that unites Scouts throughout the world.

Scout Salute

The Scout salute shows respect. Use it to salute the flag of the United States of America. You may also salute a Scout leader or another Scout.

Give the Scout salute by forming the Scout sign with your right hand and then bringing that hand upward until your forefinger touches the brim of your hat or the arc of your right eyebrow. The palm of your hand should not show.

Scout Handshake

The Scout handshake is made with the hand nearest the heart and is offered as a token of friendship. Extend your left hand to another Scout and firmly grasp his left hand. **The fingers do not interlock.**

Outdoor Code

As an American, I will do my best to—be clean in my outdoor manners, be careful with fire, be considerate in the outdoors, and be conservation-minded.

As a Webelos Scout, you'll hike and camp out. As a Boy Scout, you'll be outdoors a lot more often. The Outdoor Code is a guide all Scouts use. Read it with your Webelos den leader and discuss what it means. See page 346 for more about the Outdoor Code.

Earning the Religious Emblem of Your Faith

If you decide to earn the religious emblem of your faith as a Webelos Scout for requirement 8, you'll find information about that starting on page 68.

Earning the Compass Points Emblem

After you've earned the Webelos badge, you can earn the compass points emblem. It is awarded after you earn seven activity badges: four more in addition to the three you earned for the Webelos badge. Wear your compass points emblem attached to the button on the right pocket of your Webelos uniform shirt.

After you earn the compass points emblem, you'll receive a metal compass point for each four additional activity badges you earn. Pin these compass points on the emblem in the "E," "W," or "S" positions, in any order you choose.

You can earn the emblem and all three compass points by completing 19 activity badges, including the three required for the Webelos badge.

Compass Points Emblem Requirements

Webelos badge awarded on (date): _____

Activity badges earned for the Webelos badge:
(Earn Fitness, Citizen, and one other.)

1 _____ Fitness _____

2 _____ Citizen _____

3 _____ Aquanaut _____

Activity badges earned for the compass points emblem: (After you earn the Webelos badge, earn four additional activity badges.)

1 _____ Engineer _____

2 _____ Readyman _____

3 _____ Geologist _____

4 _____ Showman _____

Compass Points

Earn a *compass point* for each additional *four* activity badges you complete:

E

1 _____ Scientist _____

2 _____ Naturalist _____

3 _____ Sportsman _____

4 _____ Traveler _____

W

1 _____ Music _____

2 _____

3 _____

4 _____

S

1 _____

2 _____

3 _____

4 _____

Earning the Arrow of Light Award

After you have earned the Webelos badge, you can continue working on the requirements for the Arrow of Light Award, which is Cub Scouting's highest award. This award tells everyone you're ready to be a Boy Scout.

The Arrow of Light Award displays a universal symbol for the sun and, below it, an arrow. The seven rays of the sun stand for each day of the week. They remind you to do your best every day as you follow the arrow that leads to Boy Scouting.

It will be a proud day for you when you receive the Arrow of Light Award. It is the only Cub Scouting badge you can wear on your Boy Scout uniform.

The requirements are listed on the following pages.

Arrow of Light Award Requirements

Approved by

1. Be active in your Webelos den for at least six months since completing the fourth grade (or for at least six months since becoming 10 years old), and earn the Webelos badge.

2. Show your knowledge of the requirements to become a Boy Scout by doing all of these:

    - Repeat from memory and explain in your own words the Scout Oath or Promise and the 12 points of the Scout Law. Tell how you have practiced them in your everyday life.

    - Give and explain the Scout motto, slogan, sign, salute, and handshake.

    - Understand the significance of the First Class Scout badge. Describe its parts and tell what each stands for.

    - Tell how a Boy Scout uniform is different from a Webelos Scout uniform.

    - Tie the joining knot (square knot).

3. Earn five more activity badges in addition to the three you already earned for the Webelos badge. These must include:

    - Fitness (already earned for the Webelos badge)

    - Citizen (already earned for the Webelos badge)

    - Readyman

    - Outdoorsman

    - At least one from the Mental Skills group *Traveler*

    - At least one from the Technology group *Engineering*

    - One more of your choice *Naturalist* *Aquanaut*

See page 74 for the activity badge groups.

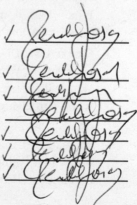

4. With your Webelos den, visit at least

- one Boy Scout troop meeting and
- one Boy Scout–oriented outdoor activity.

(If you have already done this when you earned your Outdoorsman activity badge, you may not use the same outing to fulfill requirements for your Arrow of Light Award.)

5. Participate in a Webelos overnight campout or day hike. (If you have already done this when you earned your Outdoorsman activity badge, you may not use the same outing to fulfill your Arrow of Light Award requirements.)

6. After you have completed all five of the above requirements, and after a talk with your Webelos den leader, arrange to visit, with your parent or guardian, a meeting of a Boy Scout troop you think you might like to join. Have a conference with the Scoutmaster.

7. Complete the Honesty Character Connection.

   a. **Know:** Say the Cub Scout Promise to your family. Discuss these questions with them: What is a promise? What does it mean to keep your word? What does it mean to be trustworthy? What does *honesty* mean?

   b. **Commit:** Discuss these questions with your family. Why is a promise important? Why is it important for people to trust you when you give your word? When might it be difficult to be truthful? List examples.

   c. **Practice:** Discuss with a family member why it is important to be trustworthy and honest. How can you do your best to be honest even when it is difficult?

The First Class Scout Badge

The First Class Scout badge is shown here.

The three-point design of the top part of the badge is like the north point of the compass sailors used long ago. These three points, like the three fingers in the Scout sign, stand for the three parts of the Scout Oath.

The main part of the badge shows that a Scout is able to point the right way in life as truly as the compass points north in the field.

The two stars on the right and left top points symbolize Scouting's ideals of truth and knowledge. Stars guide us by night and remind us of the Scout's outdoor life.

The eagle with the shield is the national emblem of the United States of America. It stands for freedom and readiness to defend that freedom.

The scroll with the Scout motto is turned up at the ends to suggest a Scout's smile as he does his duty.

The knot attached to the bottom of the scroll reminds you that as a Boy Scout, you promise to do a Good Turn for someone every day.

The Boy Scout Uniform

The basic Boy Scout uniform is a tan shirt and olive green trousers and Scout belt and buckle. The shirt may have either short or long sleeves. For summer you may wear the short-sleeved shirt, olive green shorts, and long (or short) socks.

Your hat will depend on the style worn by the troop you join. It may be a baseball-style cap or a broad-brimmed campaign hat.

Each troop has its own neckerchief design. Yours will be the one worn by your new troop.

Some of the insignia on your Boy Scout shirt are like those on your Webelos uniform. But on your right sleeve, you'll wear your patrol emblem. On your left shirt pocket, you'll wear the highest Boy Scout rank you've earned. Your Arrow of Light Award goes at the bottom of the left pocket. You'll wear red shoulder loops that attach to the shirt at the shoulder.

Wear your Boy Scout uniform with pride. It shows you are a good citizen and are ready and willing to help other people.

Working on the Arrow of Light Award

You must have eight activity badges to earn the Arrow of Light Award. Four of them *must* be Fitness and Citizen (which you already earned for the Webelos badge), Outdoorsman, and Readyman. Of the other four, at least one must be from the Mental Skills Group and one from the Technology Group. Activity badge groups are shown on page 74.

Remember, the activity badges you earned for the Webelos badge count in the total.

The other requirements should be easy, if you're active in your den. Be sure to attend Webelos campouts and other den activities. Be sure to go along when your den visits a Boy Scout troop meeting or other Boy Scout event.

Your Religious Duties

Webelos badge requirement 8 concerns your religious duties; it helps you learn more about your religious beliefs and how to commit to and practice ways to be closer to God. As part of the requirements you complete for the Webelos badge, you can either earn the Webelos religious emblem of your faith or in other ways explore how your religious beliefs support and are supported by the Scout Oath and the Scout Law.

If you earned your faith's religious emblem earlier in Cub Scouting and your faith does not have a Webelos religious emblem, you must complete the alternative requirement (8e).

Religious Emblems for Webelos Scouts

Talk to your pack leaders or local council to find out how to contact the religious organizations listed below about religious emblems for Webelos Scouts.

If your faith isn't listed, it didn't have a religious emblem program for Webelos Scouts at the time this book was published.

Religious Organization	*Webelos Scout Emblem*
Armenian: Diocese of the Armenian Church of America (Eastern Diocese)	Saint Gregory
Association of Unity Churches	God in Me
Baha'i	Unity of Mankind
Baptist	God and Family
Buddhist	Metta
Christian Church (Disciples of Christ)	God and Family
Churches of Christ	Joyful Servant
Church of Jesus Christ of Latter-day Saints (LDS)	Faith in God
Eastern Orthodox	Chi Rho
Eastern-Rite Catholic Churches	Parvuli Dei
Episcopal	God and Family
First Church of Christ, Scientist (Christian Science)	God and Country
Hindu	Dharma
Islamic	Bismillah
Jewish	Aleph
Lutheran	God and Family
Meher Baba	Love for God
Polish National Catholic	Love of God (Milosc Boga)
Presbyterian Church (U.S.A.)	God and Family
Protestant (available to any Christian denomination)	God and Family
Religious Society of Friends (Quakers)	That of God
Community of Christ	Light of the World
Roman Catholic	Parvuli Dei
The Salvation Army	Silver Crest, God and Family
United Church of Christ	God and Family
United Methodist	God and Family

Cub Scout World Conservation Award

As a Webelos Scout, you can earn the Cub Scout World Conservation Award. This is a special international award. (You may earn it only once while you are in Cub Scouting.) Use this page to keep track of your progress.

World Conservation Award Requirements

Webelos den leader initials

1. Earned the Forester activity badge. _____
2. Earned the Naturalist activity badge. _____
3. Earned the Outdoorsman activity badge. _____
4. Participated in a den or pack conservation project. _____

Qualified to receive the World Conservation Award:

Name _____

Date _____

Webelos den leader's signature _____

The Cub Scout Academics and Sports Program

If you were in Cub Scouting before joining your Webelos den, you already may know about earning belt loops and pins in the Cub Scout Academics and Sports program. You can earn them by learning about and playing sports like basketball or soccer, or by investigating an academic area like math or art.

You can earn some of these awards along with your pack or den. You can earn some on your own, or with your family or in your community.

The requirements for each subject are listed in the *Cub Scout Academics and Sports Program Guide,* which is available from your den leader or your local council service center.

You can earn:

Belt loops for learning about and participating in an Academics or Sports area.

Academics and Sports pins by earning the belt loop and then completing additional requirements that have you explore more about the academic or sport area you are working on.

bicycling

music

You can wear the belt loop on your navy blue uniform belt. Wear the pin on your ordinary clothes.

Some activity badges in this book ask you to earn a belt loop or pin: **Sportsman** requires two individual sports belt loops and two team sports belt loops. **Athlete** requires the Physical Fitness Sports pin. **Aquanaut** gives you a choice of earning the Swimming belt loop.

If your work on an activity badge requires you to earn an Academics or Sports belt loop or pin, previous work done as a Tiger Cub or Cub Scout won't count. You must earn the belt loop or pin again while you are a Webelos Scout for it to count toward the activity badge.

These activity badges give you the choice of earning (or require that you earn) a belt loop or pin: **Aquanaut:** Swimming; **Athlete:** Physical Fitness; **Artist:** Art; **Engineer:** Math; **Family Member:** Heritages; **Geologist:** Geology; **Naturalist:** Wildlife Conservation; **Scholar:** Language, Math, Chess; **Scientist:** Science, Weather, Astronomy; **Sportsman:** 2 individual sports, 2 team sports; **Traveler:** Geography, Map and Compass.

Cub Scouting's Leave No Trace Awareness Award

Leave No Trace is a program that helps you to be more concerned about your environment and learn to protect it for future generations. Leave No Trace applies in a backyard or local park (frontcountry) as much as it does in the wilderness (backcountry). Use page 73 to keep track of your progress.

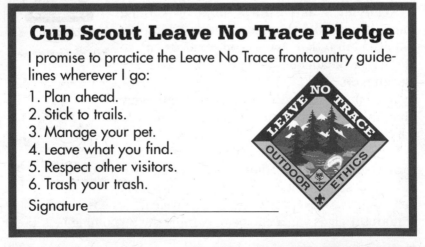

Cub Scout Leave No Trace Pledge

I promise to practice the Leave No Trace frontcountry guidelines wherever I go:

1. Plan ahead.
2. Stick to trails.
3. Manage your pet.
4. Leave what you find.
5. Respect other visitors.
6. Trash your trash.

Signature_____

Cub Scouting's
Leave No Trace Awareness
Award Requirements

Webelos den leader initials

1. Discuss with your leader or parent/guardian the importance of the Leave No Trace frontcountry guidelines. _____

2. On three separate outings, practice the frontcountry guidelines of Leave No Trace. _____

3. Earn the Outdoorsman activity badge. _____

4. Participate in a Leave No Trace–related service project. _____

5. Promise to practice the Leave No Trace frontcountry guidelines by signing the Cub Scout Leave No Trace Pledge. _____

6. Draw a poster to illustrate the Leave No Trace frontcountry guidelines and display it at a pack meeting. _____

Qualified to receive Cub Scouting's Leave No Trace Awareness Award:

Name _____

Date _____

Webelos den leader's signature _____

Earning Activity Badges

If you were in Cub Scouting before becoming a Webelos Scout, you had a chance to earn up to four badges of rank—Tiger Cub, Bobcat, Wolf, and Bear. You may also have earned Tiger Tracks, Arrow Points, and Progress Toward Ranks beads.

But as a Webelos Scout, you can earn many badges and awards! Most of the rest of this book gives you details about the 20 activity badges.

Activity badges are colorful metal emblems that you pin on your Webelos cap or Webelos colors. You can earn them by completing the requirements during den meetings and at home (with your den leader's approval).

Activity Badge Groups

All the instructions for earning activity badges are in this book. The 20 activity badges are divided into five groups.

Physical Skills			
✓Aquanaut	Athlete	✓Fitness*	Sportsman

Mental Skills			
Artist	Scholar	Showman	✓Traveler

Community			
✓Citizen*	Communicator	Family Member	✓Readyman**

Technology			
Craftsman	✓Engineer	Handyman	✓Scientist

Outdoor			
Forester	Geologist	✓Naturalist	Outdoorsman**

* Fitness and Citizen—Required for the Webelos badge
** Outdoorsman and Readyman—Required for the Arrow of Light Award

Activity Badge Tracking Chart

Aquanaut

Do all (three)
___1___2___3

Do any three
___4___5___6___7___8

Artist

Do both
___1___2

Do any five
___3___4___5___6___7___8___9___10___11

Athlete

Do all (five)
___1___2___3___4___5

Do any two
___6___7___8___9___10

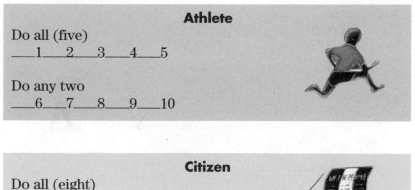

Citizen

Do all (eight)
___1___2___3___4___5___6___7___8

Do any two
___9___10___11___12___13___14___15___16___17

Communicator
Do any seven
___1___2___3___4___5___6___7___8
___9___10___11___12___13___14___15___16

Craftsman
Do all (four)
___1___2___3___4

Engineer
Do both
___1___2

Do any four
___3___4___5___6___7___8___9___10

Family Member
Do all (six)
___1___2___3___4___5___6

Do any two
___7___8___9___10___11___12___13

Fitness
Do this
___1

Do any six
___2___3___4___5___6___7___8

Forester
Do any five
___1___2___3___4___5___6___7___8___9___10

Geologist

Do any five
___1 ___2 ___3 ___4 ___5 ___6 ___7 ___8 ___9

Handyman

Do this
___1

Do any six
___2 ___3 ___4 ___5 ___6 ___7 ___8 ___9
___10 ___11 ___12 ___13 ___14 ___15 ___16 ___17

Naturalist

Do this
___1

Do any five
___2 ___3 ___4 ___5 ___6 ___7 ___8 ___9
___10 ___11 ___12 ___13

Outdoorsman

Do any two
___1 ___2 ___3 ___4

Do any five
___5 ___6 ___7 ___8 ___9 ___10 ___11 ___12

Readyman

Do all (eight)
___1 ___2 ___3 ___4 ___5 ___6 ___7 ___8

Do any two
___9 ___10 ___11 ___12 ___13 ___14 ___15

Scholar

Do this
___1

Do any three
___2___3___4___5___6___7___8

Do any three
___9___10___11___12___13

Scientist

Do all (four)
___1___2___3___4

Do any six
___5___6___7___8___9___10___11___12___13___14

Showman

Do six from any area (mark them below as well)

Do one not already done
Puppetry ___2___3___4___5___6___7

Do one not already done
Music ___8___9___10___11___12___13___14___15

Do one not already done
Drama ___16___17___18___19___20___21___22___23

Sportsman

Do all (four)
___1___2___3___4

Traveler

Do any five
___1___2___3___4___5___6___7
___8___9___10___11___12___13

On to the Adventure of Boy Scouting!

Adventure! That's what Boy Scouting is. You're standing at the doorway to the most exciting adventures you can imagine.

Step into the world of Boy Scouting, and you'll hike along trails, canoe across misty lakes, and camp under the open sky. Smell fresh rain in the woods and fill your mouth with the taste of wild strawberries. At the end of a patrol bike hike, plunge into a cool mountain lake. Cook your meals over a camp stove.

Travel the backcountry without leaving a trace and live well with only what you carry in your pockets and pack. Observe wildlife close up and study nature all around you.

Sound inviting? As a Boy Scout, you can do all this and more.

Scouting is also a doorway to friendship. Boys you know might be joining your troop, and you'll meet a lot of other Scouts along the way. Scouting is a worldwide brotherhood many millions strong. Almost anywhere you go, you'll find Scouts excited about the same activities you enjoy.

Want to learn skills you can use outdoors? Scouts know how to find their way with a map and compass, how to stay warm and dry in stormy weather, and how to give proper first aid. When you master important Scouting skills, you can teach others what you know. Everyone helping everyone else—that's part of Scouting, too.

People have always relied on Scouts to **Be Prepared** in times of need. Your troop leaders will show you meaningful ways to help your family, community, nation, and world. The acts of kindness you perform every day will improve the lives of others. In an emergency, you'll be ready to do whatever the situation requires.

Outdoor adventures, service projects, leadership in your patrol and troop—Scouting will give you experiences and responsibilities that will help you mature. The Scout Oath and the Scout Law provide the guidelines you need to become a strong, confident adult. The knowledge and attitudes you develop as a Scout will be with you the rest of your life.

And Scouting is fun. You can look around during Scouting activities and see everyone sharing and learning.

Are you ready to get in on all the fun that Scouts have? Do you want to enjoy the adventures and friendship of a troop and patrol? It's all up to you!

Becoming a Boy Scout

In order to become a Boy Scout, you must:

- Be a boy who has completed the fifth grade and is at least 10 years old, or is age 11, or has earned the Arrow of Light Award and is at least 10 years old but not yet 18.

- Find a Boy Scout troop you want to join. (It helps to visit troops in your area, and talk to the senior patrol leader or Scoutmaster while you're there.)

- Complete the requirements to join the Boy Scouts. (You already learned most of these to earn the Arrow of Light Award!)

Troops Visited

Troop	Location	Date	Time	Leader	Phone

Scoutmaster's conference to complete requirements needed to join Boy Scouts was held on (date) _____

I received my Arrow of Light Award on _____.

My graduation ceremony was conducted on _____.

Activity Badges

Physical Skills Group

A

Aquanaut
Requirements

Requirement   **Approved by**

Do these:

1. Jump into water over your head. Come to
   the surface and swim 100 feet, at least half
   of this using a backstroke.   _____DK_____

2. Stay in the water after the swim and float on
   your back and your front, and demonstrate
   survival floating.   _____DK_____

3. Put on a personal flotation device (PFD)
   that is the right size for you. Make sure it is
   properly fastened. Wearing the PFD, jump
   into water over your head. Show how the
   PFD keeps your head above water by swimming 25 feet. Get out of the water, remove
   the PFD, and hang it where it will dry.   _____DK_____

And do three of these:

4. Do a front surface dive and swim under
   water for four strokes before returning to
   the surface.   _____

5. Explain the four basic water rescue methods.
   Demonstrate reaching and throwing rescues. _____

6. With an adult on board, show that you know
   how to handle a rowboat.   _____

7. Pass the BSA "swimmer" test:

   • Jump feet-first into water over the head in
     depth, level off, and begin swimming.   _____DK_____

   • Swim 75 yards in a strong manner using
     one or more of the following strokes: side-
     stroke, breaststroke, trudgen, or crawl. _____DK_____

- Then swim 25 yards using an easy, resting backstroke. _____ DK
- After completing the swim, rest by floating. _____ DK

The 100 yards must be completed in one swim without stops and must include at least one sharp turn. _____ DK

8. While you are a Webelos Scout, earn the Cub Scout Sports belt loop for swimming. _____

A quanauts are people who are at home in and around the water. When you're an aquanaut, you enjoy the water, but you also respect it. You master the water skills you need.

Swimming, floating, snorkeling, water rescue, and boating are all skills of aquanauts.

Aquanauts know water can be dangerous. They know how to be safe in and on the water, and they never take foolish chances or break safety rules. They know that rules protect everyone. They help others enjoy the water safely and help them improve their skills.

So splash right in and become an aquanaut! The better you become at water skills, the more fun you'll have.

Are You an Aquanaut?

Practicing the skills for this activity badge will tell you whether you're an aquanaut. You'll enjoy trying them. If you can't do all of them right away, keep practicing. You'll improve all the time. The aquanaut activity badge will help you get ready for more challenging aquatics activities in Boy Scouting.

When you complete each requirement, ask your Webelos den leader or Aquanaut activity badge counselor to initial it on the previous page or this page.

Have Fun—Be Safe

Swimming and boating are lots of fun. The water skills you learn now can lead to even greater adventure as you grow up.

You'll be safe around water if you understand its dangers, always follow safety rules, and improve your swimming and boating skills.

Swimming Safety

Can you swim now? How far can you swim? And how deep is the water where you want to swim? The answers to these questions will help you swim where the water is safest for you.

- **If you can't swim,** stay in water that is not more than 3½ feet deep.
- **If you can swim 50 feet,** you may go in water that is 6 feet deep but you may not go more than 25 feet from shore.
- **If you can swim 100 yards or more,** you may swim in water that is more than 6 feet deep but you may not go more than 50 yards from shore.

Make plans to improve your swimming ability with adult supervision. Swim only when a lifeguard or an adult who is a skilled swimmer is along.

Always Swim With a Buddy

Swimming with a buddy is good common sense for people of all ages. You and your buddy can help each other if either of you gets into trouble in the water. And you'll both improve your swimming skills by making a game of practicing. The buddy system is used for all swimming in Scouting. (See "Safe Swimming" in the Readyman activity badge section, pages 384–385.)

Be Fit for Swimming

Have a fitness checkup with your family physician. If you don't have any health problems, you can practice swimming more confidently.

Rules on the waterfront protect you. Check a "Do" or "Don't" on each line to make the rules read correctly:

☐ DO ☐ DON'T swim with adult supervision.

☐ DO ☐ DON'T show off in the water.

☐ DO ☐ DON'T dive into unfamiliar or shallow waters.

☐ DO ☐ DON'T go swimming right after strenuous physical activity.

Aquanauts Are Skilled Swimmers

Aquanauts learn several different swim strokes. Each stroke has its purpose. You can learn all of them with the help of a swimming coach or teacher. Follow the pictures and directions for the right way to do the elementary backstroke, sidestroke, and crawl.

Floating on Your Back

Most boys can float on their backs. About one in 20 can't float unless he moves his arms and legs. See if you can float without moving.

Start by arching your back. Take a deep breath and hold it. Put your head back until your ears are in the water. Slowly put your arms out with palms up.

If you're a floater, your body will rise slowly to the surface. When you take a breath, do it fast to keep your lungs full of air. Try to float with as little motion as possible for one minute.

Elementary Backstroke

Start by floating on your back, arms at your sides. Keep your eyes looking down toward your feet, over the surface of the water.

Bring your cupped hands up over your chest to your shoulders. At the same time, drop your heels downward. They should be beneath your knees.

Turn your toes outward and swing your feet outward in a circular motion without stopping. At the same time, reach your arms straight out. Then sweep them down to your sides as your legs come together in a straight-out position, with toes pointed. The arm pull and leg kick happen at the same time.

You should end up the same way you were at the start.

Sidestroke

Lie on your side with one ear in the water. Stretch your bottom arm out ahead of you. Your top arm is at your side, along your leg.

Start with your feet together, and then bend your knees, pulling your heels toward your hips.

Cup your reaching hand a little. Sweep it down in front of your chest.

Move your feet apart by moving your top leg forward and your bottom leg backward.

Notice the hand and arm movement. As your lower hand pushes down, your upper hand moves toward your chest. They nearly meet.

When your legs are as far apart as possible, snap them together quickly as if closing a pair of scissors.

Your upper hand is pushing down. Your lower hand is reaching out ahead of you, returning to its starting position.

Stop your feet as they come together. Repeat arm and leg movements.

Crawl Stroke

Float face down in the water with your arms and legs extended.

Move your legs up and down. Press down on the water with the top of your foot. (This is called the *flutter kick*.)

Still kicking, pull downward with your right arm. Breathe out through your nose and mouth while your face is in the water.

As your right-arm stroke ends, begin a stroke with your left arm. Raise your face by turning your head to the right so you can breathe in through your mouth.

Reach ahead again with your right arm. At the end of the left-arm stroke, begin a new one with the right arm. Turn your face under water again to breathe out.

Keep strokes and leg kicks even.

The crawl stroke is a fast way to swim, but it's tiring. It's great for racing and for swimming a short distance.

Surface Dive

Float face down with your arms out ahead of you. Sweep your arms back toward your hips.

At the same time, bend forward sharply at the hips. Aim the top part of your body toward the bottom.

Turn your hands palms down. Push them toward the bottom. Raise your legs above the surface as high as you can.

Your head will be pointing downward. The weight of your legs in the air above the water will drive you down.

Swim underwater for four strokes before coming to the top again.

Swimming Underwater

Never overbreathe (hyperventilate) before swimming underwater. Take regular breaths. Whenever you feel you want to breathe while underwater, do so right away by coming to the surface and lifting your face out of the water. Then you won't be taking a chance on blacking out for lack of oxygen.

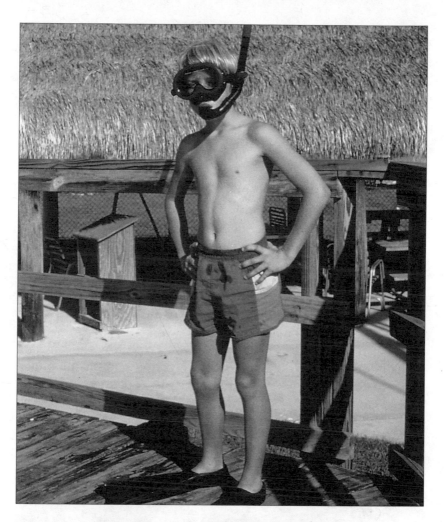

Aquanauts See More
When Snorkeling

There's a way you can move about the surface with your face underwater, see the scene beneath you, and still breathe. How? Use a snorkel. Would you like to become a "snorkeler?"—learn to use a face mask, a snorkel, and swim fins? First, you must be a good swimmer. You must be able to surface dive and swim underwater.

The Mask

Your vision is blurred underwater by the water against your eyes. A face mask puts air in front of your eyes, which helps you see clearly.

A good mask should cover only your eyes and nose. As a test, when you're out of the water, hold the mask to your

face without using the head strap. Take a breath through your nose. When you do this, a mask that fits well will cling to your face. The window should be safety glass, with a metal band to hold the glass tightly in place.

When you go underwater with a face mask, it may fog over. To minimize fogging, spit on the glass and rub the spit around. Then rinse the glass before you put on your mask.

Try out your face mask in shallow water. When you need to breathe, raise your head from the water and breathe through your mouth. This is the only way to breathe when using a face mask by itself. Your view of the underwater scene will be interrupted each time you take a breath.

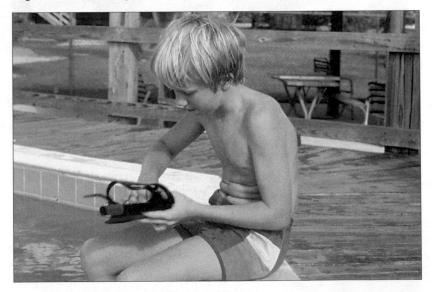

The Snorkel

The snorkel is a J-shaped tube with a soft rubber end that fits in your mouth. You breathe through your mouth, through the tube that reaches upward above the surface of the water.

When you use a snorkel, put it inside the headband of your mask. It should slope backward. Adding a snorkel should not break the seal between your face and the mask. Hold the mouthpiece in your mouth. Blow out before you breathe through your snorkel. Breathe only at the surface. Feel the back of your head to see whether the tube is out of the water. If it is, you can breathe through it.

Swim Fins

You can swim faster with swim fins. There are several kinds. Some have heel straps, and others have full foot pockets. The fins with heel straps fit any foot because you can adjust the size of the straps. The fins with pockets cost more and must be fitted to your feet. They can't be too tight or too loose. They protect your feet like shoes when you walk on sharp rocks.

With fins, your feet have more surface area in the water, giving you the swimming advantage a fish has with its tail and fins. Use slow, easy flutter kicks, keeping your knees well bent. This will move you through the water at a good speed. Don't work too hard at first. Your legs will tire quickly. Train slowly and build your ability until you can use the fins for a longer time.

Snorkeling = Swimming on the Surface

When you swim, your body is at the surface. Looking through your mask and breathing through your snorkel, you swim with your eyes and thoughts directed below. Unless you're a good swimmer, don't dive under. When you become skilled at swimming and snorkeling on the surface, you may wish to learn the sport of skin diving, which is underwater exploration using a mask and fins but not the snorkel. Then you can see many more wonderful underwater sights.

Safe Snorkeling

While snorkeling, stay near your buddy at all times. Wise aquanauts obey the chief point of all aquatic safety:

Never swim alone!
Always use the buddy system!

Aquanauts Know Water Rescue Methods

Webelos Scouts are not expected to do the rescue work of a trained adult. Still, they should know some simple rescues. You might save a person in trouble when no one else is around.

But remember, swimming rescues are for trained older people. Swimmers need to be strong and know exactly what to do to rescue someone. Therefore, never try a water rescue by swimming if you can do it another way.

The safest ways are

Reach!

Throw!

Row!

Go, with support!

An order of rescues has been determined to help boys learn safe, effective water rescues. Although Webelos Scouts only do the first two methods in water rescues, you need to be aware of all four methods. The first two methods are the easiest and safest techniques, because they do not require any swimming.

1. **REACH** toward the person in the water with whatever is available or at hand. For instance, you can use your hand or foot, a tree branch, a canoe paddle, or a towel.

2. **THROW** a line, a buoy, or a floating object (like a beach ball) to the person, to provide support.

3. **ROW** in a watercraft to the victim. A rowing rescue can only be made by a "swimmer" and one who can handle the boat. A PFD must be worn.

4. **GO, with support.** Those who "go" to the victim and make a swimming rescue must be trained in Swimming and Lifesaving. In these rare instances, when a swimming rescue must be tried, the swimmer takes with him something that can be used for flotation or can be extended to the victim to avoid direct contact.

In any water rescue, the Webelos Scout should never put himself in danger or at risk. If reaching and throwing don't work, GET HELP!

Aquanauts Are Safe Boaters

Whenever aquanauts use a rowboat, a canoe, or any other type of water craft, they keep in mind being safe and the safe ways of handling their craft.

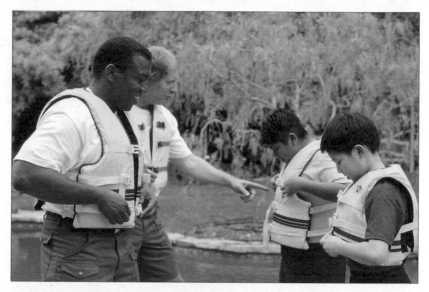

Personal Flotation Devices

Webelos Scouts participating in boating activities must use a Type I, Type II, or Type III personal flotation device (PFD). The Type I PFD provides the most buoyancy. It can be used in open, rough, or remote waters. The Type II and Type III PFDs will help keep a person in a vertical or slightly backward position in the water. They are recommended for water sports and close-to-shore operations on lakes and ponds. The BSA recommends using the Type I PFD.

Boating Safety Rules

- Know your boat—don't overload it. In a rowboat, one person per seat is a good rule.

- Put on a PFD before getting into the boat. Everyone should wear a PFD when in a boat less than 20 feet long. In some states, it's the law.

- Balance your load. Divide weight evenly from side to side and from bow (front) to stern (back).

- Step into the center of the boat when boarding or changing seats, and always keep low.

- If your boat tips over or fills with water, hang on. You can kick the boat to shore or drift in, but don't leave it. Let help come to you.

- Watch the weather. Head for shore if it begins to look bad. If you're caught on the water in bad weather, seat your passengers on the floor of the boat. Have everyone in the craft sit as low as possible. Head your boat into the waves.

- If you use a motor when boating with your family, use one that is appropriate for the boat. Too much power can damage your boat or even swamp it. Look on the boat for the capacity plate. It shows how many people the boat should hold and the recommended horsepower for the motor.

- Sharp turns are dangerous, so take it easy.

- Keep a lookout for other boaters and for swimmers.

Cub Scout Sports Participation

Recognition for Swimming

If you earned the Swimming belt loop earlier in Cub Scouting, great!

But that won't count for Aquanaut requirement 8. For requirement 8, you must earn the Swimming belt loop while you are a Webelos Scout. It should be fun—and easy, too.

swimming

A

Artist
Requirements

Requirement

Approved by

1. Talk to an artist in your area or to your art teacher about the different occupations in the art field. Make a list of them. _____

2. Create a scrapbook (portfolio) of your Artist activity badge projects and show it to your den leader. _____

And do five of these:

3. Draw or paint an original picture out-of-doors, using the art materials you prefer. Frame the picture for your room or home. _____

4. List the primary and secondary colors. Explain what happens when you combine colors. _____

5. Using a computer, make six original designs using straight lines, curved lines, or both. _____

6. Draw a profile of a member of your family. _____

7. Use clay to sculpt a simple subject. _____

8. Make a mobile, using your choice of materials. _____

9. Make an art construction, using your choice of materials. _____

10. Create a collage that expresses something about you. _____

11. While you are a Webelos Scout, earn the Cub Scout Academics belt loop for Art. _____

Paints, brushes, crayons, clay. Soft colors, bright and dark ones. Shapes you haven't tried before. When you create a work of art, you stir up a fascinating mixture of materials and ideas.

Making art is a constant experiment. You try many ways of working. Your art is like no one else's because you are unique. So are your ideas and your vision of the world around you.

Art is about making your ideas visible and even changing them as you work. It's also about playing with materials until an idea takes hold. You'll go your own individual way on this badge. When you complete each requirement, ask your Webelos den leader or activity badge counselor to sign it on page 102.

Create a Scrapbook

As you work on projects for the Artist activity badge, you can make a record of your finished projects in a scrapbook. (Professional artists call this a *portfolio*.) Some projects, such as drawings or paintings, might go straight into the scrapbook. You could add sketches or photographs of other projects, such as sculptures or mobiles. Besides the fun you'll have making your scrapbook, when you show it to your Webelos den leader, you will have completed requirement 2!

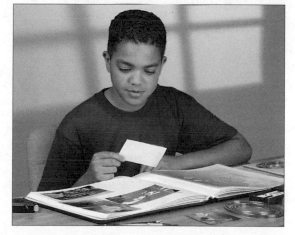

Choosing a Medium

An artist chooses a *medium* to use in creating a work of art. Watercolor paint is a medium. Pencil is a medium. So is clay. A computer is a medium. The medium is whatever you use to make art.

When you combine two or more materials, you are using *mixed media*. (*Media* means more than one *medium*.) An example of mixed media would be using crayon for the lines of a drawing and then brushing watercolor paint into some areas.

As you work on the Artist activity badge, you'll experiment with several media.

What Will It Be?

You decide what to draw or paint. The choices are endless. Ideas could come from thinking about your family, celebrations, vacations, a pet, playing basketball with friends, or anything else. Just standing outside and looking at your house or apartment building or neighborhood could give you ideas. The view from a window could give you a starting point. Something you remember or wish for could go into your drawing or painting.

A work of art doesn't have to look exactly like your actual house or your friends or your dog. It's your own personal expression, not an exact likeness. You could even decide to create a mystery of shapes, lines, and colors that makes everyone guess what it is, and each person will have a different guess.

Drawing

You could draw something from your imagination, like a dinosaur, or you could draw while you look at your subject: a person, a house, or a collection of items on a tabletop—that's called a *still life*.

A simple still life setup might include a mug, an apple, and a cereal box, to give you different shapes to draw. Or gather a few of your favorite things together.

Whether your subject is a cup or a person, notice the form—how the subject is shaped. Imagine the whole form, even the part around the back that you can't see. If you want to, you can use light pencil lines to sketch the general shapes first, as a guide.

Look for shadowed areas and see if you can shade them in. Light, medium, and dark areas help show the form, so the subject won't look flat. If you're using color, you can apply the color more heavily in the shadows and make it thinner in the light places.

Media

Some ideas for drawing media:

- Pencil
- Ink (black and other colors)
- Crayon
- Marker (fine or broad-tipped)
- Oil pastels

With pencil and ink, a fairly smooth paper gives you clean lines. With crayons and markers, use either smooth or rougher-textured paper for different effects.

Drawing a Profile

A profile is a side view of a person. Try drawing one of a member of your family.

Note the shape of the subject's head and sketch that in first. Then start adding features.

If you have trouble drawing a profile, try this. Tape your drawing paper to a wall. Ask your subject to stand in front of the paper. Then shine a bright light on him or her. The shadow will outline the profile and you can trace it.

Painting

Media

Some choices for painting (these paints clean up with soap and water):

Watercolor paint. Watercolor comes as a set in a box. Perhaps you use a set like this at school or have one at home. You can use this kind of paint for your painting. Watercolor in separate tubes or in kits is more expensive. Paint on drawing paper or watercolor paper. Watercolor paper is more expensive but also more absorbent.

Tempera paint or poster color is liquid and dries quickly. It comes in small bottles or large squeeze bottles. Paint on manila paper or heavy white drawing paper.

Acrylic paint. "School acrylic" comes in large squeeze bottles. Acrylic paint in tubes is thicker and more expensive. Paint on canvas board or heavy paper.

Because of the cost of tempera and acrylic paints, it's probably more thrifty to do this kind of painting as a den project. The cost of the paint squeeze bottles can be shared.

Comparing paint: With tempera and acrylic, you can paint over areas you want to change. Watercolor won't hide a color you've already painted, but it lets the white of the paper shine through, adding light to the color.

Compare paint prices. To start, you need only red, yellow, blue, black, and white. You can mix other colors from these. (See the color wheel on page 110.) If you buy a paint kit, it may include more than the basic colors.

Brushes: Inexpensive brushes with synthetic bristles will work for tempera or acrylic. (For acrylic, you must have synthetic bristles because the paint will ruin natural hair bristles.) Watercolor brushes are softer, and camel hair is the least expensive. It's helpful to have at least two sizes of brushes—one for larger areas and one for detail.

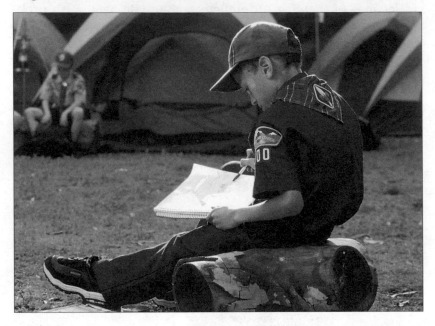

Maybe you have other art materials on hand. You decide what to use. Remember, you can combine drawing and painting materials in one picture.

Supplies

- A mixing palette or tray. You can use a large plastic lid from a food container for tube acrylics. For tempera, school acrylics, and watercolor, which are more runny, use several jar lids or buy an inexpensive plastic paint tray with wells for colors.

- For tube acrylics: a palette knife (a flexible mixing tool). For the other paints, mix colors with your brush.
- A sturdy water container for rinsing paint from brushes before using another color. (Change water often.)
- A sponge for pressing excess water from brush before dipping in paint.
- Rags for spills.

Cleanup: Make cleanup easy. If possible, work at a table with a washable surface. Before you start, cover it with layers of newspaper to protect it.

When you stop, wash brushes promptly with soap and warm water. Store them with bristles up, in a jar, can, or mug. Wash and dry all tools.

The Color Wheel and Mixing Paint

The *primary colors* are red, yellow, and blue. The secon*dary colors* are orange, green, and violet.

Look at the color wheel on the next page. You mix yellow and blue (primary colors) to make green (a secondary color). Green is on the wheel halfway between yellow and blue. If you add more yellow, you get a yellow-green. If you add more blue instead, you get a blue-green.

If you want a red-orange, you can use the wheel to find out which primary colors it lies between—red and yellow.

Using the wheel, you can find out which primary colors to use to mix the other colors.

You can use a small amount of white to lighten a color you've mixed, or black to darken it. Or try adding only water to get a

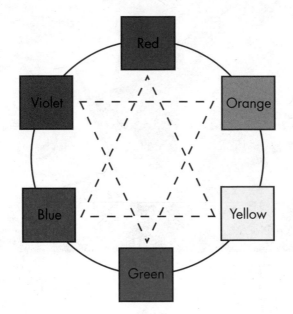

pale color. For brown, experiment with combinations of red, yellow, and blue. Try adding a little black.

If you're not sure about a color you've mixed, try it first on a piece of scrap paper. The more you paint, the more you'll remember about mixing colors.

Art supply stores sell paints in many colors. After working with the primary colors, you may decide to buy a few other colors to see what they're like.

Experiment!

You can use a brush in different ways. You know you can use it for lines, details, and larger areas of color. A wet brush makes a different pattern than a mostly dry brush. Discover other marks and textures you can make by holding the brush differently. Lay it flat, so it makes a mark the shape of its bristles. Touch the tip of it to the paper and see if it leaves a dot or a texture.

You can use tools other than brushes. A sponge dipped in paint adds texture. A string dragged through paint and pressed down on the paper or canvas leaves a line. Crumpled paper dipped in paint makes interesting patterns.

Making a Frame

You don't have to buy a frame for your drawing or painting. Make one instead. Here are three simple kinds of frames to make.

Tape or glue your picture to a piece of cardboard that is about 1 inch bigger all around than the picture. (Use glue only on the edges so the paper won't buckle.) From a second piece of cardboard, cut out the frame. Glue that to the back cardboard.

If you have a woodworking shop, you can make a wood frame.

An old weathered board makes a good frame. You have to sand the board very smooth in the area where the picture will be glued.

Two pieces of heavy cardboard

Cut frame to fit picture.

Simple wood frame with mitered corners

Glue picture on weathered board.

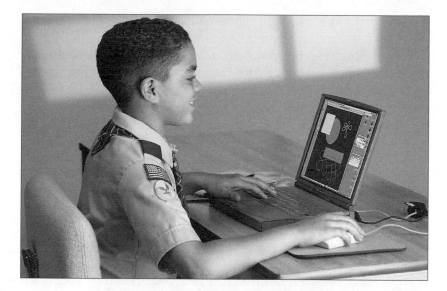

Computer Designs

When artists create designs, they think about shape, line, color, placement, the feeling they want to convey, and more.

If you do requirement 5, you'll create original designs using a computer drawing program. You'll use straight lines or curved lines or a combination of both. You could try arrangements of thin lines or marks, or use lines to make shapes that you leave empty or fill with color.

The result probably won't look like any object in the real world, although you might have been thinking about an ocean wave, a storm, a birthday party, or traveling through outer space. Sometimes a design expresses a feeling. We don't know what was on the artist's mind, but the design might make us think of a happy time, or a peaceful night, or an adventure.

Your designs can be as simple or as complicated as you want. Have fun and experiment with the drawing and painting "tools" and colors you can use. Learn how to move pieces of the design until the arrangement on the screen pleases you and feels right to you. Save and print your designs.

Sculpture

When you have a piece of clay in your hands, what happens? You squeeze it, twist it, pull it, roll it, and shape it. You are sculpting. Some sculptors say this is like "thinking with your hands."

What will you make? It could be the figure of a person, or just the head and neck. It could be an animal or a fantastic creature no one has ever seen before. You could even sculpt your own design of a futuristic car. You decide.

Media

Plasteline, a commercial modeling clay, is oily and plastic, meaning you can shape it. It never dries out. It works easily when kept at room temperature.

If you stop working, put the sculpture away until you can return to it. You'll find it is still soft and ready to be worked. Plasteline costs more than natural clay in the beginning. But you'll save money in the long run because you can use it again and again.

Moist clay comes from the earth. It can be worked easily when damp. As it dries, it becomes stiffer and is good for detail work. Because natural clay does dry out, it must be kept covered when not being worked. Use wet cloths and a plastic bag. If it dries out, you can soak it and knead it until it becomes soft again.

Self-hardening clay is a prepared clay. It costs more than the moist kind. It is as easily worked, as long as it is kept wet and soft. It is self-drying and becomes very hard. When it has dried, it cannot be softened for reuse.

Tools

Your best tools for working clay are your fingers, but some-times another tool comes in handy. Try these:

- Dull kitchen knife for cutting clay
- Tongue depressor or craft stick for detail work and smoothing
- Homemade modeling tool (See instructions below.)

Dull Knife

Craft Stick

Hairpin or Paper Clip→

⅜"

Modeling Tool

Make a modeling tool with a wooden dowel for a handle. Shape a hairpin or paper clip and attach it to the dowel by wrapping with thread. Coat the thread with model cement.

Sculpting a Head

When you start sculpting, make the head small, about 3 or 4 inches wide. This size takes less clay, but it's large enough for you to be able to work on detail.

Work in a well-lighted room. Your workbench or table should be solid. The clay should be at eye level. Do this by sitting on a low chair or stool. Or put your clay on a box on top of your workbench.

Work in a place that is easy to clean. Clay dropped on a good floor or rug leaves stains.

How to Get Started

1. Make a support. Use a 1-inch dowel 12 inches long. Have an adult drill a 1-inch hole in the center of a 6-by-6-inch block of wood.

2. Start putting clay on and around the dowel stick. Build up an egg shape about 3 to 4 inches wide.

3. Push in the eye spaces with your thumbs.

4. Note the shape of a normal head. Most beginners forget the forehead and back of the head.

5. Add bits of clay to build up the chin, nose, neck, brows, hair, and ears.

6. Refine lips, eyes, and shape of the head.

You can change clay while it is soft—take a pinch off here, add a little more there. Turn your work around and look at it from the top, sides, back, and front.

Mobiles: Sculpture in Motion

A *mobile* (MO-beel) is a hanging sculpture. It has many lightweight parts hanging from arms that move in the slightest breeze.

Making a mobile is a matter of thinking of a design, creating the parts, and balancing them as you put the mobile together.

What will your mobile be? It could be about your favorite sport—or someone else's favorite sport if the mobile is to be a gift. It could have butterflies or imaginary insects flying from it. It could simply have curious shapes of things that no one can identify. Draw a simple plan so you know how many hanging items to make. They can be different sizes.

You'll need: Several metal wire clothes hangers, heavy thread or lightweight string, flexible wire (the kind that comes on spools in craft shops), materials for making the hanging items (see below). Tools: wire cutters, pliers, a hammer or a vise.

To make the designs you'll suspend from the arms: Use cardboard, foil, thin wood, metal, or any lightweight material. You can add color to the designs if you wish.

Finding the balance point:

- You're going to make a hole at the top of each design so you can hang it. If you want the design to hang level like the designs in the fishing mobile pictured, you need to find the balance point—the right place to make the hole. Push a pin through the top of the design and hold onto the pin. The design should be loose on the pin so it can move. If your design takes a nosedive, this isn't the balance point. Move the pin until you find the balance point.

- Punch or drill a hole at the balance point. This is where the thread or string goes that will fasten your design to an arm of the mobile.

Making the wire arms:

- Use coat hanger wire for the arms. With wire cutters, cut one length each of 12 inches, 19 inches, 24 inches, and 25 inches.

- Straighten each wire arm by hammering or pressing in a vise. Then bend it into a smooth arc.

- With pliers, bend up about ½ inch from each end, making a right angle.

Putting the mobile together:

- Make a mobile from the bottom up.

- Hang a design on each end of one wire arm.

- Tie a thread or string to the center of the wire arm and slide it until the two designs balance. Make a loop in the top end of this thread. With the flexible spool wire, make a small ring through this loop.

- Slip the ring over the end of a second wire arm. Fasten another design to the other end of this second wire.

- Find the balance point of the second arm as you did for the first one by attaching a thread and sliding it. Again, make a thread loop at the top of the thread and add a ring made of spool wire.

- Add the other wire arms and designs to the mobile. You may decide to move items and rebalance arms. When it's right, bend the ends of the wire arms to keep the designs in place.

- Hang the top of the mobile from fishing line, kite string, or other strong string.

Constructions

Constructions are fun. You "build" a sculpture, using all sorts of objects. For the base, start with a handful of clay or a piece of wood.

Collect odds and ends you'd like to combine. These might be scrap items, things you've saved, things no one wants. Ideas: tongue depressors, ice cream sticks, toothpicks, bits of wood; buttons, cloth, yarn, spools, string; plastic spoons, forks, and knives; wire, chicken wire, screen wire, pipe cleaners, chenille stems, corks; straws, keys, bottle caps, egg cartons (you can cut shapes from them); seed pods, pinecones, nuts, sticks, seashells.

Clay Base

Start with your base. Experiment. You might begin by pushing a stick or a wire into the clay. Then add items to the construction; change them around; figure out how to attach things and link them together.

Wood Base

- Drill holes in the base the right size to hold any sticks or wires you want to use for main supports. Insert ends. For wire, a slight bend just above the base will help hold it in place.

- Add items; try connecting parts of the construction by crisscrossing with yarn, wire, or string. With flexible materials, try bending and twisting them. Experiment until the design pleases you.

Collages

Collage (co-LAZH) is a French word. A collage is a work of art made by gluing materials to a surface.

How do you make a collage that expresses something about yourself? It could include a small photo of yourself and pictures out of magazines that show a sport you like, your favorite food, or a place you dream of visiting. Maybe you've saved the ticket stubs after going to a movie. Maybe you have something with your name on it, like the envelope from a letter addressed to you, a photo of your family, a photo of a pet, anything you decide on.

Start with a blank poster board or a big piece of cardboard. Collect the items you want to use. Anything made of paper works well, although you can use other materials.

Arrange things on the poster board and move them around. A collage is a very casual thing—you can do whatever looks good to you. You can tilt and overlap items. You can cut your paper items in shapes you want or use them as they are. For added color, cut or tear pieces of colored paper or scraps of gift wrap and slip them in. Try to cover all or most of the surface of the poster board.

When you're ready to glue everything in place, use a glue stick that won't make ripples in the paper items when you glue them on. If you feel like your collage needs some finishing touches, consider cutting words from magazines or writing or drawing in a few places.

If you want to frame your collage, look for a simple poster frame made of a backing, a sheet of clear acrylic, and clips that hold everything together. This will work if your collage is flat, but not if you've glued anything bulky to it.

Cub Scout Academics
Belt Loop for Art

If you earned the Art belt loop earlier in Cub Scouting, great! But that won't count for requirement 11 of this Artist activity badge. You must earn the Art belt loop again while you are a Webelos Scout for it to count toward this activity badge.

art

Athlete Requirements

Requirement	Approved by

Do these:

1. With your parent, guardian, or Webelos den leader, complete the Perseverance Character Connection.

   a. **Know:** Review the requirements and decide which ones might be more difficult for you to do. Make a plan to complete one of the harder requirements. _____

   b. **Commit:** When doing the harder requirement, did you ever feel frustrated or angry? What did perseverance have to do with that? Name another type of task for which you will need to persevere. _____

   c. **Practice:** Practice perseverance by following your plan to do that requirement for the Athlete activity badge. _____

2. Explain what it means to be physically and mentally healthy. _____

3. Explain what you as a Webelos Scout can to do stay physically and mentally healthy. _____

4. Every time you work on requirement 5 below, start with at least 5 minutes of stretching warm-up activities. _____

5. Do as many as you can of the following and record your results. Show improvement in all of the activities after 30 days.

   a. Have another person hold your feet down while you do as many curl-ups as you can. _____

b. Do as many pull-ups from a bar as you can. _____

c. Do as many push-ups from the ground or floor as you can. _____

d. Do a standing long jump as far as you can. _____

e. Do a quarter-mile run or walk. _____

And do two of these:

6. Do a vertical jump and improve your reach in 30 days. _____

7. Do a 50-yard dash as fast as you can, and show a decrease in time over a 30-day period. _____

8 Ride a bike 1 mile as fast as you can, and show a decrease in time over a 30-day period. _____

9. Swim a quarter mile in a pool or lake as fast as you can, and show a decrease in time over a 30-day period. _____

10. While you are a Webelos Scout, earn the Cub Scout Sports Physical Fitness pin. _____

Strength and good health are important to you now for sports and games. They'll be important to you all your life.

Athletes know that a good training program includes exercises that build strength and endurance. Endurance means the ability to keep going in a race or in playing a sport.

See how much you can improve in each area over a 30-day period. The more you work on each skill, the more you will improve and the higher your rating should be. As you improve, this means you're growing stronger.

Keep a record of all your scores.

When you complete each requirement, ask your Webelos den leader or activity badge counselor to initial it on the previous page or this page.

Staying Physically
and Mentally Healthy

When your body feels good and you aren't sick, you are physically healthy. This means your body is strong and resists diseases. To stay physically healthy, take care of your body, exercise often, and get lots of rest. Eat balanced meals, with the right amounts of grains (whole-grain bread, cereal, rice, and pasta), fruits, vegetables, milk products, and foods rich in protein. (See the Food Guide Pyramid on page 249.)

Being physically healthy and exercising can make you feel good, and feel good about yourself. Physical health and exercise can help you be mentally healthy and help you feel less stress. When you are mentally healthy, you can be happier, enjoy being with other people, and deal with change and other difficult situations more easily.

Cub Scout Sports Pin
for Physical Fitness

If you've earned the Physical Fitness Sports pin earlier in Cub Scouting, you must earn another Physical Fitness Sports pin as a Webelos Scout for requirement 10.

Ask your Webelos den leader to get you a copy of the requirements for the Physical Fitness Sports pin from the *Cub Scout Academics and Sports Program Guide.* You'll find that to earn the pin you need to complete five of nine requirements. The requirements include such things as understanding the Food Guide Pyramid and tracking the foods you eat in a week, setting up and following an exercise program for two weeks, and visiting a local gym and talking to a trainer about exercises for young people. You'll find that you can learn a lot about physical fitness while you also have fun!

Exercise the Right Way

Before you begin the following exercises, do stretching exercises to limber up your muscles. You can learn about good stretching exercises by checking out a book from the library, reading about warming up exercises on the Web, or talking to a physical education instructor.

You can keep track of your improvement on the Athlete Record on page 132.

Curl-Ups

Starting Position: Lie on your back with your legs bent and feet flat on the floor. Cross your arms over your chest. Have a partner hold your ankles to keep your feet on the floor and count each curl-up.

Action: Sit up and touch your elbows to your thighs. Return to the starting position.

Count one curl-up each time you go back to the starting position. See how many you can do in one minute.

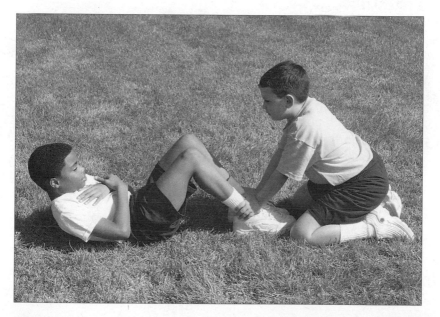

Pull-Ups

Equipment: Use a bar high enough and easy to grip.

Starting Position: Hold the bar with your thumbs facing one another. Hang with your arms and legs fully out and feet not touching the floor.

Action: Pull your body up with your arms until your chin is over the bar. Then lower your body until your arms are straight.

Rules: The pull must not be a snap movement. Don't raise your knees or kick your legs. Don't let your body swing. If this happens, your partner should stop the motion. Count one pull-up each time you place your chin over the bar.

Push-Ups

Starting Position: Lie face down on the ground or floor. Put your hands on the ground beside your shoulders.

Action: Push up with your arms, keeping your back and legs as straight as possible. Then lower your body and touch your chest to the ground. Repeat as many times as you can.

Rules: For each push-up, your body must be straight and your arms must be extended full length. Count one push-up each time your chest touches the ground.

Standing Long Jump

Equipment: You will need a level surface and a tape measure.

Starting Position: Stand with your feet apart and your toes just behind the starting line. Prepare to jump by bending your knees and swinging your arms back and forth.

Action: Jump, swinging your arms ahead and upward hard. Take off from the balls of your feet.

Rules: Three jumps are allowed. Distance is measured

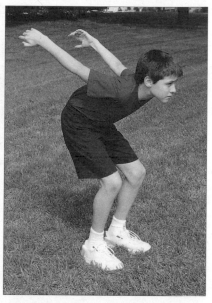

from the starting line to the place nearest the starting line that your body touches. Record the best of the three jumps.

Vertical Jump

Equipment: Chalk and a ruler or tape measure

Starting Position: Stand next to a wall with your feet flat on the floor. With the chalk in your hand, reach as high as you can and make a mark.

Action: Now jump as high as you can and make a mark above the first one. Your score is the number of inches between the two marks.

50-Yard Dash

Starting Position: Stand behind the starting line. The starter will be at the finish with a stopwatch. He will raise one hand before giving the starting signal.

Action: The starter lowers his hand and hits the side of his leg. This is the signal to start. As you cross the finish line, your time is noted.

Rules: The score is the time between the starter's signal and the instant you cross the finish line.

Quarter-Mile Run or Walk

Starting Position: Stand behind the starting line.

Action: On the signal "Ready-Go!" begin running.

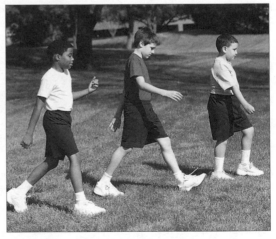

Rules: You can run or walk. However, you want to cover the distance in the shortest possible time. Record your time in minutes and seconds. Don't try to set a record the first time out. Practice each day and slowly build up your pace. Remember, you can walk.

A regular football field can be used for both running tests. The 50-yard dash would cover half the field between the goal lines. The quarter-mile run or walk would be four lengths of the field, plus the distance from a goal line to the 40-yard line.

1-Mile Bicycle Ride

For your 1-mile bicycle ride, if you have a bicycle, you may use it; otherwise, perhaps your den leader can provide a bicycle for you to use. Before your ride, review Bicycle Safety on page 386.

With your den leader, lay out a course that begins and ends at the same place. The course should be in a low-traffic area such as a park or on school or church grounds.

Each rider should complete the course individually. The ride may not be a race between members of your Webelos den, but should be an opportunity for each Webelos Scout to do his best.

Quarter-Mile Swim

Before making your quarter-mile swim, review the Aquanaut activity badge on pages 83–100.

Athlete Progress Record for Requirements 4–9

Name _____

Pack _____ Medical checkup date _____

Week	1	2	3	4	5
Date					
Minutes of stretching warm-up activities					
Curl-ups (number)					
Pull-ups (number)					
Push-ups (number)					
Standing long jump (distance)					
Quarter-mile run or walk (time)					
Vertical jump (height)					
50-yard dash (time)					
1-mile bicycle ride (time)					
Quarter-mile swim (time)					

Exercises to Make You Strong

Exercising can be fun, whether you're by yourself or with a friend. Webelos Scouts should exercise at least 20 minutes two or three times a week.

The exercises shown on these pages need little or no equipment. You can do them at home. Active games, sports, swimming, hobbies calling for action, and home chores will strengthen you, too.

Paper Crunch: This will build strong hands and fingers. Squeezing sticks, rocks, or sponge balls; and rowing boats will also develop your hands.

Biceps Builder: Push up with the right hand and arm. Push down with the left hand at the same time. Hold as you count to 10. Repeat five times for each arm.

Trunk Stretch: Strengthens the back and stretches the chest muscles. Lie face down with your hands at the back of the neck and elbows out. Raise your head and chest and hold.

Walking: Considered a perfect aerobic exercise. *Aerobic* means it helps your body use oxygen and it improves your heart and lungs. Aerobic exercise, such as walking, running, and swimming, increases your endurance and fitness. It helps prevent heart disease.

Stretcher: Done best in slow motion. Curl up your body slowly from a flat-on-your-back position until your knees touch your chin. Count to five. Return to the starting position.

All the Way: Strengthens stomach muscles for tough jobs. Lie back on the floor, with your hands above your head. With your arms and legs straight, raise your body and touch your toes.

Neck Builder: You need a bath towel. Pull it firmly across the back of your neck, using your neck muscles to push back. Hold 10 seconds and release. Repeat 10 times.

Butterfly: Strengthens the back. Lie on your stomach. Raise your arms, chest, and legs. Spread your arms and legs 10 times. Return to the starting position and repeat.

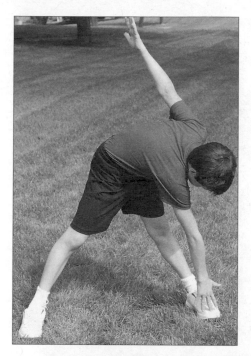

Trunk Bend: Strengthens trunk muscles. Bend sideways and down. Touch your toes—first left, then right. Spread your legs. Keep the elbows and knees straight.

Leg Stretch: Builds abdominal muscles. Raise your legs, then spread them slowly. Hold in this position 10 seconds. Bring legs together again and slowly lower to ground. Rest a few seconds. Repeat three times.

Squat Thrust: Take a squatting position with your hands in front of you on the floor. Thrust your legs back until your body is straight from the shoulders to the feet. Return to a squat. Stand up. Then repeat.

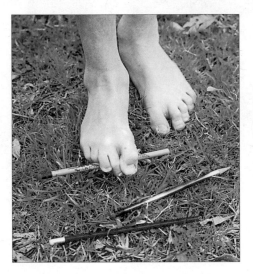

Toe Exercise: Conditions the feet. Practice walking pigeon-toed with your toes curled. Try picking up and carrying small rocks, marbles, or pencils with your toes.

Dual Contests

These two-boy contests will test your strength, balance, and ability to react quickly. **Note:** Do *not* do these contests with someone who is bigger or older than you. You and your partner should be about the same size.

Arm Wrestle: Try to force your opponent's hand to the ground or raise his elbow. You must do this without moving your own elbow. Try changing hands.

Stick Wrestle: Grip the stick firmly— left hand up, right hand down. Try to force the right end of the stick to the ground. Repeat several times.

Stick Pull: Sit on the ground facing each other. Put the soles of your shoes together. Grasping a broomstick, try to pull your opponent forward to his feet.

Pull Apart: Sit foot to foot, with your hands locked and legs spread wide apart. Try to pull your opponent forward. The winner is on his back at the end of the contest.

Duck Fight: Grasp your ankles in a low squat position. Push your opponent with your shoulders only. The winner forces his opponent to let go of his ankles or fall.

Chest Push: Start the contest between two lines, 10 feet apart. Push chest against chest, arms out, hands touching. The winner must force his opponent back over the line.

Leg Wrestle: Lie side by side on your backs, head to feet, and link inside elbows. Raise inside legs three times. On the third count, try to catch your opponent's heel and flip him.

Community Group

Citizen
Requirements

Requirement

Approved by

Do this:

1. With your parent, guardian, or Webelos den leader, complete the Citizenship Character Connection.

   _____

   a. **Know:** List some of your rights as a citizen of the United States of America. Tell ways you can show respect for the rights of others.

   _____

   b. **Commit:** Name some ways a boy your age can be a good citizen. Tell how you plan to be a good citizen and how you plan to influence others to be good citizens.

   _____

   c. **Practice:** Choose one of the requirements for this activity badge that helps you be a good citizen. Complete the requirement and tell why completing it helped you be a good citizen.

   _____

Do all of these:

2. Know the names of the president and vice president of the United States, elected governor of your state, and the head of your local government.

   _____

3. Describe the flag of the United States and give a short history of it. With another Webelos Scout helping you, show how to hoist and lower the flag, how to hang it horizontally and

vertically on a wall, and how to fold it. Tell how to retire a worn or tattered flag properly.

4. Explain why you should respect your country's flag. Tell some of the special days we fly it. Tell when to salute the flag and show how to do it.

5. Repeat the Pledge of Allegiance from memory. Explain its meaning in your own words.

6. Tell how our national anthem was written.

7. Explain the rights and duties of a citizen of the United States. Explain what a citizen should do to save our natural resources.

8. As a Webelos Scout, earn the Cub Scout Academics belt loop for Citizenship (if not already earned), or earn the pin. At a Webelos den meeting, talk about the service project Good Turn that you did.

And do two of these:

9. Tell about two things you can do that will help law enforcement agencies.

10. With your Webelos den or your family, visit a community leader. Learn about the duties of the job or office and tell what you have learned.

11. Write a short story of not less than 50 words about a former U.S. president or some other great American. Give a report on this to your Webelos den.

12. Tell about another boy you think is a good citizen. Tell what he does that makes you think he is a good citizen.

13. List the names of three people you think are good citizens. (They can be from any country.) Tell why you chose each of them.

14. Tell why we have laws. Tell why you think it is important to obey the law. Tell about three laws you obeyed this week. _____

15. Tell why we have government. Explain some ways your family helps pay for government. _____

16. List four ways in which your country helps or works with other nations. *[signature]*

17. Name three organizations, not churches or other religious organizations, in your area that help people. Tell something about what one of these organizations does. _____

I n the Cub Scout Promise, you say you will do your duty to your country. This means being a good citizen.

There are many ways to be a good citizen, not only of your country but in your community and your state, and even closer to home, in your neighborhood and school. And think about this: What does it mean to be a good citizen of the planet Earth?

As you earn the Citizen activity badge, you'll find out what it takes to be a good citizen. When you complete each requirement, ask your Webelos den leader or activity badge counselor to initial it on the previous page or this page.

Statue of Liberty's 100th birthday, 1986.

Government and You

Good citizens know what their government is doing—that means national, state, and local government. They try to find out what is happening. They read newspapers. They watch and listen to the news on television and radio.

You may not understand everything you read or hear about government in the news. Talk it over with your parent or other adult. What happens in government affects everyone's life.

Know These Names

It is important to learn the names of the president and vice president of our country, the governor of your state, and the name of the head of the government of your city, town, or county. Ask your parent or guardian what the duties of each one are. These people make decisions that affect you and your family.

The U.S. Flag

As a good citizen, you'll learn about the U. S. flag: its history, how to raise and lower it, how to hang it on a wall, how to fold it, and how to dispose of it properly, when neccesary.

History of Our Flag

Red Ensign Flag. An English flag that flew over the American colonies before the American Revolution.

Grand Union Flag. George Washington flew this flag over his army headquarters near Boston in 1776. The Revolutionary War had started the year before.

Old Glory. The first official flag of the United States. It was adopted by the Continental Congress on June 14, 1777. This is why June 14 is celebrated as Flag Day.

Star-Spangled Banner. This flag flew over Fort McHenry near Baltimore, Maryland, during the War of 1812 against Great Britain. Francis Scott Key watched it waving as the British bombarded the fort. Then he wrote our national anthem, "The Star-Spangled Banner."

Today's Flag. The 13 stripes represent the original 13 states. Each of the stars in the blue field represents one state. The 50th star—for Hawaii—was added on July 4, 1960.

Hoisting and Lowering the Flag

The flag can be attached to the halyard (the rope on the flagpole) with two half hitches or with two snap hooks, which fasten the flag more securely.

It takes two people to hoist and lower the flag correctly. One person holds the flag. The other attaches it to the halyard and hoists the flag, keeping it close to the pole by holding the line taut (see hand positions in the illustration above). He finally fastens the halyard to the cleat on the pole.

Displaying the Flag

Flag at speaker's right

Flag horizontal

Flag vertical

Flag vertical

Folding the Flag

The U.S. flag is folded in a special way until only the blue field shows. First, fold the flag lengthwise, in half, then lengthwise again with the blue starred area on the outside. Then make triangular folds, starting from the striped end, until only the blue field is showing. Tuck in the loose end. Never let the flag touch the ground, the floor, or water.

Showing Respect to the U.S. Flag

We show respect to the U.S. flag in many ways. Think about some ways you show your respect. Read on for some clues.

Flying the U.S. Flag

The U.S. flag is flown on public buildings every day when weather permits. Some citizens fly it at home every day, too.

It especially should be flown on the following days:

New Year's Day, January 1

Inauguration Day, January 20 after a presidential election

Martin Luther King Jr. Day, third Monday in January

Lincoln's Birthday, February 12

Washington's Birthday or Presidents' Day, third Monday in February

Mother's Day, second Sunday in May

Armed Forces Day, May 20

Memorial Day (half-staff until noon, full-staff to sunset), last Monday in May

Flag Day, June 14

Father's Day, third Sunday in June

Independence Day, July 4

Labor Day, first Monday in September

Constitution Day, September 17

Columbus Day, second Monday in October

Veterans Day, November 11

Thanksgiving Day, fourth Thursday in November

It is also flown on other days proclaimed by the president of the United States, on the birthdays of states (dates of admission to the Union), and on state holidays.

Saluting the U.S. Flag

If you are in uniform, give the Cub Scout salute:

- When the U.S. flag is being hoisted or lowered.
- When the U.S. flag passes by or you pass the U.S. flag. In a parade, salute just before the U.S. flag passes and hold the salute until it has gone by.
- When you recite the Pledge of Allegiance.

If you are not in uniform, greet the U.S. flag by placing your right hand over your heart. Take off your hat or cap, if you are wearing one.

Retiring Worn-Out Flags

When the U.S. flag is worn beyond repair, burn it thoroughly and completely on a modest, but blazing, fire.

This should be done in a simple manner with dignity and respect. Be sure the flag is reduced to ashes unrecognizable as a former flag.

The Meaning of the Pledge of Allegiance

When you pledge allegiance to the U.S. flag, you promise loyalty and devotion to your nation. Each part of the pledge has a deep meaning:

I pledge allegiance ... I promise to be true

... **to the flag ...** to the symbol of our country

... **of the United States of America ...** a country made up of 50 states, each with certain rights of its own

... **and to the Republic ...** a country where the people elect their fellow citizens to make laws for them

... **for which it stands, ...** the flag means the country

... **one nation under God, ...** a single country whose people believe in religious freedom

... **indivisible, ...** the country cannot be split into parts

... **with liberty and justice ...** with freedom and fairness

... **for all.** For every person in the country.

Our National Anthem

Every good citizen should learn "The Star-Spangled Banner," our national anthem. If you need to learn the words, see the *Wolf Handbook*.

How the anthem was written: From 1812 to 1815, the United States fought England in the War of 1812. In September 1814, English ships fired on Fort McHenry, near Baltimore, Maryland. The fort returned fire.

Francis Scott Key, an American lawyer and poet, was on an English ship. He had come earlier, under a truce flag, to rescue Dr. Beans of Baltimore. The battle lasted into the night.

Key anxiously awaited sunrise. The Stars and Stripes still waved proudly. The fort held out! Meanwhile, Key had begun the poem in the light of the rocket's red glare. He finished it the next night, and it was later set to music.

Your Rights and Duties

As a citizen of the United States, you have both rights and duties. Some are your rights and duties now. For others—like voting and serving on a jury—you must wait until you are an adult. Meanwhile, you can encourage your adult family members to vote and to use their other rights.

Examples of rights. As citizens, you and your family can

- Worship where you like
- Say what you think (freedom of speech)
- Join other people at "peaceful" meetings (the right to assemble)
- Own property and choose where to live
- Go to a good school
- Vote (age 18 or older)
- Have a trial by jury
- Keep people from searching your home—unless they have a special paper, called a *warrant,* issued by a judge

These are a few examples of the freedoms Americans have. Along with your many freedoms comes the responsibility to use them in ways that don't harm other people.

Examples of duties. As citizens, you and your family should

- Obey laws
- Respect the rights and property of others
- Help the police
- Keep informed on what is going on around you
- Help change things that are not good

When you are an adult, you also should

- Vote
- Pay taxes
- Serve on a jury when asked to do so

Saving Our Resources

A good citizen helps save America's natural resources. You and your den can do many conservation projects to improve our nation's air, water, and soil and to keep America beautiful. For example:

- Clear trash out of a stream or lake.
- Take part in a block cleanup campaign.

- Plant trees. Trees provide shelter and food for birds and animals. Trees also take in carbon dioxide and give off oxygen, making the air purer. (See "Photosynthesis," page 271.)
- Save water and energy at home. Fix leaks and don't use more water than necessary when you shower and brush your teeth.

Citizenship and You

Citizenship starts close to home. In fact, it begins with YOU. You know that a good citizen obeys the law, respects the rights of others, and always tries to be fair. But he does even more than that. He does a Good Turn to help other people whenever possible. A Good Turn is an extra act of kindness that you go out of your way to accomplish. (The Scout slogan is "Do a Good Turn Daily.")

What can you and your den do to help your church, mosque, synagogue, school, or community? Talk about this with your Webelos den leader and plan a Good Turn, either by yourself or with your den.

Helping the Police

The police and other law enforcement agencies need your help in fighting crime. Here's what you might do:

- Burglar-proof your home with good locks and windows that cannot be easily pried open.

- Protect the family car by always making sure the key is removed and the doors are locked.

- Safeguard your bicycle by locking it in the daytime and bringing it indoors at night.

- Report to the police any suspicious-looking people or activities you see around the neighborhood.

Learning About Your Community

Your community is where you live. It may be just a few square blocks in a big city, or perhaps your community is a small town. If you live in the country, you're part of a rural community of neighbors, even though you live some distance apart.

Wherever your community is, learn how it works. You can find out by asking a community leader.

Depending on where you live, some community leaders might be

- Mayors or city managers
- Municipal department heads
- City council members
- County commissioners
- School board members
- Service club presidents
- Municipal judges
- Ethnic group leaders
- City attorneys
- Directors of youth-serving agencies or the Red Cross
- School superintendents
- Church leaders
- Block leaders
- United Way officials

What Makes a Good Citizen?

Three of the optional requirements ask you to think about this question. For one of them, you learn about a former president of the United States or other great American. For another, you tell why a boy you know is a good citizen. For the third, you tell about three other good citizens.

How can you tell whether a person is a good citizen? Here are some signs:

- Good citizens obey the law. If they think a law is wrong, they try to have it changed. They do this by telling what they think to the people who are elected to make laws.
- Good citizens respect the rights of others. They don't try to get special privileges for themselves.
- Good citizens try to be fair and honest with everyone.
- Good citizens try to make their community, state, or nation better.
- School-aged good citizens "do their best" to learn all they can about their country.
- Adult good citizens learn all they can about their government. Then they vote on election day.

Why We Need Laws and Government

We've said a good citizen obeys the law. But why have laws or a government?

Why We Have Laws

If there were no laws, people could do anything they wanted. Does that sound wonderful? Think about it. If someone stole your bike, could you get it back? Probably not, especially if the thief were bigger than you.

Laws help us have an orderly society. Many laws are designed to protect people, property, and natural resources. There are laws against littering, driving while under the influence of alcohol, and selling certain drugs, to name a few.

Our nation has *federal laws* that are for everyone in the country. Each state has *state laws*. Cities, towns, villages, and counties have *ordinances*. If your city requires dogs to be penned up or on a leash at all times, that's a city ordinance.

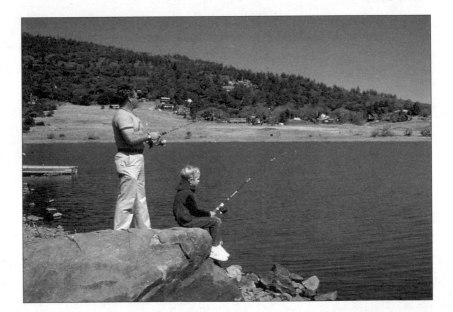

Laws You Obey

You obey laws every day of your life. Perhaps you don't even know you are doing it. Here are some times when you obey laws:

- When you're riding your bike and stop for a red traffic light or a stop sign.
- When you go to school. Your state has a law saying you must attend school unless you are sick.
- When you follow the school crossing guard's orders.
- When you cross streets only at corners when it is safe.
- When you take good care of your pet. There is a law stating that you must not mistreat or harm animals.
- When you're fishing and stop when you've caught the number of fish allowed. A law sets that limit.

These are just a few examples. Talk with an adult family member or other adult about other laws you obey.

Why We Have Government

What if there were no government? There would be no police officers to see that the laws were obeyed. There would be no firefighters to save your house if it caught fire. There would be no military to fight for our country if it were attacked. Government takes care of all these things and much more.

Paying for Government

The United States has four levels of government—federal, state, county, and city. They give us a lot of services, and they cost a lot of money. Soldiers, police officers, firefighters, teachers, and other government workers have to be paid. Roads, highways, bridges, dams, and parks are expensive to build and maintain.

All citizens help pay for these services. Most of the money comes from taxes such as income tax, sales tax, real estate tax, and property tax. Some money comes from license fees or charges for using public parks.

Citizenship in the World

Our country is full of good citizens. And it is a good citizen, too, because it helps other countries. The United States is one of the richest countries in the world. Some nations are so poor, many children go hungry and have no schools. Our country tries to help other nations in several ways. Here are some:

- By giving them food and services

- By lending money at little cost

- By buying the products other countries make and by selling them our products (this trade helps us, too)

- By sending teachers, farming advisers, doctors, scientists, and engineers to work in other countries

- By bringing students from other countries to the United States to study

Americans help in other ways, too. For example, there is the Cooperative for American Relief to Everywhere, commonly known as CARE. Our citizens give money to CARE. CARE sends food and clothing to poor people in other countries. The Boy Scouts of America helps other countries through its own World Friendship Fund. Cub Scouts, Boy Scouts, Varsity Scouts, and Venturers give money to help Scouting groups around the world.

Citizenship in Your Town

Many people in your community show good citizenship by working without pay. They are volunteers. They care about other people, and they find their work enjoyable and worthwhile. These are some volunteer groups that may make your community a better place:

- Volunteer fire department
- Rescue squad
- Red Cross
- Hospital volunteers
- Recreation associations
- United Way
- Humane Society
- The Salvation Army
- Boy Scouts of America
- Girl Scouts of the United States of America

Many people help these volunteer organizations by donating money to them.

Rescue team at work

C

COMMUNICATOR

Communicator Requirements

Requirement	Approved by

Do seven of these:

1. Play the Body Language Game with your den. _____

2. Prepare and give a three-minute talk to your den on a subject of your choice. _____

3. Invent a sign language or a picture writing language and use it to tell someone a story. _____

4. Identify and discuss with your den as many different methods of communication as you can (at least six different methods). _____

5. Invent your own den secret code and send one of your den members a secret message. _____

6. With your den or your family, visit a library and talk to a librarian. Learn how books are cataloged to make them easy to find. Sign up for a library card, if you don't already have one. _____

7. Visit the newsroom of a newspaper or a radio or television station and find out how they receive information. _____

8. Write an article about a den activity for your pack newsletter or Web site, your local newspaper, or your school newsletter, newspaper, or Web site. _____

9. Invite a person with a visual, speaking, or hearing impairment to visit your den. Ask about the special ways he or she communicates. Discover how well you can communicate with him or her. _____

10. With your parent or guardian or your Webelos den leader, invite a person who speaks another language (such as Spanish, French, Arabic, Hebrew, etc.) as well as English to visit your den. Ask questions about the other language (its background, where it is spoken, etc.), discuss words in that language that den members are already familiar with, or ask about ways to learn another language. _____

11. Use a personal computer to write a letter to a friend or relative. Create your letter, check it for grammar and spelling, and save it to a disk. Print it. _____

12. Under the supervision of a parent or other trusted adult, search the Internet and connect to five Web sites that interest you. _____

13. Under the supervision of a parent or other trusted adult, exchange e-mail with a friend or relative. _____

14. While you are a Webelos Scout, earn the Academics belt loop for Computers. _____

15. While you are a Webelos Scout, earn the Academics belt loop for Communicating. _____

16. Find out about jobs in communications. Tell your den what you learn. _____

A communicator is a person who shares information. We all do that constantly. We tell or show what we know, how we feel, and what we think.

When you speak or write, you communicate. And when you yawn, smile, or frown, you're showing other people that you're sleepy, happy, or unhappy. You can communicate by drawing pictures and by using sign language and codes.

We communicate over long distances by mail, telephone and computer. Communications keep our personal, business, and government worlds going.

As you earn this activity badge, you'll learn about the many careers in communications. When you complete each requirement, ask your Webelos den leader or activity badge counselor to sign it on pages 166–167.

Body Language

We often send messages without meaning to do it. People can see how we feel by our frown or smile or by a shrug of our shoulders. Such facial expressions and gestures are called *body language*.

Animals use body language, too. When a dog wags its tail, you know the

dog is happy. When a cat arches its back or bares its claws, you know the cat is prepared to fight.

Body Language Game

To play this game, give your den members paper and pencils. Ask them to think about feelings they can show by body language only—without making a sound. Have them make a list of at least five feelings they can show.

Den members take turns showing these feelings. The others try to guess what the feelings are. The den leader or den chief can be referee and decide whether the body language really does show the feeling.

If a den member guesses correctly, he gets one point. If nobody guesses correctly, the boy who performed the body language gets one point. The final winner is the boy with the most points.

Here are examples of feelings that you can show with body language. Probably you can think of other body language that shows feelings.

Happiness or pleasure—big smile, straight posture

Fear—wide eyes, moving back

Indifference—shrugging shoulders

Anger—frown and stare

Sadness—mouth turned down and eyes lowered

Sleepiness—yawning

Puzzlement—scratching head and frowning

Anxiety—tensed body and slight frown

Boredom—slouched and looking blank

Giving a Talk

Most of our communication is done through speaking and listening. It's important to learn to speak well so that everyone understands what you're saying, and you need to listen carefully when others are speaking. It's also important to ask questions when you don't understand or want more information.

For requirement 2, you'll give a three-minute talk in front of your den. This could be a story about something you have done. You can answer questions after the talk.

Suppose you plan to tell the den about an exciting soccer game you played recently. Would the story sound like this?

"Did we have a great game Saturday! In the last seconds, I passed off to Jason, and he kicked the winning goal. It was great!"

Your listeners will know it was a soccer game and your team won by one goal, but they're going to have questions if that is all you say. What teams were playing? What was the final score? Who is Jason? How far was he from the goal when he scored? Where were the defenders and goalkeeper? This story could have had a few more details in it.

Think through your story before you tell it. You might even make a list of the important points to fix them in your mind. You don't have to tell *everything* that happened, but include the basic information, the highlights, and why the game was exciting.

Try to avoid using words and phrases that don't move your story along. Expressions like "you know?" just slow it down.

What will *your* story be? Will it be about an exciting game, or a holiday with your family, or an outdoor adventure? After you decide, practice your talk and time it.

Sign Language and Picture Writing

If you met a French boy, how could you communicate with him? You couldn't talk with him unless he knew English or you knew French.

You would try signs or gestures. Maybe you would draw pictures, too. That's what American Indians did when they wanted to communicate with people from a tribe that spoke a different language.

If you have a *Wolf Handbook*, look in it for American Sign Language, the language used by people with hearing impairments. You'll also find signs used by American Indians and samples of picture writing. On pages 181 to 185 in this book, you'll find the Cub Scout Promise in sign language.

Now see if you can invent your own sign language or picture writing and use it to communicate with your den. First explain the meaning of each sign or picture. Then tell a simple story using them.

Here is a sample story in an invented sign language.

I

Am Hungry

Give

Me

Ice Cream Cone

Thank

You

Tastes Good

Methods of Communication

Each day, you share your thoughts and ideas with other people. You ask questions and answer them. You receive information from all sorts of sources. It's all communication. How many methods of communication touch your life?

Spoken words: Talking directly or by telephone, cellular telephone, CB radio, ham radio, announcements on the school public address system; translating spoken words from one language to another.

Signed words: Communicating with sign language to someone who is deaf.

Written words: Notes, letters, newspapers, magazines, school books, fiction books, nonfiction books, computer e-mail, posters, notices on bulletin boards, braille books; translating written words from one language to another.

Recorded words: Compact disks, tape recordings of books or instructions.

Audiovisual: Motion pictures, videos, television.

What important messages do signs on the street give you? Do they all use words? Do you get information from radio programs? Can art and music communicate? Can a look from a person communicate? What else do you know that is a form of communication?

Secret Codes

Secret codes are fun. Perhaps you learned how to make and figure out secret codes for elective 1 in the *Wolf Handbook*.

You can invent a secret code that only your den members know. Send them a short message and see if they can decode it.

Here's a simple code that is tough to break, unless you know the secret. The secret: Pick out every third letter.

ATWRQESNBZTELULCAOPVSCLSBTCRVONMUZOT
GXSRUHMFAHIVWNEYFFDRUTMN

WEBELOSSCOUTSHAVEFUN
Webelos Scouts have fun.

For a tougher code to crack, try this grid code device. On a square piece of paper, draw lines to make a grid. Put a second piece of paper under the first. Now use a paper punch to make a hole through both sheets in each of the squares. Make curved marks above and below some of the holes on both sheets as shown.

Give one sheet of the code device to another den member. Place the other code sheet over a blank piece of paper. Now you are ready to scramble a message. Let's say you want to code the message, "BILL IS AN ENEMY SPY."

Starting at the top left box with the ⌒ over it, fill in the first five letters of the message in the holes marked ⌒. Fill in the next five letters in the holes marked ⌣. Then fill in the six remaining letters in the unmarked holes.

If an "enemy agent" found the coded message, this is what he would see:

All your den members have to do is put their code device over the sheet. Presto! They are in on the secret.

Using a Library

You've probably visited a library. Do you know how to use the library's computer catalog or card catalog to find a book you want? If you don't, learn now. It's a skill you'll need all through school.

Libraries have separate sections for fiction, biographies, and nonfiction. Usually, fiction books are arranged alphabetically by the last name of the author, and biographies are shelved alphabetically by the last name of the subject.

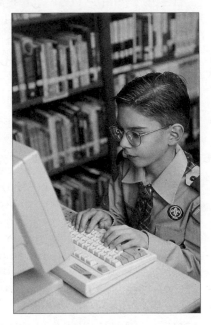

Nonfiction books are grouped by subject. Many libraries use the Dewey decimal system to group nonfiction books. All sports books, for example, have numbers beginning with 796 on the spines of the books. After you find a book's number in the catalog, you can go to the right shelf. Another way of numbering and shelving books is with the Library of Congress classification system.

When you visit the library with your den, find out which system it uses. Then see if you can find books with the computer or card catalog. Find out whether the computer catalog can be accessed from a home computer.

Libraries lend magazines, videos, CDs, and books on tape, too.

The library is a great place to go for almost any kind of information. In most city libraries, you can use telephone books from other cities, encyclopedias, and newspapers from many places. Some libraries have computers you can use for writing or to get on the Internet.

You need a library card to check out books and other materials. If your family doesn't have a card, ask your parent or guardian about getting one.

Visiting a Newsroom

Where does the news come from? Ask your Webelos den leader to help you find out by arranging a den visit to the newsroom of a newspaper, television station, or radio station.

All newspapers and broadcast stations have reporters who cover the news in their areas. For news from farther away, they rely on Internet and satellite communication. The largest news gathering organization is the Associated Press (AP). You may see the words Associated Press at the top of newspaper stories.

Computers in the newsroom receive thousands of stories and pictures every day. Editors decide which stories and pictures to use in the paper, to broadcast, or to post on a Web site. Talk to an editor to find out how these decisions are made.

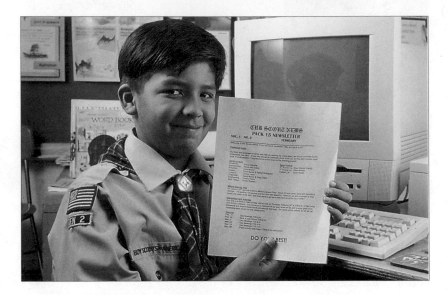

Writing a News Story

If you've ever been a reporter for your school newspaper, you know something about writing news stories. If you haven't, you can learn how.

You can write a news article about a Webelos den activity for your pack newsletter or Web site or for a local newspaper. It will be great to see your article published!

Decide what you'll write about. A special hike? Or a regular Webelos den meeting where you worked on a project, like making hand puppets for the Showman activity badge?

First, write the *lead*. The lead is the first sentence or paragraph of the article. It tells the "five Ws": *Who? What? Where? When?* and *Why?* Here's a sample lead:

> Webelos Den 1 visited Boy Scout
> Troop 10 at Green Tree Park Saturday
> to find out about Boy Scouting.

Look for the five Ws in this lead. *Who?* Webelos Den 1. *What?* Visited Boy Scout Troop 10. *Where?* At Green Tree Park. *When?* Saturday. *Why?* To find out about Boy Scouting.

Next, write about the most important parts of the activity.

> The Boy Scouts showed the Webelos
> Scouts how to set up a tent and build a
> cooking fire.
> Everyone helped cook. Lunch
> included meat and vegetables wrapped
> in foil and cherry cobbler baked in a
> Dutch oven.
> After lunch, the troop and den went
> on a nature hike together. They saw
> two red-tailed hawks and raccoon
> tracks by a creek.

Newspapers use short paragraphs, so instead of putting everything in one big paragraph, write your story in short ones. Many times, a newspaper paragraph is only one sentence long.

Double-space your article. This is easy if you're using a computer. If you're writing with pencil or pen on lined paper, leave every other line blank. This gives you space to make corrections.

Be sure to turn your article in on time. If you miss the deadline, your article may not be published. Include your name, address, and phone number. The person who receives it may have questions only you can answer.

Maybe you'll get a *byline*—your name at the top of the article when it's published!

Other Avenues of Communication

People who are unable to see, hear, or speak learn ways of sharing information that work for them. Many consider themselves *differently abled*.

A person who has a visual impairment may listen to recordings of books or read braille books. Braille is a system of raised dots on a page. A small pattern of dots stands for one letter in a word. Some patterns stand for combinations of letters, like *sh*, or whole words, like *the*. The reader reads by feeling the dots with his or her fingers.

A person who is deaf or hard of hearing may not be able to hear people speak but may be able to read lips. Some people who have been deaf since birth learn to speak, although their speech may not be clear. Others may write messages instead. People who lost their hearing after learning to speak will communicate by speaking.

Many people who cannot hear know sign language and can communicate quickly and expressively with others who know the language. And hearing people also learn sign language so they can communicate with people who are deaf or hard of hearing.

People who are mute are unable to speak. If they can hear, they can listen to you and reply by writing.

If you or someone in your den knows a person who is differently abled, invite him or her to a den meeting. Learn about the ways he or she communicates and deals with a world that offers many challenges.

The Cub Scout Promise in Sign Language

I

Promise

To

Do

My

Best

To

Do

My

Duty

To

God

And

My

Country

To

Help

Other

People

And

To

Obey

The

Law

Of

The

Pack

Other Languages

Learning other languages can be fun, and it will help you throughout your life. More and more, people all over the world visit and live in countries other than the one where they were born, and often it's a country with a different language. Many U.S. companies do business in countries where the main language is not English. Knowing another language can help you when you travel, when you meet people from other countries, and even in the job you do as an adult. Find out about learning other languages from someone who speaks two or more languages.

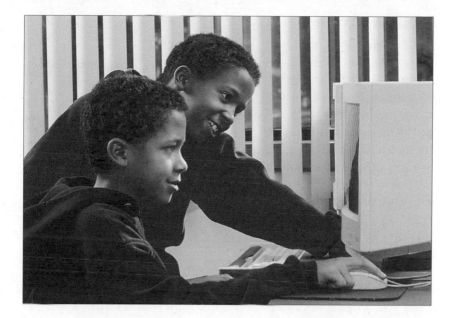

Computer Communication

You probably use a computer at school or home or both. School computers have programs (called *software*) that can help you learn math, English, and other subjects. A home computer could have programs that help you learn, as well as programs for the family's budget, recipes, games, and much more.

You can use word-processing software to write a school report or a letter. You can even check the spelling and grammar before printing it. It's still a good idea to read your work carefully, though, because the spelling checker will accept the word *here* even though you meant *hear.*

CDs and DVDs

CD drives are standard equipment on most home computers. *CD* stands for Compact Disk. The CD drive uses a laser to "read" patterns of tiny bumps on an inside layer of the CD.

CDs offer games, interactive picture books, cookbooks, encyclopedias, and information on all sorts of subjects. Many CDs are multimedia. That means they present information you can read, pictures (still and moving), recorded voices, music, and other sounds. Some CDs help you work and create on the computer. You could use a CD to make your own greeting cards.

With CDs, you can keep a lot of programs and information on hand that you couldn't keep in your computer for lack of space on the computer's hard disk.

Some computers can read a DVD (digital video disk) that has been formatted to hold data (words and pictures) instead of a movie. A DVD formatted this way can hold more than six CDs can hold.

Computer Talk

Computers use their own languages to talk to each other, just as people do. Of course, people write the languages and instruct the computers in using them. A job in computer communication might be what someone in your family does, or what you choose to do someday.

Networks

Computers are connected to other computers by telephone lines and cable speed communications in our personal, business, and government worlds every day. Computer talk goes on between computers in one office, across the country, and around the world—almost instantly!

The computers at your school, at a family member's workplace, or in your home might be on a network. A network links only "member" computers together. Computers on the network may be connected by phone lines or cables. The network might even be wireless, using radio waves for communication between the computers. This is a **local area network** (LAN). Larger **wide area networks** (WANs) link member computers in different locations, across the street or anywhere in the world. A group of businesses or organizations may communicate through an *extranet*. Members of one organization or company may communication through an *intranet*. Extranets and intranets work like the Internet, but each is private and only links members.

A worldwide network links bank computers, allowing customers to use automatic teller machines (ATMs) to withdraw cash from their accounts, even when they're far from home.

Some people "telecommute." Instead of traveling to a job, they work at home and use a computer to communicate with their employer. They can get company information, exchange messages with the staff, and send their work in—either from their homes or while they travel for the employer.

A Modem Is the Key

To communicate with others, a computer (or its network) must be connected to or equipped with a *modem*. A computer sends data in the form of electronic pulses, but a telephone system sends data in the form of waves. The modem changes the computer's pulses into waves that the phone system can use.

At the other end of the line, the receiving computer has a modem that translates the waves back into pulses. Many computers have built-in modems, but a separate modem can be purchased for a computer that doesn't have one.

Computers connected by cable, ISDN, or DSL use a *router* instead of a modem.

Computer Health

Just as you need to take care of your own health, you need to take care of your computer's health if you want it to last a long time and work well. Instructions that came with your computer should include the routine tasks you need to do, like removing old files you no longer use. If you keep up with these tasks, your computer will continue to perform well.

Virus Protection

People protect themselves from viruses by doing things like eating healthy foods, taking vitamins, and washing their hands. Computers have their own kinds of "viruses," and you need to help your computer stay virus-free, too. A virus might enter your computer from an e-mail message, from a Web site you visit, or from a disk you put into the computer. Some computer viruses are mostly harmless, but some can wreck your computer. A good virus protection program will recognize a virus and destroy it before it can damage your computer. You have several choices for virus-protection software; some are free and some charge a fee. The best virus protection programs keep up with new and changed viruses and offer a new download at least monthly, so your computer is better protected.

Making Choices

You can learn about choices for hardware, software, and service providers by visiting local computer stores and reading current computer magazines and computer company catalogs.

You and the Internet: Get Set to Surf

Have you visited cyberspace? It isn't really one place. *Cyberspace* is the word someone dreamed up for where you "are" when you use your computer to communicate with another— whether those computers are close together or oceans apart.

When you surf (explore) the Net (the Internet), you're in cyberspace. You can "visit" places, watch videos, play games, listen to spoken words and music, and even talk to other people anywhere in the world—all from your computer.

What do you need for surfing the Net? Computer technology changes so fast, new ways to get on the Net can become available at any time. When your *Webelos Handbook* was published, this is what was needed to get on the Internet using a computer:

- **A computer.** The best situation is to have a fast computer with a lot of memory, so you can surf efficiently. But you can still surf the Net without having the latest and greatest computer. Your Internet service provider (see below) can tell you how much speed and memory your computer needs.

- **A modem or router.** Having one of the faster modems or a router is an advantage. It will save you time in receiving information on your screen and getting information and new programs from other computers to yours (called *downloading*).

- **A connection.** This means signing up with a provider of your choice and paying a monthly or annual fee. An Internet service provider (or ISP) gives you a connection to the Internet and may provide e-mail and a few other services.

- **A Web browser.** This software guides your exploration of the Internet's World Wide Web. There are only a few main Web browsers, but you do have choices. There is no charge for a Web browser. You can download the one you want to use with a computer that already has a connection and browser, then save the program to a CD or disk so you can load it onto your computer. If you buy a new computer, it should come with a browser already loaded and ready to use.

Safety on the Internet

Just as you have safety rules at home, you and your family should have safety rules for using the Net. That's why requirement 12 says that when you use the Internet to work on the requirement, you must do so with a parent or other adult present.

You should have your parent's or guardian's approval any time you use the Net because not all sites are suitable for kids. Your family may have rules about whether you can look at certain types of sites. Here are some safety tips:

- Never give out your name, address, telephone number, or school location or send your picture without your parent's OK.

- Never plan to meet in person anyone you meet online, unless your parent approves and goes with you and the meeting is in a public place.

- Always tell an adult family member if anything you find or anyone you "chat" with makes you uncomfortable.

It's important that both you and your adult family members think about safety on the Internet. Have your parent or guardian read the section "Your Child's Safety on the Net" and then discuss it with you.

Your Child's Safety on the Net

You need to know that

- The content of some Web sites is not suitable for young people.

- Newsgroups (where anyone can type in a message) and chat rooms (where people "talk" live) are public; anyone can use them, say what they like, and leave addresses for Web sites you might not want your child to visit.

- If you subscribe to an online service, it may offer monitored chat rooms for kids. If you allow your child to participate, he or she should use a *screen name*, not his or her actual name.

- Access control and filtering software can be used to block access to selected sites or content. Some Internet service providers make such software available for their users.

Exploring the Net

What can you do on the Internet? It's impossible to describe it all here, but here are two of the main activities:

- **World Wide Web (WWW).** The Web is made up of Web sites you can look at (or *access*) by using browser software. You can find sites for homework help, neat science experiments, space shuttle topics, live tropical fish swimming around, pets, robots, games, video game tips—to name only the very tip of the Web iceberg. Scouting has a Web site at http://www.scouting.org.

Web sites are more than single pages. They're like magazines full of pictures and information, and they may direct you to additional pages within the site or to other Web sites. You move around by clicking on highlighted areas on the screen called *links*.

Each Web site has its own computer address called a URL (Uniform Resource Locator). You type the URL to get to the Web site. URLs are long, but you can use the browser to create a "bookmark" for a site. Then you can revisit the site quickly by using its bookmark instead of typing the address.

You can look for a subject you want to explore by using a *search engine*, which is an index. Type in a subject or some key words, and you'll get a list of sites to visit.

- **Electronic mail (e-mail)** is a way of exchanging messages with other people. All Internet e-mail participants have a unique e-mail address with their Internet service provider.

If you know a person's address, you can send e-mail no matter which service he or she uses. The messages can contain Web links, files, pictures, sounds, and other features. You write it and send it, and then it waits in the other person's mailbox until he or she checks the mail.

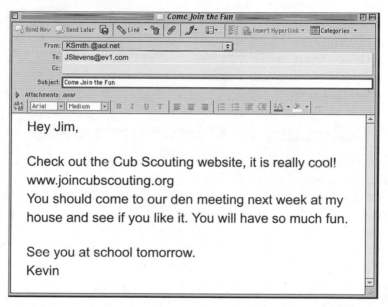

Cub Scout Academics
Belt Loops for Computers
and Communicating

If you earned the Communication or Computers Academics belt loop earlier in Cub Scouting, great! But that won't count for requirement 14 or 15 of this Communicator activity badge.

You must earn the Computers (requirement 14) or Communicating (requirement 15) belt loop again while you are a Webelos Scout for it to count toward this activity badge.

Careers in Communication

Next time you're at the library, choose a book about a career field in communications. Read the book you choose and tell your den what you learned about the field. You could also visit a person who works in communications—a newspaper reporter, an editor, a writer, a webmaster, a print buyer—and share with your den what you learn from talking to him or her.

C

CRAFTSMAN

Craftsman Requirements

Requirement   **Approved by**

Do these:

1. Explain how to safely handle the tools that
   you will use for this activity badge.   _____

2. With adult supervision and using hand tools,
   construct two different wooden objects you
   and your Webelos den leader agree on, such
   as the items listed below. Use a coping
   saw or jigsaw for these projects. Put them
   together with glue, nails, or screws. Paint or
   stain them.   _____

Book rack	Napkin holder
Shelf	Animal cutouts
Bulletin board	Garden tool rack
Weather vane	Lid holder
Tie rack	Mailbox
Letter holder	Birdhouse
Notepad holder	Desk nameplate
Toolbox	Letter, bill, and pencil
Towel rack	holder
Recipe holder	Bread box
Lamp stand	Key rack
Kitchen knife rack	Measuring cup rack
Kitchen utensil rack	Measuring spoon rack

3. Make a display stand or box to be used to
   display a model or an award. Or make a
   frame for a photo or painting. Use suitable
   material.   _____

4. Make four useful items using materials other than wood that you and your Webelos den leader agree on, such as clay, plastic, leather, metal, paper, rubber, or rope. These should be challenging items and must involve several operations.

                                             _____

Many people use tools every day in their work. Think about the tools used by carpenters, automotive technicians, machinists who make precision metal parts, furniture makers, potters who create vases and bowls.

Other people become experts at using tools so they can enjoy hobbies. For example, a person whose hobby is woodworking might design and build a table for his or her home.

In working on the Craftsman activity badge, you'll become good at handling a variety of tools. You'll use wood to make some of your projects. For others, you'll decide to work with leather, metal, or other materials. When you complete each requirement, ask your Webelos den leader or activity badge counselor to sign it on the previous page or this page.

Using Tools Safely

Whether you are working with wood, leather, plastic, or some other material, you will need certain tools. Handle each one as if it could hurt you—because it could!

Tools that cut materials—such as saws, knives, and shears—should be kept sharp. If they are dull, you may have to use too much force and they may slip and cut your hand.

Keep your hands away from saw teeth and knife blades so that if the tool slips, you won't get hurt. Be careful when you're hammering. If you miss the nail head, you sure don't want to hit your thumb!

Practice using your materials and tools until you know how to handle them well.

Protect your tools. When you're through working, put them back in place.

Keep your workshop in order. A clean bench makes a safer place to work.

Practicing good safety skills with hand tools as a Webelos Scout will help prepare you for the greater challenge of using power tools when you are a Boy Scout.

Choosing Projects

Plans for some projects are shown on these pages. You can find many more in books in your public library. Look under "Crafts" in the library card catalog or computer catalog.

Or try making your own plans. Think about what you want to make. Draw a simple picture of it. Decide how big it should be. Write the dimensions on the drawing. Keep your costs down by using scrap material if you can.

Then, with adult supervision, go to work!

Woodworking Projects

These are some of the tools you need for woodworking projects:

Hammer
Saws (ripsaw, crosscut saw, coping saw)
Pliers
Screwdrivers
Chisels
Awl
Wood clamp

Set of knives
Pocket knife
Whetstone
Sandpaper and sanding block
File and/or rasp
Nails
Drill and drill bits

Weather Vane

Cut the bird's body and legs from thin wood with a coping saw. Bolt the legs on. Fasten the bird to a 1-by-6-by-12-inch board. Fasten the board to the top of a post with washers and a bolt so the board can turn.

Worm of rubber →

Bolt

Post →

Letter Holder

Draw the duck on a 6-by-8-inch piece of ½-inch plywood. Make sure you draw its feet and out-spread wings.

Cut them out with a coping saw. Fasten them to a piece of 1-by-2-by-6-inch wood with glue, nails, or screws.

Necktie Rack

To enlarge the pattern for this Scout badge tie rack, use the grid method. With a ruler, make a 12-by-13-inch grid of 1-inch squares on a large sheet of paper.

Draw the badge by copying the badge outline from the small grid to the large one, square by square. Cut out your paper pattern and trace around it on ¼-inch-thick plywood.

Cut the badge shape out with a coping saw. Sand it smooth. Drill holes for ¼-inch dowels 2½ inches long and glue them in. Paint or decorate the rack as you like and fasten a hanger to the back.

4"

Front

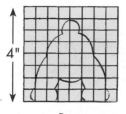

4"

Rear

Doggie Letter Holder

Enlarge the patterns. (See the grid method explained in the necktie rack instructions on the previous page.) Trace them on ¾-inch pine and cut out.

The letter holder is a spiral of coat hanger wire between the doggie pieces. To make the spiral, first straighten a coat hanger. Now wrap the wire as tightly as you can around a soup can, with ½ inch between spirals.

Then use two pliers to bend ½ inch of each end of the wire at right angles to the spirals.

The wire ends are then cemented into small holes drilled into the back of the doggie's front piece and the front of the rear piece. Paint the wood pieces.

Wall Shelf

Draw a half circle with a protractor on a piece of 1-by-4-by-8-inch pine. Cut out with a coping saw.

1"×4"×8"

Coping saw

Protractor

Make the brace by sawing diagonally through another piece, 1-by-4-by-6-inches. Sand both pieces smooth.

1"×4"×6"
Cut diagonally

Use glue and brads to fasten the brace to the shelf.

Brads

Glue 4-inch edge of this piece.

Glue

Screw 1-inch angle irons to the bottom of the shelf at the back edge. With adult help, use wall fasteners to attach your shelf to the wall.

1" Angle irons

Nail about ½" above post; → Saw off head.

Place car on nail.

2"×2" Piece about 5" long

½" Plywood

4½" Square

For engraved plate, glue piece of 2"×3" plywood to post.

Display Stands and Frames

Use any material you like to make a picture frame or a display stand or box.

Maybe you'll decide to make a wooden frame for a painting you made for the Artist activity badge. Or you might make a display stand for your favorite pinewood derby car. One type of stand is shown here.

Leatherworking

There are special tool kits for working with leather. You can buy them at hobby stores, or you can buy the Leathercraft Workshop from your Scouting distributor.

Your leatherworking tools might include some of the following:

Eyelet setter
Lacing fid
Rivet setter
French skiver
Shears
Wing divider
Punch set
Arkansas stone

Tooling board
Skiving knife
Mallet
Thonging chisel
Adjustable creaser
Circle edge slicker

For your first projects, use calfskin leather. It's easy to cut and tool. Look for it at arts and crafts supply stores. Try designing and making simple projects like a key case, eyeglass case, coin purse, or drawstring purse.

Beginning a Project

First make a pattern of the article you plan to make. Draw it on a piece of paper in its exact size. Use a ruler or steel square for straight lines.

Cut out your paper pattern and draw dotted lines where folds will be. Fold the pattern to make sure it looks right.

Make a template by tracing around the paper pattern on a piece of fairly heavy cardboard. Cut the cardboard, following the tracing lines. Then place the template on the piece of leather.

Cutting Leather

Place the leather on a softwood cutting block, with the rough side down. Put your template on the leather and hold it firmly. Draw its outline on the leather with a tracer or awl. Now use a very sharp knife to cut through the leather. Use a steel square or ruler to cut along straight lines.

Tooling Leather

Tooling is the most common way of making designs on leather. A modeling tool is used to press the design into the leather. The leather must be moist. Dampen a sponge with water and hold it on the top side of the leather for about three seconds. Make your design on the leather with the modeling tool. If you don't have one, use an orangewood manicure stick or an awl.

Lacing

To make holes for lacing leather pieces together, use a tool called a drive punch or a large nail. Use a mallet or light hammer to drive the punch or nail. For lacing, you can use a leather thong or plastic laces. The drawings show two common lacing stitches.

Running Stitch

Whipstitch

Clay Projects

Unless you know someone who has a potter's kiln, use oven-firing clay for your clay projects. Regular clay must be fired (baked) in a kiln, which gets much hotter than your kitchen oven. But you can fire oven-firing clay in your kitchen.

Go to a hobby store for oven-firing clay and glazes in powder or liquid form. The glaze, which comes in different colors, will give your projects a shiny finish.

Experiment with two basic methods of working in clay. Use the *coil method* to make bowls, cups, mugs, and other items with circular tops. Try the *slab method* to make boxes and other things with corners.

Coil Method

Suppose you want to make a small bowl. First flatten a big chunk of clay until it is about ½ inch thick. You can do this with a rolling pin. Cut out a circle about 3 inches across. This is the bottom of the bowl.

Coil Method

For the first coil, make a long smooth rope of clay with your hands. It should be just slightly longer than the bottom of the bowl is around—about 10 inches. Coil the rope around the bottom. Cement it to the bottom with *slip*—a thin mixture of clay and water. Smooth the seam with your fingers.

Make more coils and cement them on with slip. Each one should be a little longer than the last so the bowl will slope outward and get wider as you build toward the top.

Use your fingers and a kitchen knife to smooth the sides. Make sure there are no holes in the bowl. Let it dry for an hour or two before decorating, glazing, and firing.

Slab Method

In this method, you make slabs of clay and join them together with slip.

Let's say you are going to make a small box. The sides and bottom will be ⅜ inch thick. Find two flat wooden sticks of that thickness and lay them on your worktable with the clay between them. Use a rolling pin, with its edges on the two sticks, to roll out the slab.

Slab Method

Cut out pieces for the bottom, sides, and top. Join the sides and bottom with slip, using your fingers and a kitchen knife to smooth the seams. Let the box dry an hour or two before decorating, glazing, and firing.

Decorating, Glazing, and Firing

Use a pencil, an orangewood manicure stick, and a tongue depressor to press designs into the sides of the bowl or box.

For glazing and firing your projects, follow the directions that came with the glaze and clay.

Technology Group

ENGINEER

Engineer Requirements

Requirement	Approved by

Do both of these:

1. Talk to an engineer, surveyor, or architect in your area about the different occupations in engineering. Create a list that tells what they do. *DWM*

2. Draw a floor plan of your home. Include doors, windows, and stairways.

And do four of these:

3. Visit a construction site. Look at a set of plans used to build the facility or product. Tell your Webelos den leader about these. (Get permission before you visit.)

4. Visit a civil engineer or surveyor to learn how to measure the length of a property line. Explain how property lines are determined.

5. Tell about how electricity is generated and then gets to your home.

6. Construct a simple working electrical circuit using a flashlight battery, a switch, and a light.

> 7. Make drawings of three kinds of bridges and explain their differences. Construct a model bridge of your choice.

8. Make a simple crane using a block and tackle and explain how the block and tackle is used in everyday life.

> 9. Build a catapult and show how it works.

10. While you are a Webelos Scout, and if you have not earned it for another activity badge, earn the Cub Scout Academics belt loop for Mathematics.

Engineers designed your school bus, the cars on the road, the road itself, and the bridges you cross. Engineers designed all the different kinds of computers you see at school, in offices, and at home.

Almost anything you use that was manufactured was probably designed by an engineer. Not only that, but engineers designed the machines that workers used to make the product and the factory building where it was made.

Airplanes, space shuttles, space stations—all designed by engineers. Engineers work in many exciting and challenging fields.

While you earn this activity badge, you can work on engineering projects like bridge models, a catapult, and an electrical circuit. When you complete each requirement, ask your Webelos den leader or activity badge counselor to sign it on page 212.

What Engineers Do

Engineering is a specialized profession, which means there are almost as many types of engineers as there are engineering jobs to be done. Here are some of the types of engineers and a few examples of the work they do:

Civil engineers design construction projects like bridges, dams, stadiums, highways, and wastewater treatment plants.

Mechanical engineers design automobiles, engines, refrigeration and heating systems, and machines.

Electrical engineers design computers, motors, television sets, telephones, and communications systems.

There are engineers in aerospace work, industry, agriculture, chemistry, and many other areas.

Engineers write the *specifications* for their designs. Specifications are the rules that the project has to follow. They describe how the project is going to perform, what materials go into it, and exactly how the materials are to be put together.

Engineers also may investigate problems like traffic flow, water and air pollution, and river flooding. Then they work on plans to solve the problems.

Drawing Floor Plans

An architectural engineer draws plans for buildings and houses. He or she designs the plans to make the best use of standard sizes of building materials, like drywall for the interior walls. The engineer includes specifications for materials, including types of doors and windows.

See if you can draw a floor plan of your house or apartment. You don't have to show measurements on your floor plan, but if the living room is twice as big as the kitchen, your floor plan should show it, so you might want to check measurements in each room.

Show doors, windows, and stairways. Use a ruler to make your plan neat.

Visiting a Construction Site

Engineers super-vise the work that puts their designs into action. The engineer checks to see that the correct materials are used and the engi-neering plans—the specifications—are followed.

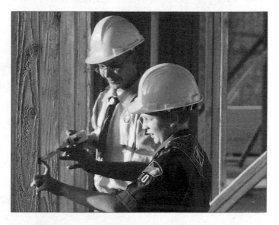

Good examples are construction jobs like buildings, roads, and dams. With your parent or den, arrange to visit a construction site and talk to an engineer. Ask him or her to show you plans for the job.

Checking Property Lines

In any construction job, whether it's a building, a highway, or an electrical power line, civil engineers have to know where construction will take place in relation to the property lines around it.

Highways and utility projects are constructed on pathways across property that are called *easements*. Engineers have to know where the boundaries of the easements are.

Surveyors use laser equipment to determine the location of the property and easement lines, how long they are, and where corners are. Once the lines are determined, a civil engineer can use the information to draw plans and supervise construction. If you talk with a civil engineer for requirement 4, you'll learn more about this.

Property lines are important to anyone who owns a home, a building, farmland, or a vacant lot. A homeowner who wants to put up a fence around a backyard may have the lot surveyed to find out exactly where the boundary lines are located.

You can use a tape measure or yardstick to measure one of the lot lines around your house or apartment building.

Power Plant Generator

Step-up Transformer

Transmission Lines

Distribution Lines

Step-down Transformer

Electric Power

An electric current is created when a magnet is spun rapidly inside a coil of wire. The huge generators in a power plant work on that principle. The turbines that spin the magnet are powered by water, steam, or wind power.

Electricity moves along wires like water running through a pipe. The electricity generated by a power plant moves over wires to a nearby *step-up transformer*. There, the voltage is raised so that the electricity can go efficiently over long distances.

A high-voltage line carries electricity to your town. But the voltage must be reduced by a *step-down transformer* before you can use the electricity in your home.

Electrical Circuits

An electrical circuit is the route by which electricity moves from an electrical source to the point where it is used and back again. In the house or building where you live, electrical circuits

Metal Contacts

Electric Switch

This switch is in the "off" position. There is a gap in the path for electricity. When the switch is turned on, the metal contacts come together so the electricity can flow.

supply electricity to different parts of the building. In lamps and appliances, when a switch is turned to the "on" position, it closes (completes) the circuit and allows electricity to flow to, for instance, the light bulb or the toaster.

You can make a simple electric circuit. You will need

- A "D" size flashlight battery
- A holder for a small light bulb
- A light bulb that fits the holder
- An on/off switch
- Wire to connect it all together

When the switch is off, the circuit is open, which means there is a gap in the circuit. Electricity cannot flow to the light bulb. When the switch is on, it closes the circuit. The circuit is complete, and electricity reaches the bulb.

Be Safe With Electricity

Even low-voltage electricity is strong enough to kill you. It can give you a hard shock or a bad burn. For your safety's sake:

- Don't touch a switch with wet hands or while standing on a damp floor.
- Don't touch anything electrical while taking a bath.
- Plug only one cord into each electrical outlet. Overloading causes fires.
- Don't put electric wires under rugs and carpets. Walking on wires wears off the insulation. This causes short circuits.
- Newer homes have circuit breakers. But if your home has a fuse box, use the correct size fuse in it.
- Don't get under a tree during a thunderstorm. Lightning could hit the tree.
- Get out of the swimming pool or lake when you see a storm or lightning, even in the distance.

Bridges

The best way to learn about bridges is to study the way they are made. Then you can build model bridges, the way civil engineers do. You can use bricks, wooden blocks, and heavy paper.

Start with a *plank bridge.* Set up two bricks. Lay a heavy piece of paper on them to go over "the river" beneath. What happens when you put a toy car on the bridge?

Plank Bridge

Activity Badges

What would you do to hold the middle? Putting a wooden block under it helps. This is called a *pier bridge*.

Pier Bridge

Beam Bridge

Take another piece of paper and fold the sides up 1 inch. Set this on the bricks. How much weight does this hold? More than the flat piece of paper? This is called a *beam bridge*.

You may have seen beam bridges on railroads. They hold up a heavy weight over a short distance.

Curve a piece of heavy paper to form an arch. Slip it between two bricks. Set a piece of heavy paper on top of it and the bricks. This is called an *arch bridge*. Does it hold more weight than the others?

Arch Bridge

Engineers know about shapes and how much weight each one will hold. Make a square out of four drinking straws, fastening the corners with straight pins. Stand it up. Is it rigid? Does it want to fold up? The square will move.

Now make a triangle out of three straws. Does it move out of shape?

In building very long bridges, engineers use a whole row of triangles. These are called *truss bridges*. Railroad bridges over rivers are truss bridges.

Truss Bridge

Suspension cable bridges are the largest. The Golden Gate Bridge in San Francisco, California, is a suspension bridge.

The Golden Gate Bridge is a suspension bridge.

Block and Tackle

A block and tackle is used to lift heavy objects easily. A crane is a huge block and tackle.

If you have ever watched the end of a crane while it was picking something up, or if you have ever used an engine hoist or a come-along, or if you have ever watched the rigging on a sailboat when the sails are being hoisted or lowered, then you have seen a block and tackle at work.

In a block and tackle, a rope or cable runs over a pulley, which is a small wheel with a grooved rim. The block and tackle is attached to something that must be lifted. A power source pulls the rope and lifts the object. It takes less force to lift this way than it would to try to lift the object without the block and tackle.

Some block and tackles have more than one pulley. Some of the ways a block and tackle can be rigged are shown here.

Runner   Luff   Gun Tackle

Spanish Burton   Twofold   Single Whip

F = Force   W = Weight

Making a Single Whip Block and Tackle

To make a pulley, you need a large spool and a coat hanger. Cut the hanger as shown and bend the ends at right angles through the spool. Then bend down the ends so the hanger won't spread apart. Make sure the spool turns easily.

Testing the Block and Tackle

Use a spring scale to see how much force is needed to lift a weight with and without a block and tackle. If you don't have a spring scale, you can make one as shown.

A cardboard tube from a roll of paper towels or something similar will make a good scale. Suspend rubber band and wire as shown.

This *runner* block and tackle is lifting several pieces of wood. The boys at either side support the rod to which one end of the block and tackle's rope is attached. The rope goes around the pulley. The other end of the rope is attached to the spring scale, and the boy in the center is holding the scale and lifting, providing the force. The scale measures the force required to lift the object. By attaching the same object directly to the scale, the boys can then measure the force required without a block and tackle.

Catapult

Catapults were once war machines used to throw huge rocks over castle walls. Today, a type of catapult is used to launch planes from aircraft carriers. A slingshot is also a kind of catapult.

Here's a simple catapult you can make. When using it, be sure everyone is out of the way, behind you.

Marshmallow Catapult

To make this marshmallow-throwing catapult, you will need a clean, empty half-gallon milk carton, a 1-inch and a 3-inch rubber band, two pencils, a toothpick, a plastic spoon, tape, and some small marshmallows, or you can use cotton balls or small pieces of dry sponge.

1. Lay a paper milk carton on its side. Cut off one side and the top of the milk carton so it looks like the diagram. Cut holes the size of a pencil in both sides and in the bottom.

2. Fold down and tape the end of the carton. Push a rubber band through the bottom hole. Put the toothpick through it on the bottom, and tape it to hold the rubber band in place. Push a pencil through the side holes.

3. Tape the plastic spoon onto one end of the second pencil. Put the small rubber band on the spoon pencil, lay it across the top of the first pencil, and use the small rubber band to securely attach (lash) the two pencils together. Attach the bottom rubber band to the other end of the spoon pencil.

4. Test your catapult to be sure it works properly: Place a marshmallow in the spoon, pull back the pencil, and release it. Adjust and modify your catapult as needed to make it work better.

Computers in Engineering

Engineers use computers in many ways:

- To make calculations. Many advanced technological problems require a huge number of calculations to be solved. Hundreds of people working on the problem by hand might not be able to do them fast enough.

- To design and draw plans using a computer-aided design (CAD) program. CAD is especially useful to architectural and civil engineers in designing and building complicated bridges and other structures. During the design stage, computers can produce models of the structure that even look three-dimensional on a computer screen. These models can be changed and tested before building ever begins. The computer can analyze things such as the strength and weight of each part of the structure, as well as its cost and availability. For a building, the computer can determine whether there will be enough vertical braces, such as walls and columns, to keep a roof up.

- To calculate and store cost estimates and plan budgets for projects.

- To schedule work.

- To write business letters.

Cub Scout Academics
Belt Loop for Mathematics

If you earned the Mathematics belt loop earlier in Cub Scouting, great! But that won't count for requirement 10 of this Engineer activity badge. You must earn the Mathematics belt loop again while you are a Webelos Scout for it to count toward this activity badge. (And if you already earned it for another activity badge, that cannot count for Engineer; you should choose another requirement, instead.)

mathematics

Community Group

FAMILY MEMBER

Family Member Requirements

Requirement   **Approved by**

Do all of these:

1. Tell what are meant by family, duty to family, and family meetings. _____

2. Make a chart showing the jobs you and other family members have at home. Talk with your family about other jobs you can do for the next two months. _____

3. Make a list of some things for which your family spends money. Tell how you can help your family save money. _____

4. Plan your own budget for 30 days. Keep track of your daily expenses for seven days. _____

5. Take part in at least four family meetings and help make decisions. The meetings might involve plans for family activities, or they might be about serious topics that your parent wants you to know about. _____

6. With the help of an adult, inspect your home and surroundings. Make a list of hazards or lack of security that you find. Correct one problem that you found and tell what you did. _____

And do two of these:

7. With the help of an adult, prepare a family energy-saving plan. Explain what you did to carry it out. _____

8. Tell what your family does for fun. Make a list of fun things your family might do for little or no cost. Plan a family fun night. _____

9. Learn how to clean your home properly. With adult supervision, help do it for one month. _____

10. Show that you know how to take care of your clothes. With adult supervision, help at least twice with the family laundry. _____

11. With adult supervision, help plan the meals for your family for one week. Help buy the food and help prepare three meals for your family. _____

12. While you are a Webelos Scout, earn the Academics belt loop for Heritages. _____

13. Explain why garbage and trash must be disposed of properly. _____

A family is a group of people who care for one another and share their lives and their love.

There are many different kinds of families. Some families have a father, a mother, and children. In other families, children live with one parent. A grandparent or a guardian with a child—that's a family too. And children belong to families in foster homes or boarding schools.

As you earn the Family Member activity badge, you'll discover new ways to take part in family life and show your family you care about them. When you complete each requirement, ask an adult member of your family to sign it on the previous page or this page.

You and Your Family

What Is a Family?

Did you read what is written above? It tells what really makes a family, so be sure to read it.

Your Duty to Family

Living in a family means you get support and love. You give support and love, too. When you care about others' feelings and when you listen to their problems and try to help, you're being a good family member.

Being in a family also means doing everyday things like clearing the table after a meal or picking up your belongings. When you hang up your coat and put school books away in your room, that helps everyone else and makes life more pleasant.

Doing your share and helping others is an important part of living together in a family.

What Are Family Meetings?

A family meeting happens when the whole family takes time to talk about what is happening in their lives and about plans and decisions they need to make together. Maybe your family makes plans around the dinner table, and it doesn't seem like a meeting at all.

Sometimes a family may set a special time to plan the coming weekend or talk about family rules. You can read more about family meetings on pages 242–243.

Family Jobs

What are some of the jobs a family does?

Someone cooks the meals, or maybe several people pitch in to help. Family members may take turns setting the table and taking the trash and garbage out. Does one person clean the house, or does each person clean part of it? Then there's lawn mowing and other outdoor chores. All these jobs are important, and they may be shared by family members who are old enough to do them.

For requirement 2, list all your family's jobs around the house. Who does each job? Write in those names beside the jobs. Now you can discuss with your family some other ways you can help out.

Be Neat and Clean

As a family member, your first job is to take care of yourself and your room. If you don't do that, you could add to the work of other family members.

Keep yourself clean. Of course you will get dirty when you play outside or work around the house. Nobody minds that, IF you take a bath or shower afterward.

Brush your teeth regularly. Clean your nails. Don't forget to comb your hair. These simple things show other family members that you care about yourself and want them to be proud of you.

Is your room a mess? Do you just drop your clothes on the floor and expect other family members to pick them up? If you do, what does that tell them about you?

It isn't hard to keep your room neat. Pick up after yourself. Put your books, games, and sports equipment where they belong. Learn to make your bed—and do it every morning.

Doing these things shows you care about others in your family.

Be Safe at Home

A lot of people are hurt or even killed in accidents in their own homes each year. Most of these accidents could be prevented.

Make your home safe by checking it for dangers. Then do something about the dangers.

Other safety tips: If there are young children in the house, add special safety latches to kitchen and bathroom cabinets. They're easy for you and adults to open.

When cooking, use the back burners when you can. Turn pot handles toward the back of the stove so young children can't reach them.

Make sure all purses and briefcases, including those belonging to visitors, are placed out of children's reach.

Home Safety Checklist

Place	Danger	What You Can Do
Living Room	Toys on Floor	Put toys away.
	Furniture blocking easy passage	Rearrange furniture.
	Electric cords under rugs; worn cords can cause shock, fire	Move cords so people don't walk over them.
	Curtain cords dangling	Keep cords out of children's reach.
Kitchen	Matches in reach of children	Move matches to safe place.
	Knives in reach of young children	Put knives in holder or special drawer.
	Cleaning fluids and other poisons exposed	Put all poisons out of children's reach; in locked area if necessary.
	Spilled grease or water	Wipe up immediately.
Bathroom	Medicines in reach of young children	Put medicines in locked cabinet (in child-resistant containers.)
	Radio, hair dryer, or other electrical device near water source	Move away from sink, bathtub, and toilet.
	Toilet lid open	Keep closed when not in use.
	Water too hot	Ask adult to lower water temperature.
Stairways	Boxes, toys, and other items left on stairs	Remove anything people might trip over.
	Handrail loose	Tighten handrail screws.
	Stair covering loose	Tack down covering.
	Light bulb out	Replace bulb.
Work area	Tools left out	Put away, out of children's reach.
Furnace area	Waste paper, rubbish near furnace	Move flammable items far away from furnace or throw away.
Outside	Trash, garbage	Keep in tightly covered containers.
	Sandbox, wading pool	Cover when not in use.

Garbage and Trash

Garbage can be a health problem unless you dispose of it properly. It can attract flies, roaches, mice, or other pests that carry diseases. It should be taken out of your home and put in garbage cans with tight lids or in sealed plastic bags. The cans or bags should be carried out for each garbage collection day. You can help with this chore.

If your community has a recycling program, recycle glass, metal, plastic, and paper.

Trash and litter outside a home make it look like no one cares. It's also a fire hazard and can cause falls and injuries. Clean it up and get rid of it!

Helping Your Family Save Money

It takes a lot of money to run a household and buy food for a family. Here are a few ways you can help your family hold down the costs.

- If you are given a weekly allowance, make it last for a week and try to save some of it. Don't spend it quickly and then ask for more. If you need more money, perhaps you could do jobs for neighbors: rake lawns, shovel snow, walk dogs.

- Take good care of your clothes and shoes. They will last much longer, and that saves money.

- The monthly bills for utilities—gas, electricity, and water—are a big part of a family's expenses. Turn off lights when you leave a room, and don't waste hot water when you wash or shower. Run the cold water only as long as you need it, too.

Talk with the adults in your family about other ways you can save money for the family.

Your Budget for a Month

A family needs to plan ahead to pay for food, clothing, shelter, activities, and all its other expenses. You can plan ahead for some of your own expenses.

For requirement 4, you'll map out a budget for the month ahead, week by week. First, think about these things:

- How much money will you have for each week? Do you receive an allowance, payment for a paper route or neighborhood jobs, or money from a parent for certain expenses like school lunches?

- What are your usual expenses? Think about lunches, school supplies, den dues, snacks, a weekly offering for your church or other religious group.

- What special expenses are coming up? A gift for a family birthday, a donation to a charity, items for Webelos Scout activities, a movie with friends?

The money you have to spend depends on the way your family handles children's expenses. In some families, a parent gives a child money as each expense comes up. The child also might have a small allowance to spend as he or she wishes.

In other families, a parent gives a child an allowance to cover lunches and other expenses, and the child has to budget carefully to make the money last.

Because of these differences between families, your budget probably won't look like anyone else's. Plan your month's budget to show the amount of money you expect to have each week and the expenses you will pay out.

How to Plan Your Budget

In planning any budget, it's good to think about *priorities*. A priority is something that comes first. It has to be paid, like your lunch money, so you put it first.

Try planning a budget for the first week. Here's a sample you can fill in, or make a chart of your own:

Where my money will come from:

Allowance.. $ _____

Jobs.. $ _____

Savings... $ _____

Total money... **$** _____

Where my money will go:

School lunches (1 week) .... $ _____

Den dues .... $ _____

Other expenses

_____ .... $ _____

_____ .... $ _____

Total expenses... **$** _____

Add up the total money available to you, and then add up the total expenses. If you're not going to have enough money for the first week, decide where you can cut down on expenses. If you expect to have more than enough money, you can increase your savings for another category. Plan the second, third, and fourth weeks. Be sure to include any special expenses you expect and make plans to save for them ahead of time if you can.

Requirement 4 also asks you to keep a record of the money you spend for one week. Each time you spend money, write down what you spent it for and the amount.

When you add up your actual expenses for a week, you'll know whether your budget is working out. You may have to adjust your budget if you didn't include all your expenses, or you may have to cut down your spending so you don't run out of money.

Saving Energy

Saving energy helps your family save money. It also helps conserve our natural resources. Requirement 7 asks you to prepare an energy-saving plan for your family. Check the list below to see what ideas need to go in your plan. Maybe you know other ways to save energy around your home.

- Close heating or air-conditioning vents in unused rooms.

- In winter, close the fireplace damper when the fireplace is not in use, because warm air in the house can be drawn up the chimney.

- Set the thermostat at the lowest comfortable level in winter and highest comfortable level in summer.

- In winter, lower the heat at night.

- Keep windows and outside doors closed when heating or air conditioning is on.

- Don't keep the refrigerator open more than needed.

- Cook several foods at one time. For example, if you cook two things in the oven at one time, the oven doesn't have to be on as long.

- Don't let water run when it isn't needed.

- Use lower wattage bulbs where less light is needed.

Family Fun

A family can have fun together in many ways. Some ways may cost no money, others cost a lot. Try to think of some inexpensive activities your family can do for fun. Here are some ideas:

- Play a new game together
- Make crafts with your family
- Go on a picnic
- Visit a museum, zoo, or park
- Do some community activities together
- Go swimming
- Go on a fishing trip

What are some other things you can do with your family?

Helping With Cleaning

Nobody likes living in a dirty home. It looks bad, and it can even be dangerous to your health because germs breed in dirt, trash, and garbage.

There is no magic way to keep your home clean. Everyone must do his or her part to vacuum or sweep floors, dust and polish furniture, and clean sinks, bathtubs, and toilets.

Cleaning may not be anyone's favorite activity, but when you're done, it's satisfying to have a clean home to live in and enjoy. You are old enough to help, so pitch in willingly. This is another way of showing you care about your family and your home.

Helping With Laundry

Do you take care of your own clothes? When they're dirty, do you put them in the laundry hamper? Once they're clean, do you fold them and put them in drawers or hang them on hangers in the closet?

There is no trick to doing these things. You can learn to fold clothes in about two minutes.

Why not help with the laundry? You'll learn how to operate the family's washing machine or the large machines at the self-service laundry. It will be one more step in showing that you can share in your family's jobs.

Feeding the Family

Everyone likes to eat. But a lot has to happen before the food gets to the table. Planning what to buy, shopping, preparing each dish—that's all part of creating a meal. And cleaning up, too! When you share in this, you learn a lot, and being with your family in the kitchen can be fun.

For requirement 11, you'll help plan at least one week's meals, help shop for the food, and help prepare at least three meals.

Planning Meals

Do you think it would be great to have a hamburger, French fries, and soda for every meal? You'd soon get bored with it, and a diet like that wouldn't do your body any good.

To stay healthy, you need a balanced diet and a variety of foods. When you help an adult in your family plan meals for requirement 11, look at the Food Guide Pyramid on page 249 and the section on meal planning, pages 248–256 (Fitness activity badge). That will tell you about a balanced diet and give you ideas for a variety of foods to choose for your plan.

Shopping for Food

Before you go to the store for food, make a list of the items you'll need for the meals you've planned. This is very important. If you just grab off the shelves the things that look good, you may not have what you need for complete meals. You also need to look for ways to save money on your purchases.

It's a good idea to check the store ads in the newspaper before you shop. Often they will have "specials" that can save you money. An adult member of your family can help you decide whether they are good buys.

In the store, remember to use your list. Ask the adult family member who is with you to help you compare prices. If an 8-ounce can of tomato sauce is 59 cents and a 15-ounce can is 89 cents, which is the better buy? See if you can figure it out. Smart shoppers compare prices.

Price isn't everything, though. Your family may like one brand best, even if it costs more.

Preparing Meals

Have an adult member of your family with you when you prepare meals. He or she can help if you don't understand the cookbook recipe or the directions on a box.

For requirement 11, you'll help with at least three meals. Will they be three different breakfasts? Or a breakfast, a lunch, and a dinner?

Getting a meal ready to eat shouldn't be difficult. Maybe you already prepare your own breakfast cereal. But this requirement asks you to help prepare three meals for the whole family. So you might be cooking hot cereal and adding chopped apple to it, or mixing up pancakes to serve with blueberries. Don't forget the other items on your menu plan, like milk and fruit juice.

Lunch can be easy, especially when you know exactly what to get ready. Washing fruit and putting it in a bowl on the table can take just a few minutes. If you get out all the ingredients for the family's favorite sandwiches before you start, you can put them together quickly.

Dinner may take more planning. Since some foods take longer to cook than others, ask an adult to help you decide when to start cooking each dish so everything is ready at about the same time. Or maybe you'll plan a dish you can make earlier in the day, and you can prepare the remaining items just before dinner.

If you use a recipe, read it carefully. Then read it again. Follow it exactly. If the recipe calls for 1 teaspoon of salt and you put in a tablespoon, your dinner will be a disaster!

After dinner, when everyone compliments your good food, you'll feel great. But there's still one thing to do. Clean up! Wouldn't this be a good time for everyone to help?

Family Meetings

Requirement 5 asks you to take part in at least four family meetings. Most families don't have formal meetings, but when your family is at the dinner table, you probably talk about school and events coming up. You make plans for a weekend or a trip. That's one type of meeting that is more like a conversation.

Sometimes families need to sit down and talk at a special time about plans and ideas they need to work out together. These are family meetings, too. The meeting might involve plans for fun, or it might be about serious topics that a parent wants children to know about. Here are some of the subjects that might come up at a meeting like this:

- A schedule to get everyone to music lessons, religious instruction, sports practices, Webelos den meetings, and home again
- Plans for a weekend camping trip or a vacation during the summer
- Family volunteering, like a bike ride for charity or a litter cleanup in your community
- Deciding what to make or buy as a gift for a relative or family friend
- Current events, what is in the news
- Family rules
- Ideas for helping each other
- What everyone needs to know about child abuse, alcoholism, drug abuse, and crime prevention

In the meeting, it's important to listen as well as to talk about your ideas and opinions.

If other family members disagree with you, don't get angry about it. Remember, they have their own interests and ideas, just as you do. Afterward, do your best to do your part in whatever is decided.

Family meetings are important. Talking about things brings all family members closer together.

Cub Scout Academics
Belt Loop for Heritages

If you earned the Heritages belt loop earlier in Cub Scouting, great! But that won't count for requirement 12 of this Family Member activity badge. You must earn the Heritages belt loop again while you are a Webelos Scout for it to count toward this activity badge.

heritages

Fitness Requirements

Requirement	Approved by

Do this:

1. With your parent, guardian, or Webelos den leader, complete the Health and Fitness Character Connection.

   a. **Know:** Tell why is it important to be healthy, clean, and fit.

   b. **Commit:** Tell when it is difficult for you to stick with good health habits. Tell where you can go to be with others who encourage you to be healthy, clean, and fit.

   c. **Practice:** Practice good health habits while doing the requirements for this activity badge. _10-27-1_

And do six of these:

2. With a parent or other adult family member, complete a safety notebook, which is discussed in the booklet "How to Protect Your Children from Child Abuse" that comes with this book.

3. Read the meal planning information in this chapter. With a parent or other family member, plan a week of meals. Explain what kinds of meals are best for you and why.

4. Keep a record of your daily meals and snacks for a week. Decide whether you have been eating foods that are good for you.

5. Tell an adult member of your family about the bad effects smoking or chewing tobacco would have on your body.

6. Tell an adult member of your family four reasons why you should not use alcohol and how it could affect you.

7. Tell an adult member of your family what drugs could do to your body and how they would affect your ability to think clearly.

8. Read the booklet *Take a Stand Against Drugs!* Discuss it with an adult and show that you understand the material.

What does *fitness* mean? It means being healthy and in good physical and mental shape.

One of your jobs in life is taking care of your wonderful and complex body. You need to become an expert at keeping it working at its best.

That means you must have a healthy diet and plenty of exercise and rest. You must avoid harmful substances.

You can earn the Fitness activity badge at home, on your own and with a family member. You'll learn about taking care of yourself, so you'll be your best when you work, play, and learn. When you have completed each requirement, ask an adult member of your family to sign it on the previous page or this page.

Your Safety Notebook

Part of taking care of yourself is knowing how to be safe and how to react in an emergency. In requirement 2, when you make a safety notebook with your parent or other adult family member, you'll have a place to keep emergency telephone numbers, your parent's work number, and other important numbers to have on hand. You'll write down the safety rules that you and your family follow. For more details on requirement 2, you and your parent can check the booklet "How to Protect Your Children from Child Abuse" that comes as a pull-out section with this book.

How to Plan Meals

There's a great advantage to requirement 3: You help choose the menus for meals you might eat for a whole week! But choose wisely and include foods that are best for you.

How to start? You'll find what you need for planning right here:

- The MyPyramid Plan, explained below and on page 249, shows you types of foods to include and tells how much of each you need each day.

- The sample serving list gives you examples of foods to include and tells how much equals an ounce (grains and meats) or cup (vegetables, fruits, milks).

- The sample menu for a day on page 253 gives you an idea how meal planning is done. It's really easy if you use the tools on www.mypyramid.gov.

Plan your menus with a parent or family member. If you or any family member has any dietary restrictions, keep those in mind.

In this chapter, you'll also find out how to read labels on food packages so you can compare foods.

MyPyramid Helps You Plan

In 2005, the U.S. Department of Agriculture (USDA) replaced their Food Guide Pyramid with the MyPyramid Plan. Because one size *doesn't* fit all, MyPyramid Plan can help you choose the foods and amounts that are right for *you*. All you have to do to find out what and how much you need to eat is go to www.mypyramid.gov and enter your age, sex, and activity level.

MyPyramid.gov has tools to help you plan your meals, and can also give you a detailed assessment of your own food intake and physical activity level over time with MyPyramid Tracker.

You can use the advice "Inside MyPyramid" to help you make smart choices from every food group, find your best balance between food and physical activity, and get the most nutrition out of your calories.

Every member of your family has different nutritional needs, and each of them can go to mypyramid.gov to find out what those are. (Or you can do it for them.) That information is what you need to be ready to plan family meals.

By using MyPyramid, you'll plan a balanced diet that includes protein, vitamins, minerals, carbohydrates, and fiber. You need all of these to grow and stay healthy and strong. See the pyramid on the next page. You need the most each day from the widest areas of the pyramid, and the least amounts from the narrowest areas.

Grains—Make half your grains whole. Eat at least 3 ounces of whole-grain cereals, breads, crackers, rice, or pasta every day. One ounce is about 1 slice of bread, about 1 cup of breakfast cereal, or ½ cup of cooked rice, cereal, or pasta.

Vegetables—Vary your veggies. Eat more dark-green veggies like broccoli, spinach, and other dark leafy greens. Eat more orange vegetables like carrots and sweet potatoes. Eat more dry beans and peas like pinto beans, kidney beans, and lentils.

Fruits—Focus on fruits. Eat a variety of fruit. Choose fresh, frozen, canned, or dried fruit. Go easy on fruit juices (they are high in sugar and low in fiber).

Milk—Get your calcium-rich foods. Go low-fat or fat-free when you choose milk, yogurt, and other milk products. If you don't or can't consume milk, choose lactose-free products or other calcium sources such as fortified foods and beverages.

Meat and beans—Go lean with protein. Choose low-fat or lean meats and poultry. Bake it, broil it, or grill it (don't fry it). Vary your protein routine—choose more fish, beans, peas, nuts, and seeds.

Fats, sugars, and salt (sodium)—Choose these with caution. Get most of your fat from fish, nuts, and vegetable oils. Limit solid fats like butter, stick margarine, shortening, and lard. Check nutrition labels to keep your intake low on saturated fats, trans fats, and sodium. Choose foods and beverages that are low in added sugar.

Water—Not on the pyramid. but essential. Be sure you drink plenty of water, too, especially if you've been playing hard, hiking, or exercising.

Source: www.mypyramid.gov

How Much at a Meal?

The serving size for a meal can vary for different foods and different people. MyPyramid tells you how many ounces of grains and meats you need daily, and it uses cups to measure vegetables, fruits, and milk. As you plan your meals, check the following list of examples from each food group. The list may give you ideas for meals, too.

If five or six ounces from the bread, cereal, rice, and pasta group seems like a lot, look at the list carefully. You already may be eating that much, because you get two servings in a sandwich or in one cup of pasta.

Some dishes are combinations. Pizza combines a bread crust, cheese, tomato sauce, and possibly vegetables and meat. You'll have to guess at the serving sizes in a piece of pizza.

Grains (Bread, Cereal, Rice, and Pasta)

These are examples of what to count as one ounce:
- 1 slice of bread (a sandwich has two servings)
- 1 tortilla
- ½ cup cooked rice, pasta, or cereal
- 1 ounce ready-to-eat cereal
- ½ hamburger bun, bagel, or English muffin (one whole bun has two servings)
- 3 to 4 plain crackers (small)
- 1 pancake (a stack of three pancakes has three servings)
- ½ doughnut or Danish (medium)
- $\frac{1}{16}$ cake (average)
- 2 cookies (medium)
- $\frac{1}{12}$ pie (two-crust)

Vegetables

These are equivalent to a half cup of vegetables:
- ½ cup chopped raw or cooked vegetables
- 1 cup raw, leafy vegetables

- ¾ cup vegetable juice
- ½ baked potato

Fruits

These are equivalent to a half cup of fruit:

- 1 apple, banana, orange, pear, nectarine, peach, or melon wedge
- ¾ cup fruit juice
- ½ cup chopped, cooked, or canned fruit
- ¼ cup dried fruit

Milk

These are equivalent to a cup of milk:
- 1 cup low-fat or skim milk
- 1 cup yogurt
- 1½ ounces natural cheese
- 2 ounces processed cheese
- ½ cups cottage cheese
- 1 cup frozen yogurt

Meat and Beans

These are equal to 1 ounce of meat, poultry, or fish:
- ½ cup cooked beans
- 1 egg
- 2 tablespoons peanut butter
- ⅓ cup nuts

Fats, Sugars, and Salt

Use sparingly. Examples of fats and oils in your diet are:
- One pat (1 tablespoon) butter or margarine
- Oils used in cooking
- Shortening used in pastry
- Salad dressings (read the label) Fat-free dressings are available.

Sweets include most desserts, cookies, candy, cakes, pies, puddings, and syrups. Some reduced-fat and reduced-sugar products are available.

What About Snacks?

Everyone likes snacks! You'll want to include a couple of healthful snacks in each day's plan. A snack can provide nutrients and give you energy between meals. The low-fat snacks listed below are good choices.

Fruits

- 1 apple, banana, orange, pear, nectarine, or peach
- ¾ cup orange or grape juice
- ½ cup pineapple or grapes
- ¼ cup prunes or raisins

Vegetables

- 1 carrot
- ¾ cup mixed vegetable juice
- 1 stalk celery (1 cup chopped)

Grains

- 1 graham cracker, wheat cracker, ½ English muffin, or rice cake
- ½ bagel
- 1 low-fat granola bar
- 1 cup popcorn, light (not much fat added)
- 1 ounce pretzels

Milk

- 1 ounce skim mozzarella cheese
- 1 cup of 1 percent chocolate milk
- 1 cup powdered breakfast drink made with skim milk
- 1 cup skim milk
- 8 ounces yogurt with fruit

Mixtures

- 1 cup low-sodium (low-salt) chicken noodle or vegetable soup
- 1 cup low-sodium (low-salt) chicken broth

Sugars

- 1 slice angel food cake (bread group)
- 3 gingersnaps or vanilla wafers (bread group)
- ½ cup ice milk (milk group)
- 1 juice bar (fruit group)

A Sample Menu

Make different daily plans with a variety of foods. Check to see if you have enough servings from each food group.

Sample Menu for a 2,000-Calorie/Day Diet

	Group				
	Grains	Vegetables	Fruits	Milk	Meat and Beans
Breakfast					
Orange			½ medium		
Milk				1 cup	
Cereal with raisins	½ cup		(¼ cup in cereal)		
Whole-grain toast	1 slice				
Lunch					
Ham sandwich on whole-grain bread	2 slices bread	Lettuce leaf			2.5 oz. ham
Carrot sticks		½ cup			
Apple			1 medium		
Milk				1 cup	
Afternoon Snack					
Celery		1 stalk			
Dinner					
Chicken					3 oz.
Peas		½ cup			
Brown rice	½ cup				
Tossed salad		1 cup			
Low-fat salad dressing					
Ice milk				1 cup	
Evening Snack					
Popcorn	½ cup				
Daily Total	6 ounces	2.5 cups	2 cups	3 cups	5.5 ounces

The amounts you need may be different than these. See www.mypyramid.gov to find out your daily amounts of each food group.

What About Fat?

You hear and read a lot about people avoiding fat in foods. But our bodies actually need some fat in our diets, and we can't avoid fat altogether, anyway.

But a diet high in fat can be harmful in terms of weight gain and health. A good rule is to eat a balanced diet, be aware of high-fat foods, and make low-fat choices when you can.

Apples, bananas, and other fruits are obvious low-fat choices for snacks. Skim milk has very little fat compared with whole milk. Although children younger than 2 years need whole milk, a better choice for older children, teens, and adults is low-fat or skim milk.

If you make good choices every day, an occasional higher-fat choice, like fast food or real ice cream, shouldn't be a problem.

One way to identify high-fat foods—and learn more about foods you eat—is to read food labels.

Read Those Labels

You can learn a lot from a food label. Compare these labels from two snack food products.

Look at each label. What makes one serving for each? Is that about the amount you might eat for a snack, or would you eat more?

A *calorie* is a unit of energy stored in food. Notice the calories in one serving and the number of calories from fat. In one serving of the cheese-flavored snack are 150 calories, and 90 of those calories come from fat. That's 60 percent of the calories from fat. You can figure it this way:

90 (calories from fat) ÷ 150 (calories per serving) = 0.60 (60% of calories from fat)

(Note: If the label lists only grams of fat, you can figure calories yourself: 1 gram fat = 9 calories.)

Experts say we should get no more than 20 percent to 35 percent of our daily calories from fat. You can see how a person who eats many high-fat items in a day may end up getting too many of his calories from fat. In other words, he's not getting the most nutrition out of his calories.

Fat-free pretzels

Nutrition Facts

Serving Size 1 oz. (28g/About 12 pretzels)
Servings Per Container 15

Amount Per Serving

Calories 110   Calories from Fat 0

	% Daily Value*
Total Fat 0g	0%
Saturated Fat 0g	0%
Cholesterol 0mg	0%
Sodium 520mg	22%
Total Carbohydrate 23g	8%
Dietary Fiber 1g	5%
Sugars less than 1g	
Protein 2g	

Vitamin A 0%	•	Vitamin C 0%
Calcium 0%	•	Iron 10%

*Percent Daily Values are based on a 2,000 calorie diet. Your daily values may be higher or lower depending on your calories needs.

Calories:		2,000	2,500
Total Fat	Less than	65g	80g
Sat Fat	Less than	20g	25g
Cholesterol	Less than	300mg	300mg
Sodium	Less than	2,400mg	2,400mg
Total Carbohydrate		300g	375g
Dietary Fiber		25g	30g

Calories per gram:
Fat 9   •   Carbohydrate 4   •   Protein 4

Cheese-flavored snack food

Nutrition Facts

Serving Size 1 oz. (28g/About 12 pieces)
Servings Per Container 10

Amount Per Serving

Calories 150   Calories from Fat 90

	% Daily Value*
Total Fat 10g	15%
Saturated Fat 2.5g	12%
Cholesterol less than 5mg	1%
Sodium 350mg	14%
Total Carbohydrate 15g	5%
Dietary Fiber less than 1g	1%
Sugars 1g	
Protein 2g	

Vitamin A 0%	•	Vitamin C 0%
Calcium 2%	•	Iron 2%

*Percent Daily Values are based on a 2,000 calorie diet. Your daily values may be higher or lower depending on your calories needs.

Calories:		2,000	2,500
Total Fat	Less than	65g	80g
Sat Fat	Less than	20g	25g
Cholesterol	Less than	300mg	300mg
Sodium	Less than	2,400mg	2,400mg
Total Carbohydrate		300g	375g
Dietary Fiber		25g	30g

Calories per gram:
Fat 9   •   Carbohydrate 4   •   Protein 4

If you read labels, you begin to get an idea of the nutritional content of different types of foods. Some have higher sodium (salt) content than others. Some products have protein, potassium, vitamins A and C, calcium, and iron, and some have little or none. Some have fiber, and some don't. Some have extra sugars that add calories but few nutrients. Read the ingredient list and make sure that added sugars (with names like sucrose, glucose, and high fructose corn syrup) aren't one of the first few ingredients.

Eating right is a kind of balancing act. What you don't get from one food you may get from another. The more you learn about what your body needs, the better prepared you'll be to make wise choices about food.

The Dangers of Tobacco

Why do some kids smoke or chew tobacco? They do it because they think it makes them more grown up.

In fact, smoking and using chewing tobacco are bad choices for anyone—child, teen, and adult. Many adults have given up smoking and chewing tobacco because scientists have shown that these habits are very harmful to health.

Cigarette smoking has these bad effects:

- It causes lung cancer, heart disease, and other ailments.
- It reduces a person's ability to breathe deeply. Athletes who smoke cannot play as hard or as long as those who don't.
- Smoke may irritate the eyes, making them red and sore.
- Smoke stains teeth and fingers.

Chewing tobacco is as dangerous as smoking.

- The tobacco may damage the delicate tissues of your mouth.
- It causes diseases.
- It certainly will stain your teeth.

Using tobacco is like putting sand in the gas tank of a new car. The beautiful car won't run, and the engine will be ruined.

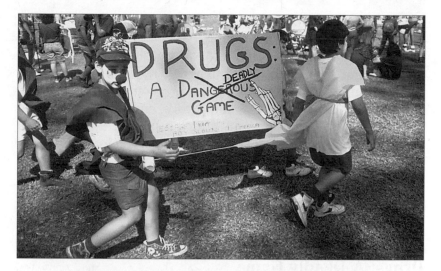

The Dangers of Alcohol, Other Drugs, and Inhalants

Drinking alcoholic beverages and doing drugs are even more dangerous than smoking because these actions can have terrible consequences the very first time a person tries them.

The effects of alcohol: Perhaps you have seen someone unsteady on their feet because of drinking too much beer, wine, or liquor. Alcohol slows down the brain and body. It destroys balance. It may make a person see double or even pass out.

Alcohol makes some people do bad things they would never consider doing when they are sober. Drunk drivers are responsible for thousands of deaths on our nation's streets and highways every year.

A person who drinks too much for several years may suffer from serious illnesses of the liver and other organs.

The effects of drugs: Some drugs are prescribed by doctors to ease pain or relieve symptoms of disease, but prescription drugs are dangerous if they are misused. You should never take a prescription drug unless it is prescribed for you by a doctor. All other drugs are dangerous for you—whether they have been legally prescribed for someone else or sold illegally on the street.

The effects of inhalants: Sniffing glue and inhaling the fumes of paint thinner or gasoline can be dangerous and even fatal. These substances contain toxins that can affect the liver, kidneys, and muscular system. Inhaling these poisonous substances can also cause psychological problems.

Stay away from inhalants and drugs and people who sell them. Marijuana, cocaine and "crack," heroin, "speed," "pep pills," LSD, and other illegal drugs bring nothing but trouble.

Some drugs make people drowsy. Some make it hard to know what is real and what is a dream. Others make people feel so awake and active that they cannot relax and rest. Overdoses are often fatal.

All illegal drugs are bad news.

Drugs: A Deadly Game

Requirement 8 asks you to read a booklet called *Take a Stand Against Drugs!* It's meant to be another reminder about the dangers of drugs—*all drugs*—including cigarettes and beer. Maybe you'll learn something you didn't know about drugs. You can discuss what you learn with adults or members of your den. You can never know too much about the bad news of drugs.

Note: Take a Stand Against Drugs materials may be obtained through your local council service center.

F

FORESTER

Forester Requirements

Requirement	Approved by

Do five of these:

1. Make a map of the United States. Show the types of forests growing in different parts of the country. Name some kinds of trees that grow in these forests.

2. Draw a picture to show the plant and tree layers of a forest in your area. Label the different layers. (If you don't live in an area that has forests, choose an area that does and draw a picture of that forest.)

3. Identify six forest trees common to the area where you live. Tell how both wildlife and humans use them. (If you don't live in a region that has forests, read about one type of forest and name six of its trees and their uses.)

4. Identify six forest plants (other than trees) that are useful to wildlife. Tell which animals use them and for what purposes.

5. Draw a picture showing

   • how water and minerals in the soil help a tree grow

   • how the tree uses sunlight to help it grow

6. Make a poster showing a tree's growth rings or examine the growth rings of a tree stump. Explain how the rings tell its life history.

7. Collect pieces of three kinds of wood used for building houses. Tell what kinds of wood they are and one place each of them might be used.   _____

8. Plant 20 forest tree seedlings. Tell how you planted them and what you did to take care of them after planting.   _____

9. Describe both the benefits and the harm wildfires can cause in a forest ecosystem. Tell how you can help prevent wildfire.   _____ .

10. Draw your own urban forestry plan for adding trees to a street, yard, or park near your home. Show what types of trees you would like to see planted.   _____

Trees and other forest plants are important parts of the interconnected life on Earth. A forester's work—taking care of trees and managing forest land—is important to the well-being of the planet. You'll learn why when you earn the Forester activity badge.

Wherever you live, on a farm, in a small town, in a large city—or even in the middle of a forest—you can learn about identifying trees and planting new trees.

You might visit a forest with your Webelos den. Take your time and notice everything—all kinds of trees and other plants, animals, birds, and insects. The forest is a fascinating place.

Learning about forests will help you understand more about how all the living things on our planet work together to keep each other healthy. Forests provide much more than building material and shade. They help keep a livable climate for us and other animals. We learn to make medicines from studying forest plants. Learning about forests is important because we need to manage our forests wisely to keep them healthy. When you complete each requirement, ask your Webelos den leader or activity badge counselor to sign it on pages 260–261.

Forest Regions of the United States

Most trees grow best in certain kinds of places. Each type of tree needs a certain range of climate, rainfall, and soil. The United States has several different kinds of forests.

West coast forest: Mild climate, lots of rain. Some of the trees are Douglas fir, ponderosa pine, redwood, giant sequoia.

Western forest: Chiefly on mountain slopes. Cold winters, short summers, dryness in summer in the southern part. Typical trees are ponderosa pine, blue spruce, western larch, quaking aspen. Pinyon pine in the southwest.

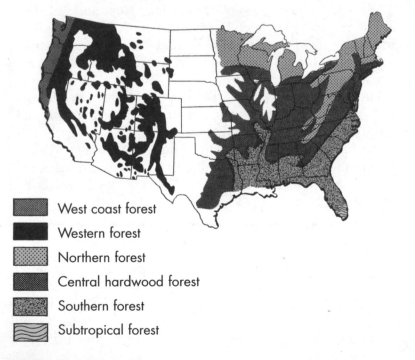

West coast forest
Western forest
Northern forest
Central hardwood forest
Southern forest
Subtropical forest

Northern forest: Low temperatures, short growing season. Common trees are eastern white pine, northern white cedar, white and black spruces, paper birch, sugar maple, northern red oak.

Central hardwood forest: Climate varies from north to south. Rich soils. Good rainfall, usually. Some of the trees are red, white, and black oak; black walnut; sycamore; sweetgum; silver maple; poplar; hickory. Hardwood trees lose their leaves in the fall. Some conifers (trees that have cones) also grow in this region.

Southern forest: Drier soils, but usually enough rainfall. Typical trees are shortleaf and longleaf pines, magnolia, red and white oak, pecan, poplar, overcup oak, holly. In swamps, bald cypress and gums.

Subtropical forest: Warm climate and humid (damp). Common trees are West Indies mahogany, mangroves, palms.

What Is a Riparian Forest?

Forests along streams and wetlands are called *riparian forests*. They are very much influenced by how close they are to water and have unique vegetation compared with areas farther away from water.

The plant life in the rich soil and the aquatic life in the water attract more kinds of birds, insects, and small animals to the riparian forest, compared with other kinds of forests.

The combination of forest and water attracts some species of birds that migrate in the fall and spring and is important to their survival.

Forest Structure

Did you know a forest has *layers*? Here are the five basic forest layers, from top to bottom.

The canopy: The canopy of a forest is made up of the tops of the tallest trees. It's like the roof of the forest. This layer gets the most sunlight, so it often produces the most food for wildlife. Birds, squirrels, reptiles, and insects live here.

The understory: Shorter trees grow in the understory of the forest. They get less sunlight, but they also produce food and habitat for animals, birds, and insects.

The shrub layer: Shrubs are woody plants, smaller than trees, that have more than one stem. Mammals, birds, and insects live and feed in the shrub layer.

The herb layer: These plants are small and have softer stems that are not woody. Depending on the type of forest and the amount of sunlight at this level, you'd find ferns, grasses, and wildflowers here. Insects, mice, other small animals, and snakes live here.

Large animals like deer and bears depend on the food in the understory, shrub layer, and herb layer.

The forest floor: This bottom layer collects dead leaves and plants, fallen trees, animal droppings, dead animals—and returns them to the soil in a process called *decomposition*. Earthworms, fungi, and insects, along with bacteria and other microscopic organisms, gradually break down the materials. The plants of the forest absorb the nutrients released by decomposition.

Look for plants in the different forest layers in your area (or in a forest area in your state). What kinds of trees are the tallest? Which trees are in the understory? In an eastern hardwood forest, the tallest trees might be oak and hickory. The understory could contain flowering dogwood, redbud, sassafras, and sumac. The shrub layer might have blackberry and wild grape. In a western conifer forest, the tallest trees might be Douglas fir, western hemlock, and western red cedar. The understory might have Pacific yew, dogwood, and ocean spray. The shrub layer might have salal and sword fern. The forest you study could have entirely different trees and plants.

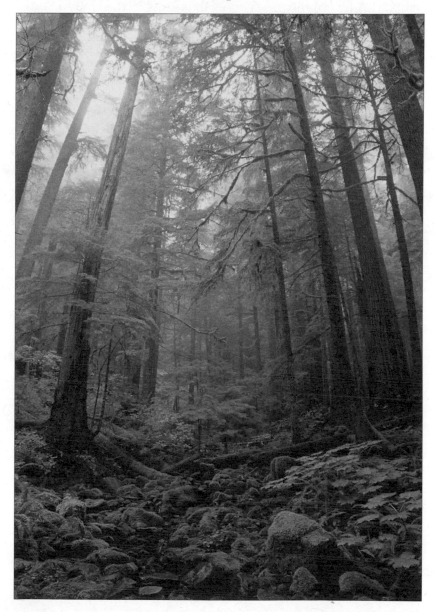

Forest Trees

Foresters learn everything about the many kinds of trees, smaller plants, and animals that grow and live in the forests they manage. A few of the forest trees that grow in the United States are shown on these pages.

Douglas Fir
Pacific Northwest coast and Rocky Mountains
Height: 100–250 feet
Used for lumber, plywood, paper.

Sweetgum
Southeastern states and north to Connecticut, New York, Ohio, Illinois, Missouri, Oklahoma
Height: 80–120 feet
Used for veneer, furniture, cabinets, and woodwork. (Veneer is a thin layer of wood used to make furniture surfaces.)

Eastern White Pine
Northeastern states
Height: 50–100 feet
Used for cabinets, interior lumber, woodenware.

Ponderosa Pine
All western states, into southern Canada and northern Mexico
Height: 60–200 feet
Used for lumber, fences, railroad ties; very important for millwork.

Shagbark Hickory
Eastern half of the United States
Height: 60–80 feet
Used for furniture, wall paneling, tool handles, cooking fuel; provides nuts for wildlife.

Walnut
Eastern half of the United States
Height: 80–100 feet
Used for furniture, gunstocks, doors, and cabinets; wildlife and humans eat the nuts.

White Oak
Eastern half of the United States
Height: 60–120 feet
Used for lumber, furniture, boats, fuel wood; the acorns are important food for wildlife.

Hemlock
Northeast (eastern hemlock)
Far west (western and mountain hemlocks)
Height: 60–100 feet (mountain hemlock); 125–200 feet (western hemlock)
Used for lumber, pulpwood for paper, and railroad ties.

Longleaf Pine
Southeastern coastal states
Height: 100–120 feet
Once used for turpentines and resins; now used for lumber and framing.

Animals and Humans Depend on Forests

Many kinds of trees are used for building materials and wood for furniture. Foresters know which types of trees are best for building and which are more useful for making paper—or which are important for *both* building and making paper.

Trees like walnut and pecan supply nuts to use in baking cookies and pies. Wild plums and other fruits grow on forest trees. People often pick wild blackberries, huckleberries, and gooseberries, which grow on shrubs in the shrub layer.

Animals find even more to eat in the forest than humans do. Think about seeds, acorns, grasses, tree leaves—do you know which animals eat them?

Here are a few more ways wildlife and humans use forest plants.

Wildlife uses:

- Bluebirds, catbirds, and mockingbirds eat the red berries of the holly tree.
- Deer eat tree bark, leaving marks. Deer also eat tree leaves, stems, and other green plants.
- Bears mark their territory by clawing and biting tree trunks. Mountain lions sharpen their claws on trees.
- Moose, elk, and deer use tree trunks or flexible saplings to rub the velvet off their antlers.
- Beavers eat the bark and cut down trees to build dams and homes for themselves.

Human uses:

- Hickory and white ash are used to make baseball bats and tool handles.
- Western red cedar is used to make porches, decks, and shingles for roofs.

- Mesquite and hickory chips on cooking fires flavor food.
- Candles are made from the waxy covering of the southern bayberry fruit.
- Maple syrup is made from the sap of sugar maples harvested in the early spring.

Identifying Forest Trees and Plants

A forest is a community of plants, from the tallest trees down to the smallest mosses and lichens that you have to kneel on the ground to see.

When you visit a wooded area or forest, take along a tree field guide. A wildflower guide is handy, too. Your public library may have these books.

Take time to look closely at everything. Use a magnifying glass to study tiny details.

When you're looking at trees, check for:

- Type of leaf. Feel it. Is it smooth or rough? Notice the shape.
- Leaf edges—smooth or toothed?
- Type of bark—smooth or rough, peeling, light or dark?
- Unusual features—thorns, flowers, berries. Some trees will have more than one leaf shape. The sassafras has three leaf shapes.
- With conifers, notice the length, shape, and grouping of the needles. Spruce needles are sharp and short, with four sides, and they grow separately on the twigs. Pine needles grow in bundles, so count the number in a bundle for a clue to the kind of pine it is. Needles of a longleaf pine could be 18 inches long,

but jack pine needles are only about 1 inch long. The size and type of cone will also provide clues to the identity of the tree.

The tree supports much life. Look for woodpecker holes, insects hiding under the bark, mistletoe rooted in the branches, fungi growing on the bark, and the nests of birds and squirrels. Move slowly and quietly so you can have a chance to see birds, squirrels, and other animals.

How a Tree Grows

The tree grows in its roots, trunk, and crown (its top, where all the branches and leaves are). The tree needs food to grow, and its roots and leaves play a part in the process of making food.

Roots: Roots anchor the tree in the earth. They soak up the water, minerals, and nitrogen from the soil that the leaves need to make food for the tree. A layer of growth cells at root tips makes new roots each year. Tree roots help slow erosion by holding soil in place.

Trunk: The trunk is a pathway for water and minerals to move from the soil upward to the leaves. It grows outward each year. (See "The Inside Story of a Tree," page 272.) As the trunk grows taller, the crown of the tree grows higher in search of more sunlight. In trees used for lumber, the trunk produces most of the useful wood.

Crown: The crown is the upper part of the tree, including the branches and leaves. The leaves take in sunlight and use it to make food for the tree in a process called *photosynthesis* (discussed on the next page).

The crown of the tree grows each year by adding a new growth of leaves and twigs. This growth comes from young cells in buds on the twigs.

Tree Bud

Photosynthesis

Trees, like all plants with green leaves, use sunlight to make food from air and water, in a chemical process called *photosynthesis*. The food *(carbohydrate)* is made in the leaves.

Carbon dioxide from the air comes through pores in the leaves. Water and

Carbon dioxide from the air.

Chlorophyll captures the sun's energy.

Oxygen and moisture are released into the air.

Water and minerals from the roots.

minerals come up through the roots in tubelike pathways in the tree to the veins in the leaves. (You can see these tubes on the branch and in the stem when you detach a leaf.)

Chlorophyll is what makes a leaf green. It also captures the sun's energy and uses it to process carbon dioxide and water, making liquid sugar. This flows to every living part of the tree, nourishing it and helping it grow.

Some of the oxygen taken from the water is left over. The tree doesn't need all the leftover oxygen, so the leaves release excess oxygen and also water, keeping the air around the trees damp and cool.

The Inside Story of a Tree

Inner Bark: Carries food made in the leaves down to the branches, trunk, and roots. It consists of hollow tubes.

Fire Scar: A tree can be damaged by fire even if it is not burned down. Disease and insects can enter through fire scars.

Outer Bark: Protects the tree from injuries.

Thinning: At this point, nearby trees were cut down, giving the tree more light. There were 20 years of growth before thinning, and 10 years of growth after.

Sapwood: Carries sap from roots to leaves.

Heartwood: Originally sapwood, inactive; gives strength to a tree.

Cambium: This thin layer of cells between bark and wood is where the trunk grows. Each year it forms a ring of new wood toward the inside of the trunk and new inner bark toward the outside of the trunk.

Collecting Wood Samples

Many kinds of wood are used in building houses. In any house, you are likely to find oak, pine, and cedar as part of the structure, decoration, or furniture.

You may be able to get scraps of these woods and others by visiting a lumberyard.

Show the grain from four different angles by cutting each sample as shown here. Sand each surface with sandpaper. You may want to lacquer or varnish half of each surface. This shows what the wood looks like when it's finished.

Tree Planting

Planting new trees is the key to *sustainable forestry*. Sustainable forestry means that people in the future will have the same abundant forests that we enjoy today.

- Carry seedlings in a bucket or box. Keep the roots damp.

- Plant them at least 6 feet apart.

- Dig holes just deep enough to hold the roots. Loosen the sides and bottom of the hole so that tiny roots can push into the soil. The roots should not be stuffed into the hole, or the tree's chances of surviving are low.

- A seedling should be planted so that its old ground line is about ¼ inch below the new ground level. (The *ground line* is the dark mark on the trunk.)

- A seedling should be planted with its trunk straight up and the hole filled with soil even with the ground. The soil should not be sunk in or mounded up above the ground.

- Press the soil down firmly around the roots to prevent air pockets. If you don't, the roots will dry out and the tree will probably die.
- A newly planted seedling needs lots of water, so soak the soil around the seedling with water, and then soak it again.
- Cover the ground around the base of the seedling with several inches of *mulch*—composted leaves, wood chips, grass cuttings, straw, or sawdust. This holds in moisture and helps make the soil richer for the new tree.

Fire in the Forest

Fire can both benefit and destroy a forest. A cool fire burning slowly along the ground does not hurt the trees. By burning away excess brush, the fire provides nutrients and space for new trees to grow. A new, young forest then provides habitat for many animals and birds.

But a hot wildfire burns high into the tree crowns and can injure and kill many trees. A wildfire in a forest can do much more than destroy trees. It also destroys food and cover for

Fall Color

Why do some hardwood tree leaves change color and fall off the tree? Chlorophyll production stops in the fall, revealing the yellow and orange pigments that were hidden by the green of the chlorophyll. Reds and purplish colors also develop in leaves rich in sugar, in trees like hard maples, dogwoods, and sweetgums.

As winter approaches, days grow shorter. The place where the leaf stem is connected to the branch weakens. Wind and frost can cause the connections to break, and the leaves fall.

wildlife. Sometimes it destroys the animals themselves. And, as more people build their homes near or in forests, more and more homes are at risk of being destroyed by wildfire.

Wildfire can burn the plant cover that protects the soil and sometimes might cause erosion. When soil and ashes wash into streams and lakes, good fishing may be spoiled. Campsites and other recreation areas may be destroyed by fire.

You can help prevent wildfire in these ways:

- Be extremely careful with any fire you build in the outdoors.

- Always build your fire in a safe place and watch it at all times.

- Don't leave a fire until it is out and *cold*. If you can still feel heat through the ashes, the fire is not completely out. (Be careful not to burn your hands!)

- If you see a fire, report it immediately to the nearest fire warden or fire department.

Because some kinds of fires can help the forest, foresters sometimes intentionally set controlled fires (called *prescribed fires*) or allow a "natural fire" caused by lightning to burn in order to reduce the buildup of deadwood or leaves on the forest floor. When this material gets too deep, a wildfire will burn hotter, increasing the destruction.

Foresters also use prescribed fires to maintain savannas, which are grasslands with scattered trees and shrubs. Fires help control the invasion of too many trees into the grassland.

The lodgepole pine, which grows in the west from Alaska to Baja, California, actually needs fire to release its seeds. Its cones stay closed and attached to the tree for years. When a ground fire comes through the forest, the heat causes the cones to open and release the seeds.

Urban Forestry

Foresters work in cities, too. That's called urban forestry. These foresters know what kinds of trees grow well in a city environment.

Planting trees in cities helps in these ways:

- New trees beautify streets and show that people care about the way their city looks. People enjoy walking along tree-lined, shady sidewalks. Trees in front of businesses make the property more attractive to customers.

- Flowering trees put on a show in the spring. Fall leaf colors brighten the city in autumn.

- Adding trees in parks creates shady places to play and picnic.

- Shade trees can be located to shade pavement and buildings, cooling them in summer and cutting down on air-conditioning costs.

- A grove of trees can shelter an area from winter winds.

- Trees provide habitat and food for birds and other wildlife in the city.

- Trees purify air by taking in carbon dioxide and releasing oxygen.

Urban foresters plan tree-planting projects, decide what kinds of trees to plant, and supervise crews of workers who plant and care for new trees. The foresters also may advise volunteer groups working on community tree-planting projects.

G

GEOLOGIST

Geologist
Requirements

Requirement	Approved by

Do five of these:

1. Collect five geologic specimens that have important uses.

2. Rocks and minerals are used in metals, glass, jewelry, road-building products, and fertilizer. Give examples of minerals used in these products.

3. Make a scale of mineral hardness for objects found at home. Show how to use the scale by finding the relative hardness of three samples.

4. List some of the geologic materials used in building your home.

5. Make a drawing that shows the cause of a volcano, a geyser, or an earthquake.

6. Explain one way in which mountains are formed.

7. Describe what a fossil is. How is it used to tell how old a formation is? Find two examples of fossils in your area.

8. Take a field trip to a geological site, geological laboratory, or rock show. Discuss what you learned at your next Webelos den meeting.

9. While you are a Webelos Scout, earn the Cub Scout Academics belt loop for Geology.

6/22/12

A geologist is a person who studies the history of the earth and its life. In this case, the history books are rocks. Geologists are interested in learning how the earth is made.

Geologists study rock formations at the tops of mountains and deep in the earth's crust. They investigate earthquakes, volcanoes, and geysers. They know about the uses of rocks and minerals. Some geologists search for mineral deposits like gold, diamonds, coal, and oil.

In earning this activity badge, you'll find out how the earth is formed and what is in it. You'll find out what fossils are. You'll learn what they can tell us about the earth millions of years ago. When you complete each requirement, ask your Webelos den leader or activity badge counselor to sign it on page 280.

Rocks and Pebbles

Your own backyard and neighborhood are good places to begin collecting rocks. Use a guide to rocks and minerals to help you identify the rocks you pick up. (See more about collecting on pages 286–287.)

While you're examining a rock, think about the rock you can't see and pick up. It's under your feet, under your yard, and it runs deep into the planet. It's the earth's *crust*.

Rhyolite

Granite

Shale layer on sandstone

The Earth's Crust and Core

The earth's crust is up to 65 miles thick and is made up of many kinds of rock, formed in layers at different times. In places, the layers are broken or have been folded, pushed up, or dropped down in blocks. In some places, the crust is fractured along a line called a *fault*. (See page 293.) Some faults run for hundreds of miles.

When you see mountain peaks, rock cliffs along rivers, or layers of rock where a highway has been cut through, you're seeing the upper parts of the earth's crust.

Below the crust is the *mantle*, which is about 1,750 miles deep. The upper part of the mantle (the *asthenosphere*) is partly molten (melted). Below that the mantle is solid.

While we don't yet know, the most widely accepted theory is that below the mantle is an *outer core* of iron and nickel melted together in a hot liquid, and an *inner core* at the center of the planet; a solid ball of iron and nickel.

Crust

Mantle

Outer core

Inner core

Three Kinds of Rock

All rocks belong to one of the three main groups making up the earth's crust: igneous, sedimentary, and metamorphic rocks.

Igneous Rock

Igneous rock is any rock made by the cooling of magma or lava. Magma is molten material that flows under the earth's crust. Sometimes it finds a weak spot and breaks through to form great areas of rock called flood basalts, or it may erupt as a volcano. Besides basalt, examples of igneous rock are granite and obsidian.

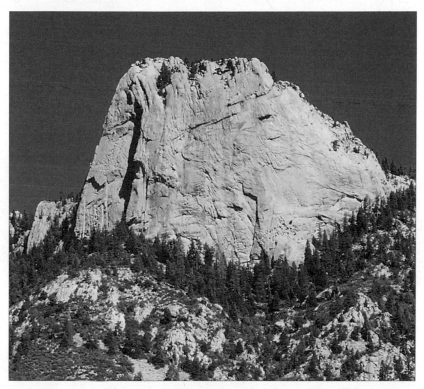

The Tooth of Time at Philmont Scout Ranch is an example of igneous rock formed by volcanic action 22 to 40 million years ago.

Sedimentary Rock

Sediment is gravel, sand, clay, or soil that settles out of water in riverbeds, ponds, lakes, and oceans. Sediment may contain shells and skeletons. Sedimentary rock is formed in layers, like a giant cake, after sediment has been under great pressure for millions of years. If the sediment was originally sand, it becomes sandstone. Clay turns into shale. Shells and skeletons make limestone. Small pebbles and sand form conglomerate.

Metamorphic Rock

Metamorphic rock has been through a process much like baking. (*Meta* means changed, and *morphic* means form.) The change is caused by intense heat and great pressure deep in the earth. Under these conditions, sedimentary limestone becomes marble. Sedimentary sandstone turns into quartzite. Igneous granite changes into gneiss (pronounced "nice").

How Rocks Break Down

Wind, water, heat, and cold are all strong forces in the world. They slowly break down any rock, no matter how hard it is. The result is sand, gravel, clay, and soil.

Lichens growing on rock also break it down, slowly loosening rock particles.

When material from decayed plants and animals mixes with the broken-down rock, soil forms. Rock is always being broken down, very slowly.

Useful Minerals

The earth contains useful minerals. Some, like silica (sand), are easy to see and collect. Others, like iron and zinc, are found in rocks. They must be removed from the rock by a process called *smelting* or *refining*.

There are three classes of useful minerals—metals, nonmetallic minerals, and fuels. Here are some examples.

Metals	Nonmetallic Minerals		Fuels
	Used in building materials and supplies	Precious and semiprecious stones	
Iron	Gypsum	Turquoise	Coal
Tin	Potash	Topaz	Natural gas
Platinum	Limestone	Garnet	Petroleum
Zinc	Sand	Tourmaline	Uranium (used for nuclear fuel)
Mercury	Borax	Diamond	
Aluminum	Talc	Zircon	
Lead	Quartz	Sapphire	
Gold		Ruby	
Uranium			
Copper			
Silver			
Magnesium			

Precious and Semiprecious Stones

Minerals Used in Tools

Some precious stones are used in scientific and industrial tools. Examples are the diamond, which is so hard that it is used to make the most effective cutting and grinding tools, and ruby, which focuses the light in high-powered lasers used by scientists.

Collecting Specimens

One way to begin a collection of geologic specimens is to visit a business that sells building stone or one that makes gravestones. These businesses might have small scraps of marble, granite, sandstone, limestone, pumice, shale, or slate that they will give you.

Or, go on a field trip. If possible, go with a collector who knows a lot about rocks (called a *rock hound*). A rock hound will know which rocks contain useful materials.

Look for minerals in gravel or sand pits, road cuts, diggings, mountains, hills, and stream banks. But stay away from dangerous areas like quarries, mine dump heaps, and old mines. Always have an adult with you. Be careful when climbing on rocks or cliffs.

Watch out for snakes. They may crawl under rocks, so learn to poke around a rock with a stick before reaching under it.

Keep your rock samples small. Small ones are easier to carry and easier to care for.

Collecting rocks is not allowed in national parks and in many state parks. Ask permission before you collect anywhere.

Geologist's Equipment

- Safety glasses to protect your eyes.
- A pocket magnifier for seeing things up close.
- Geologist's hammer for pulling rocks out of hillsides and breaking them open.
- Cold chisel, ½-inch to 1-inch wide, for chipping stone with a hammer and for digging things loose.
- Small notebook and pencil for recording where and when you found a sample. Number each sample in the notebook.
- Clear plastic food storage bags. Write the number of the rock sample on paper and slip it into the bag with the rock sample.
- Heavy gloves for rough work.
- A small day pack for carrying equipment and rocks.

Your Collection

You can display your rock collection by putting specimens in egg cartons, or you can make dividers for boxes.

Specimen Boxes

Egg Carton

Cigar Box With Dividers

On each specimen, paint a spot of quick-drying white enamel. When it is dry, write a number on the spot with a dark felt-tip pen.

For each specimen, keep a card with that number. The card should tell what the specimen is and where and when you found it.

Identifying Rocks and Minerals

Rocks and minerals are often hard to identify. You can get help by borrowing a field guide to rocks and minerals from a library. Or arrange to show your specimens to a high school science teacher. He or she may be able to help identify them.

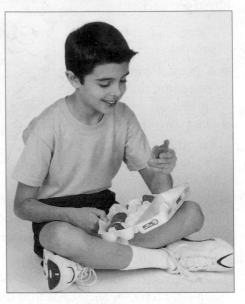

Geologists use the following tests to identify minerals.

Color Clue: Scratch the specimen on a plate of unglazed porcelain or the back of a piece of tile. The color that appears helps to identify it.

Luster Clue: How does the specimen look when light is reflected from it? Is it shiny, dull, or greasy?

Cleavage Clue: How does it split or break up? Does it turn into powder? Split in layers? If it breaks into crystals, how many sides does a crystal have?

Chemical Clue: Does it contain limestone? If a drop of vinegar bubbles on it, the answer is yes.

Hardness Clue: How hard is it? See the hardness scale.

Hardness Scale for Minerals

Scale No.	Mineral Example	Scratch Test
1	Talc	Easily with fingernail
2	Gypsum	Barely with fingernail
3	Calcite	Barely with copper penny
4	Fluorite	Easily with knife blade
5	Apatite	Barely with knife blade
6	Feldspar	Not by blade; easily with glass
7	Quartz	Easily marks steel and hard glass
8	Topaz	Harder than common minerals
9	Corundum	Scratches topaz
10	Diamond	Scratches corundum; hardest mineral

Geologic Materials in Construction

Here are some of the geologic materials used in construction. Maybe you can add others.

Ore	Metal	Use
Hematite Limonite Magnetite	Iron	Beams, girders, posts, nails, machines, screws
Azurite Malachite Chalcocite	Copper	Electric wiring, gutters, roofing, pipes
Sphalerite	Zinc	Galvanizing pipe, sheet metal
Bauxite	Aluminum	Siding, windows, doors, roofs
Quartz	Silicon	Glass
Kernite Borax	Boron	Glass
Limestone	Calcium	Cement, building stone

Volcanoes

Volcanoes are simply vents in the ground formed by the pressure of magma building up. They come in many sizes and shapes. The streams of melted rock that pour out of the earth during some volcanic eruptions are called *lava*.

Lava changes the earth's shape as it flows and cools. In time, it may build up into a mountain peak with a vent up the center. From this chimney comes smoke, steam, and gas mixed with melted minerals.

As lava pours out, it spreads over the country-side and keeps building up. Geologists say that in some places this mineral rock may be thousands of feet deep.

Mount St. Helens in Washington state erupted in 1980.

Cool lava becomes igneous rock. The foaming surface of lava forms lightweight pumice stone, which is used as an abrasive cleanser or polish.

Capulin Volcano

Capulin Volcano, an extinct volcano in northeastern New Mexico, is more than 1,000 feet high from its base to the crater rim. Long ago, wagon trains traveling west used it as a landmark. From its rim you can see parts of five states: New Mexico, Oklahoma, Texas, Kansas, and Colorado.

Capulin Volcano National Monument is not far from Philmont Scout Ranch. If you visit Philmont, maybe you'll have a chance to see Capulin Volcano, too.

Capulin Volcano is one of the United States' largest recent cinder cones. But that's "recent" in geologic terms: Geologists estimate that it was active about 7,000 years ago. The cone is also one of the most perfectly shaped. The rim is 1 mile around, and the center is 415 feet below the rim.

Geysers

Geysers form when underground water meets hot gases and molten rock deep in the earth. This water is partly changed into steam by the red-hot magma. The steam gathers in the geyser's tube. When enough pressure builds, a column of steam and boiling water erupts into the air.

Old Faithful geyser is in Yellowstone National Park. It shoots 100 to 150 feet into the air. Until 1959, this occurred about every 70 minutes. Since then, its timing has been affected by several earthquakes, making it less predictable.

In some geysers, the steam pours out in a steady cloud.

Underground hot water and steam are also present in areas around geysers called *geothermal fields*. In some places, steam from the geo-thermal field is piped to power plants and used to make electricity, but this often kills the nearby geysers.

In some geysers there is so much water it isn't turned into steam. This heated water flows out as a hot spring. Because the water is hot, it dissolves minerals from the rocks it passes over. Some of these mineral springs have become health resorts.

Old Faithful geyser in Yellowstone National Park

Fault

A fault is a fracture in the earth's crust. Earthquakes may occur along a fault.

Earthquakes

The earth's rock crust is not in one piece like an unbroken shell around the planet. It's made up of parts called *plates*. The plates that are mostly land are called continental plates, and the plates under oceans are called oceanic plates.

The plates are huge, and they are moving all the time. They move slowly, perhaps 1 inch a year, but they have great force.

Most earthquakes occur along plate boundaries, when the edges of two plates slide into each other or past each other. Far below the surface, the rocks are strained to the limit by this pressure and finally break up, sending out vibrations called *seismic waves*. The seismic waves reach the surface, causing anything from a short, light shaking to violent tremors that can wreck a city.

In California, many earthquakes have happened along the San Andreas fault. The San Andreas fault lies over the place where the North American plate meets the Pacific plate.

An earthquake may happen near the surface of the earth, or it may be as much as 400 miles down. Scientists use a machine called a *seismograph* to measure the force of vibrations in the earth's crust.

How Mountains are Formed

Crustal uplift
Rocky Mountains

Volcanic action
Mt. Rainier

Erosion
Buttes and mesas

Mountains have been formed over millions of years. There are three basic ways this has been done.

First, mountains are formed when the plates in the earth's crust collide. Over a very long time, the crust will fold or arch up, resulting in mountains caused by *crustal uplift*. The Rocky Mountains were formed this way.

In the Great Basin area of the western United States, which includes most of Nevada and parts of its neighboring states, the crust was pushed upward and then pulled apart. Huge sections of the crust, called fault blocks, dropped downward, making broad valleys between mountain ranges.

Volcanic action also makes mountains, as you read on page 290. This action happens along the moving edges of the plates. Mount Rainier in Washington state is an example of a mountain made out of cooled lava and volcanic debris.

Finally, *erosion* makes mountains, usually lower ones. Softer rocks erode, or get worn away by wind and water, more quickly than harder rocks. This results in certain kinds of mountains, such as the flat-topped mesas or buttes in parts of the western and southwestern United States. Also, parts of the Ozark Mountains in Arkansas and Missouri and some mountains in the eastern United States were created by the forces of erosion.

Fossils Are Fun!

You may find fossils while you are looking for rock specimens. If you do, why not collect them, too?

A fossil is a trace of animal or plant life from millions of years ago that has hardened in rock. Sedimentary rock usually contains fossils. A fossil may be a print of a shell or the skeleton of a fish or bird. It may be a dinosaur's track or a leaf or flower print.

Would you believe that fossils from the sea can be found in a desert? It's true. And fossils have been discovered on top of mountains! This means that the spot where they were found was once an ocean floor.

Certain plants and animals live in hot climates, but their fossils have been found in cold countries. This means that these areas were not always cold. Geologists study the rock layer in which the fossils were found. Then they can tell when the country was warm and for how long.

Fossils show us what plants and trees lived millions of years ago and where. They show the changes that have happened through the years.

An unusual type of fossil is petrified wood or bone. A chemical known as silica replaced each cell of the original matter. Slowly the material turned to stone. Today it looks just as it did millions of years ago.

You probably can find fossils in your own neighborhood. Look in diggings, road cuts, or stream banks. Look wherever cuts have been made through layers of sedimentary rock.

If you don't know a good place to hunt for fossils, ask your teacher or write to a college geology department in your state.

Geologist in the City

Is it hard to find rocks in the heart of a huge city? They're all around you. You're walking on rock. You're looking at rock. When you go inside downtown office buildings and department stores, you're entering enclosures built of rock.

A city may have more rock samples than any plot of ground out in the countryside. You can hunt for them, even if you can't take them home.

Here are a few places to look for some types of rocks in the city:

Granite. This strong igneous rock is used often in city buildings. Look for it on the outside of buildings. It can be gray, pink, or a deeper rose color. It has a speckled pattern. The darkest flecks are mica crystals, and the glasslike areas are quartz. The feldspar in it is smooth. You can find both rough and polished granite in buildings.

Sandstone. In eastern cities, many older homes, called *brownstones*, were built of brick and then covered with brown sandstone blocks.

Slate. This metamorphic rock, changed by heat and pressure, was once clay. It can be split into slabs. You might find an old sidewalk made of gray slate. Chalkboards in schools used to be made of smooth black slate. Some roofs are made of slate.

Marble. Look for marble in the lobbies of office buildings and banks. A streaky, swirling pattern of mixed color and a smooth, shiny surface will be the main clues. Marble comes in many different colors. The main color might be black, gray, green, pink, or white.

You can find marble in museums and parks, too. Pure white marble is often used for sculptures, statues, and monuments.

Cub Scout Academics Belt Loop for Geology

geology

If you earned the Geology belt loop earlier in Cub Scouting, great! But that won't count for requirement 9 of the Geologist activity badge. You must earn the Geology belt loop again while you are a Webelos Scout for it to count toward this activity badge.

Technology Group

HANDYMAN

Handyman
Requirements

Requirement   **Approved by**

Do these:

1. With your parent, guardian, or Webelos den leader, complete the Responsibility Character Connection.

   a. **Know:** List all the tasks you can think
      of that are necessary in keeping a house-
      hold in good shape. Name the tasks that
      are your responsibility. Tell what it means
      to be responsible for these tasks. _____

   b. **Commit:** Talk about what happens
      when people don't do their jobs. Tell why
      it is important to be helpful and to be
      responsible. List ways that you can be
      more responsible on your own. _____

   c. **Practice:** Choose one of the require-
      ments and show how you are responsible
      by doing that task well for two weeks. _____

And do six of these:

2. With adult supervision, wash a car. _____

3. Help an adult change a tire on a car. _____

4. With adult supervision, replace a bulb in
   the taillight, turn signal, or parking light or
   replace a headlight on a car. _____

5. With adult supervision, show how to check
   the oil level and tire pressure of a car. _____

6. Make a repair to a bicycle, such as tightening
   the chain, fixing a flat tire, or adjusting the
   seat or handlebars. _____

7. Properly lubricate the chain on a bicycle. _____

8. Properly inflate the tires on a bicycle. _____

9. Change the wheels on a skateboard or pair of inline skates. _____

10. Replace a light bulb in a fixture or a lamp. _____

11. With adult supervision, arrange a storage area for household cleaners and other dangerous materials where small children cannot reach them. _____

12. Build a sawhorse or stool to be used around your home. _____

13. Help take care of the lawn. _____

14. Arrange a storage area for hand tools or lawn and garden tools. _____

15. Clean and properly store hand tools or lawn and garden tools in their storage areas. _____

16. Label hand tools or lawn and garden tools. _____

17. Put together a toolbox for common repairs around the house. Be sure the toolbox and tools are stored safely. _____

A handyman can do many different jobs. He knows how to take care of a car and a bike. He uses tools to make repairs around the house, and he takes care of the lawn.

When you work on this activity badge, you can learn a lot about keeping a car, bike, and home in good shape. You can find out how to change a flat tire. You might even build a sawhorse or a step stool.

Keep adding to this knowledge after you earn this activity badge. Your handyman skills will always be useful to you and your family. When you complete each requirement, ask an adult member of your family, your Webelos den leader, or your activity badge counselor to sign it on the previous page or this page.

Taking Care of a Car

In just a few years you'll be old enough to drive a car. Now is the time to start learning how to take care of one.

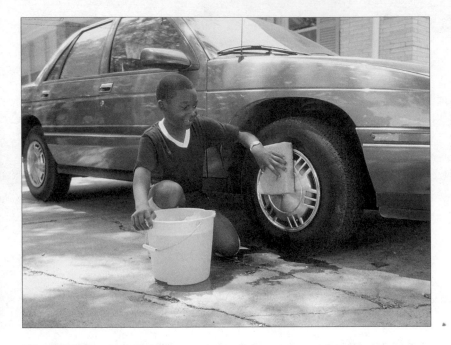

Washing a Car

Use an automatic shut-off nozzle on the hose so you don't waste water while you are washing the car.

Use products specifically designed for washing your car. Use a sponge or clean cloth for a scrubber. Check the car owner's manual for any instructions on caring for the finish.

Close the car windows so wash water won't drip inside. Rinse the car with plain water. Start washing the top of the car and work down so the suds and dirty water won't streak areas you have already washed. Do a small area—about 3 feet square—at a time. Then rinse by spraying.

You can let the car drip dry, but wiping it dry with a dry, clean cloth prevents water spots.

Changing a Tire

Don't try to change a car tire unless an adult is with you.

First, set the parking brake as tight as you can. If the car has an automatic transmission, put it in "park." If it has a manual transmission, put it in first gear. Put wedges in front and back of the wheel diagonally opposite the tire you are going to change. These steps will keep the car from moving forward or backward when you jack it up.

Before using the jack, use the sharp end of the lug wrench (found with the jack) to pry off the wheel cover (if your car has wheel covers). You'll see the nuts that hold the wheel on the axle. With the other end of the wrench, loosen the nuts one turn. If they are tight, you may need the adult's help.

You'll find instructions for using the car's jack in the instruction manual. Follow the instructions exactly. If the jack is not placed properly under the car, you could damage the car when you jack it up, or the car could fall off the jack and injure you.

Use the jack to lift the car so that the flat tire just clears the ground. Remove the nuts and pull the wheel off. Slip the spare tire wheel on over the bolts. Screw the nuts on until all of them are fairly tight. Carefully lower the jack until it is free of the car.

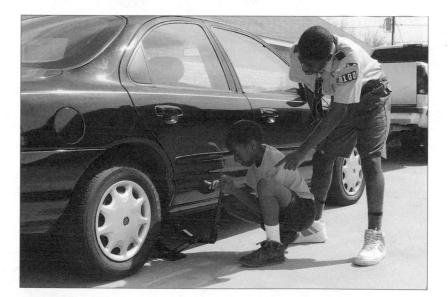

Then, with the lug wrench, tighten one nut as tight as you can make it. Next, tighten the nut opposite the first. Then tighten all the others. Finally, go around the circle again, tightening each nut as hard as you can. Ask the adult to check.

Fit the wheel cover back into its brackets and push it into place. Put the jack, lug wrench, and flat tire back in the trunk of the car.

The job is done, but remind the car's owner to have the flat tire fixed!

Replacing a Taillight or Headlight

Each car model is different, so it's a good idea to have an adult advise you how to replace a taillight or headlight. On many cars the rear lights can be replaced from inside the trunk. See the owner's manual on how to change a taillight, because taillight bulbs and installation methods aren't the same for all cars.

Headlights take a little more work and may require special tools. Because headlights and headlight bulbs aren't the same for all cars, follow the directions in the owner's manual and have an adult advise you on how to change a headlight.

Taillight

Socket

Headlight

Checking Oil and Tire Pressure

Oil allows the parts of the car's engine to move easily and helps keep the car's engine from over-heating. It is important to have enough oil in the engine at all times.

You can check the oil by using a metal rod called a *dipstick*. **Ask an adult to help you find the oil dipstick in the engine.**

Dipstick

While the engine is cool, pull out the oil dipstick and wipe it clean with a rag. Then put it back, all the way in. Pull it out again and look at the markings.

Tire Gauge

If the oil level is below the "add" line, the car needs oil. Put the dipstick back in. Tell the owner that the car needs oil.

You need a tire gauge to check tire pressure. **When the tires are cool,** take the cap off the tire's valve stem. Push the tire gauge hard against the valve. The gauge's scale will show the tire's pressure. The recommended pressure is shown on a sticker usually attached to the edge of the car door. You can also find the recommended pressure in the owner's manual. Check all tires, including the spare.

If any of the tires need more air, tell the car's owner.

Taking Care of a Bicycle

A bicycle is a lot simpler to maintain than a car. But it is a machine, too, so it needs to be taken care of just as a car does.

Adjusting a Bike Chain

If the chain needs tightening, turn the bicycle upside down. Loosen the two axle nuts on the rear wheel with a wrench. A combination or socket wrench is best so that you don't wear down the nuts over time. If the bicycle has a coaster brake, loosen the brake arm mounting nuts, too.

Now pull the wheel back until the chain has about ½ inch of play in its center. Tighten the axle nut on the chain side. Make sure that the wheel is centered between the chain stays. Then tighten the other axle nut and the coaster brake arm mounting nuts. Don't try to adjust the chain on a multispeed bike that has a derailleur.

Fixing a Flat

To fix a flat tire, you need a tire repair kit. Some kits have a scraper or sandpaper, patches, and cement. Other kits have patches that don't need cement.

Take the wheel off the bicycle, and then take off the tire and tube. Taking off the tire can be tricky. You might have to use tools called *tire levers*. Ask an adult to help you the first time if you have trouble.

If you can't see where the hole in the tube is, pump air into the tube. Dunk it into a tub of water. Bubbles will show where the air is escaping. Dry off the area around the hole.

Use the scraper or sandpaper to rough up the tube around the hole. If your repair kit has cement, put a light coating of cement around the hole and quickly wipe it off. Then put on another coat of cement and let it get tacky. If you have glueless patches, you don't need to use any cement.

Remove the coating from a patch and smooth the patch over the hole. Press the patch hard to spread the cement evenly and make a tight seal.

Put the tube back in the tire and position the tire carefully on the wheel before you inflate it.

Adjusting the Seat and Handlebars

To adjust the seat (also called the saddle) or handlebars of your bike, all you need is the right wrench. For some bikes, you'll need a combination wrench, and for others, an Allen wrench.

To change the height of the seat, loosen the bolt that keeps the seat post tight in the frame and then raise or lower the seat post to the height you need. Make sure that at least 2 inches of the seat post is in the frame.

You can raise and lower the handlebars on your bike and also change the position of the handlebars. Look at your bike and find the bolts that control these adjustments. Loosen the bolts to make the adjustments.

Seat post bolt
Loosen to adjust seat, then tighten bolt.

Seat post
At least 2" must be in the frame.

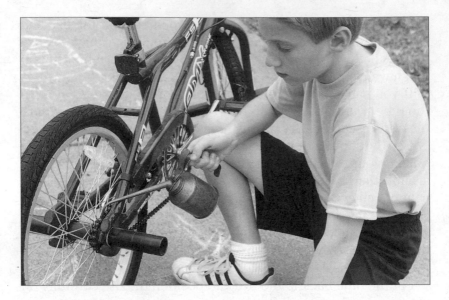

Lubricating a Bicycle

Oil prevents rust and helps to keep a bicycle running smoothly.

To lubricate the chain, turn the bicycle upside down. Use the pedals to make the crank turn, and then drip lightweight oil on the chain. The oil will spread over the chain as you turn the crank.

When all the links of the chain have a light coating of oil, the job is done. Wipe any extra oil from the chain and sprocket with a clean rag.

Inflating the Tires

A bicycle's tires should be kept at the correct pressure. The pressure may be stamped on the side of the tire. If it isn't, check the bicycle owner's manual.

Use a bicycle tire gauge to check the pressure. (Many bike tires require higher pressure than a car tire gauge can read.) You can inflate tires with a hand pump. Keep checking the pressure until it is right.

Taking Care of Skateboards and Skates

Check your equipment before skating or skateboarding. Be sure all fittings are tight and that all skates and skateboards are well maintained and in good repair consistent with the manufacturer's recommendations.

Handyman Around the House

You can make life easier for your family by helping with minor repairs and other jobs. Requirements 10 through 17 cover some ways you can help.

Replacing a Light Bulb

This is just about the simplest job there is.

But you can learn an important lesson as you do it. That lesson is: Whenever you are working on an electrical appliance, **first turn off the switch if it has one, and then pull the plug or turn off the circuit breaker.**

Wait for the old bulb to cool if it has just burned out. Then all you have to do is screw out the old bulb and screw in the new one. Use the correct wattage bulb for the fixture. Now put the plug back in the outlet or turn on the circuit breaker. Turn on the switch to test the light.

Storing Dangerous Materials

Household cleaning materials are full of poisons. Young children do not know that. If they get the chance, they will play with poisons and may even try to drink them.

So if you have a little brother or sister, check to see whether cleaning supplies are in a safe storage area. If not, you might arrange to store them out of the reach of small children.

Or you could buy a small lock and install it on the present storage area. Directions for installing the lock will be on the package.

Woodworking Jobs

If you like working with wood, try making a sawhorse or stool. Either one will be useful around your house.

The carpenter's best friend is the sawhorse—or better, two sawhorses. Using sawhorses, a carpenter has his or her work at a comfortable height for sawing, planing, and nailing boards.

Easy-to-Make Sawhorse

The easiest sawhorse uses two steel brackets. You can buy them at a hardware store. Use two-by-four lumber for the legs and crosspiece. Cut four legs, each 2 feet long. Cut a crosspiece about 30 inches long.

Fit the legs and crosspiece into the steel brackets, and you have a strong sawhorse.

1. Clamp bracket to crosspiece.

2. Insert legs in bracket slots.

3. Spread legs, forcing bracket teeth to bite into the wood.

4. Tighten wing nut.   5. Ready to use.

All-Wood Sawhorse

The main crosspiece
is a two-by-four, cut 30
inches long. Set it on
edge and nail a 30-inch
one-by-four to its top.
This will be the top sur-
face of the sawhorse.
Turn it over and nail
another 30-inch one-by-
four to the bottom.

Cut the four legs
from one-by-fours. Each
should be 21 inches
long. Nail the legs to the
two-by-four crosspiece,
just under the top, and

again to the edge of the bottom one-by-four board, as shown.

Cut the braces to fit. Nail on the braces, and the job is done.

Making a Stool

To make a stool (or bench), you need about 36 inches of 1" × 12" wood (pine or ¾" plywood). See the drawing below. You will cut five pieces from this one board. Measure carefully so you don't waste any of the wood.

Cut the top of the stool: 1" × 12" × 18".

Cut two 8" × 8" pieces for the legs. Clamp the two leg pieces together, mark where you will cut the notch, and saw them out. This will make the legs exactly the same so the stool won't wobble.

Cut two ¾" × 2" × 14" pieces for the side braces.

Nail the stool together with finishing nails. Note that the legs are set 2 inches in from the ends of the top. Measure carefully before you drive the top nails into the legs to be sure they go into the legs.

Countersink the top nails. (That is, use another nail to tap them just below the surface.) Fill the nail holes with wood putty.

Nail the side braces to the legs. Fit them just under the top of the stool. The side braces will keep your stool stable.

Sand the stool all over. Be sure to clean any grit from the stool before applying the finish. You can stain the stool to match other furniture, or you can paint it any color you like.

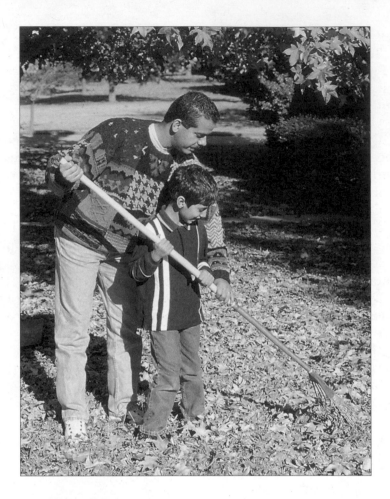

Outdoor Jobs

If your home has a lawn, you can help take care of it by raking the leaves and grass clippings.

If the grass isn't too long, don't rake up the clippings. They will rot and enrich the soil.

If the clippings are very long, you may have to rake them up because they could damage the grass by cutting off sunlight. Put them on a compost pile. If you don't have a compost pile, dispose of the clippings by whatever method allowed by law in your community.

Taking Care of Tools

Your family may already have a storage area for hand tools and lawn and garden tools. Perhaps you can make it neater.

For hand tools, you can build a rack from pegboard. Use special pegboard hangers to store saws, hammers, augers, and other tools.

For lawn and garden tools like rakes, hoes, and trowels, do this: Nail a length of one-by-four to a wall in a convenient place. Tap two long nails into the board to support each tool.

Cleaning Tools, Putting Them Away, and Marking Them

Whenever you want to use a tool, your job goes much faster if the tool is clean and in its place. After you use tools, clean them: Carefully remove sawdust from woodworking tools; clean dirt off gardening tools. If your family's tools aren't ready to use, spend a little time cleaning them and storing them for the next use. Mark tools with waterproof ink for identification. Or use a plastic tape machine to put your family's name on tools.

Put a Toolbox Together

If you gather most of the hand tools you will need for jobs around the house and put them in a toolbox, you can take care of many smaller handyman jobs easily and quickly. First, gather the tools you want to put in your toolbox. A basic handyman toolbox might include small and medium slotted screwdrivers, a medium Phillips screwdriver, a shop knife, a putty knife, a pair of scissors, a pair of pliers, a pair of needle-nose pliers, a hammer, some duct tape, and a few screws and nails.

Then make or choose a box that will hold them all (with a little open space left for tools that you later find out you need in the toolbox). You may have made a toolbox when you were a Bear Cub Scout. Plans for a toolbox are in the *Bear Handbook*.

The handle is a broomstick piece or dowel.

18"

Cut two pieces 17½ inches long for the sides and one 16 inches long for the bottom.

1" x 6" boards

|←———— 17½" ————→|

|←——— 16" ———→|

2"

1¾"

10"

|←— 5½" —→| Cut two ends.

Put your toolbox together with wood screws.

Naturalist
Requirements

Requirement	Approved by

Do this:

1. With your parent, guardian, or Webelos den leader, complete the Respect Character Connection.

   a. **Know:** Tell what interested you most when completing the requirements for this activity badge. Tell what you learned about how you can show appreciation and respect for wildlife.

   b. **Commit:** Tell things some people have done that show a lack of respect for wildlife. Name ways you will show respect for and protect wildlife.

   c. **Practice:** Explain how completing the requirements for this activity badge gives you the opportunity to show respect.

And do five of these:

2. Keep an "insect zoo" that you have collected. You might have crickets, ants, or grasshoppers. Study them for a while and then release them. Share your experience with your Webelos den.

3. Set up an aquarium or terrarium. Keep it for at least a month. Share your experience with your Webelos den by showing them photos or drawings of your project, or having them visit to see your project.

4. Visit a museum of natural history, a nature center, or a zoo with your family, Webelos den, or pack. Tell what you saw.

5. Watch for birds in your yard, neighborhood, or town for one week. Identify the birds you see and write down where and when you saw them.

6. Learn about the bird flyways closest to your home. Find out which birds use these flyways.

7. Learn to identify poisonous plants and venomous reptiles found in your area.

8. Watch six wild animals (snakes, turtles, fish, birds, or mammals) in the wild. Describe the kind of place (forest, field, marsh, yard, or park) where you saw them. Tell what they were doing.

9. Give examples of

- A producer, a consumer, and a decomposer in the food chain of an ecosystem

- One way humans have changed the balance of nature

- How you can help protect the balance of nature

10. Identify a plant, bird, or wild animal that is found only in your area of the country. Tell why it survives only in your area.

11. Learn about aquatic ecosystems and wetlands in your area. Discuss with your Webelos den leader or activity badge counselor the important role aquatic ecosystems and wetlands play in supporting lifecycles of wildlife and humans.

12. Look around your neighborhood and identify how litter might be dangerous to the birds and other animals. Clean up the litter. Identify what else you might do to make your neighborhood safer for animals. _____

13. While you are a Webelos Scout, earn the Cub Scout Academics belt loop for Wildlife Conservation. _____

If you like watching wildlife, you're already a naturalist. A naturalist studies living creatures and plants in the wild. When you visit a nature center to learn about birds, reptiles, mammals, trees, and wildflowers, your guide is a naturalist.

For this activity badge, you might keep an insect zoo, watch tadpoles change into frogs, or make a terrarium for wild plants. Perhaps your den will visit a real zoo or take a nature walk in the woods.

Naturalists have a great love for nature. They notice details that other people miss. They know that the well-being of all living things is interconnected. When you complete each requirement, ask your Webelos den leader or activity badge counselor to sign it on the previous page or this page.

Your Insect Zoo

Keeping an insect allows you to study it closely and get to know what it does. Get a book from the library about the insect you keep.

It will need your care each day. Consider it a visitor and release it back to its natural outdoor habitat after a while.

Summer is the best time to keep an insect zoo because insects are most active then. Here are tips on finding and caring for different insects.

Crickets

Sink a small plastic jar or can into the ground so its rim is level with the surface. Put a sweet, gooey mixture in the jar. It might be a mixture of two parts molasses and one part water or a mashed pulp of overripe fruit.

The sweet smell will attract crickets and beetles, and they will tumble in.

Or you can look for crickets under rocks and logs. You have to be quick to catch a cricket. Crickets don't bite, but they do jump.

Cricket home

You can use a large, wide-mouthed plastic jar as a cricket home. Have an adult help you punch air holes in the jar lid, or if the lid is too hard, make a lid out of fiberglass screenwire and put a rubber band around it.

Put 1 inch of moist soil in the bottom. (Soil from the place you found the cricket should be good.) Put in a bottle cap for drinking water and a rock or small piece of wood. Crickets like to crawl underneath rocks or other objects.

Don't place the jar where it will get direct sunlight, as it will heat up inside and the cricket may die.

Food: Try lettuce, a small wedge of raw potato, or a bit of dry dog or cat food—fresh food each day. Keep the house clean by removing leftover food and droppings.

Expect some chirping! Your cricket guest may keep you awake or sing you to sleep.

Ants

To capture ants you need a 2-foot-square piece of white cloth or paper, two large-mouth bottles with lids, a piece of cardboard, and a trowel. Now find an anthill or ant nest under rocks. **Caution:** Don't try to collect fire ants or other biting ants. Stay away from them.

Stir the anthill gently with your trowel. When the ants come out to investigate, use the cardboard to guide them into one jar. Put some dirt from the anthill in with them. Some ants may be carrying white objects, which are the larvae and pupae, two stages of ant development. Collect some of these too.

Now find the colony's queen—if you can. Some ant queens live very deep in the ground, and when the nest is disturbed, the other ants carry her off to safety. That is because the queen produces all of the colony's young. She will be larger than the other ants. As you look for the queen, spread the dirt on the white cloth, and she should show up against the white background.

Put the queen into the second bottle and add some dirt.

Ant house

You can use a wide-mouthed jar with screenwire (if the holes are small enough to keep ants from climbing out) or cheese-cloth on top to let in air. Put your ant colony in it, including the queen, along with the dirt from the anthill. Add ordinary soil until the jar is about two- thirds full. Keep the soil moist, but not wet, by putting in a few drops of water when it looks dry. Fill a bottle cap with water for the ants to drink.

Keep the house covered when you aren't watching the ants at work. Ants like to work in the dark. You can cover it with black paper or cloth held on by rubber bands. Handle the house with care, and don't jar or jiggle it.

Food: Small bits of sugar, peanuts, apples, and bananas every few days. Remove uneaten food each time you put in new food.

Praying Mantises, Grasshoppers, and Walkingsticks

Praying mantises and grasshoppers are usually found on grass and in grain fields. Look for walkingsticks on trees. Sometimes you can pick up these insects with your fingers, but a collecting net like the one shown below is useful.

You can also catch many types of insects by using a stick to shake a bush so they will fall off. Hold an umbrella upside down under the bush or spread a large cloth on the ground to catch them. To catch night-flying moths and other insects, hang up an old sheet and shine a flashlight on it. The insects will be attracted to the light and land on the sheet.

Bent wire

Notch

Broomstick

Tape

Mosquito net

Cage for a praying mantis

You'll need metal screening and a large round tin can with a plastic lid. The screening will be the top of the cage. Cut the screening so it is 12 inches high and long enough to go around the can and overlap 1 inch. Make a tube from the screening, to fit inside the can. Lace it together with wire.

Set the wire tube in the can. Fill the bottom of the can with plaster of paris. Push a branch into the plaster of paris before it hardens. The can's plastic lid goes on top of the screen tube.

Food: Flies, small insects, tiny bits of raw liver, chopped meat. The mantis prefers live food.

Water: Put in a bottle cap.

Note: In some states it is against the law to confine a praying mantis. Make sure that, with the help of your parent, guardian, or Webelos den leader, you check your state's laws.

Grasshoppers and walkingsticks

Cover the bottom of a plastic jar with 1 inch of soil. Cover this with grass sod. (Water the grass occasionally.) Punch air holes in the cover.

Food: Grass for grasshoppers. Walkingsticks eat the leaves of oak, locust, cherry, and walnut trees. Supply water, too.

Moths and Butterflies

These amazing insects have four stages in their lives.

1. **Egg.** Egg masses are on the undersides of leaves or grass blades.
2. **Larva.** A larva (caterpillar) emerges from the egg.
3. **Pupa.** During this stage, the larva develops into an insect with wings. There is a difference between moths and butterflies in the pupal stage:

   • A typical moth caterpillar spins a soft silky covering around itself and becomes dormant (goes to sleep). The covering is called a *cocoon*. (See page 327.) Some cocoons have twigs or leaves attached to the outside.

   • A butterfly larva doesn't spin a cocoon (except for a few kinds of butterflies, like the skippers). The butterfly's body changes, forming a firm outer case called the *chrysalis*. It is also dormant.

Monarch Butterfly

4. **Moth or butterfly.** In the spring or summer, an adult moth or butterfly emerges. Butterflies come out more quickly than moths.

Collecting moth and butterfly larvae

Many larvae blend in with their surroundings, so look closely to find a green larva on a leaf. Other larvae may have bold patterns, like the monarch butterfly larva with its black, yellow, and white stripes. Some larvae have hairs or spines sticking out. Be careful, because in some species the hairs can irritate your skin or the spines can sting.

Use a wide-mouthed jar with a screw top. Punch air holes in the top. Put in a branch or twig and some leaves of the tree or shrub on which you found the larva. Keep a fresh supply of the same leaves in the jar until the larva stops eating. Then it will enter the pupal stage (cocoon or chrysalis). Later it will emerge as a butterfly or moth. Be prepared to release it at that time.

Starting with a cocoon or chrysalis

Look for the cocoons of moths and the chrysalises of butterflies in early spring before trees and shrubs have leaves. You'll find them hanging from branches or twigs. Cut away part of the twig.

Keep the cocoon in a clean, covered jar. Punch air holes in the cover. Soon you'll see a miracle—a moth or butterfly emerging. Release the butterfly or moth very soon so that it can find the food it needs.

Moth Cocoon

Aquariums

Perhaps you already have an aquarium for tropical fish at home. Even if you do, it's fun to make one for fish or water animals you have collected from a stream or pond.

Jointed Handle, 4½' to 5½' Long

Dip Net, ½" Mesh

Bait can or jar full of pond water for collecting tadpoles.

Use a fish bowl or a square-sided aquarium. Make a dip net to catch small fish along the edge of a pond and put them in your aquarium with water from the pond.

Tadpoles

In the spring, you can catch tadpoles in ponds and watch them grow into frogs or toads in your aquarium. Prepare your aquarium by putting a layer of sand and rocks on the bottom. Plant a few aquatic plants in the sand. You can buy them at tropical fish stores. Fill the aquarium with water from a pond. Put in some rocks—they'll be needed later.

Catch two or three tadpoles and put them in. As the tadpoles grow, you'll see the first hint of legs. Feed the tadpoles soft insects, earthworms, grasshoppers, flies, and crickets.

Tadpole's Growth

Before legs appear

Hind legs developed

Frog

Watch for the legs to appear, because when your tadpoles start looking like frogs or toads, they can no longer breathe in the water. Lower the water level so they can climb out on the rocks. Feed the maturing frogs or toads mealworms, which you can buy at pet shops.

Make a support for your terrarium. Use lathing strips and nail them to a wood block.

Terrariums

One kind of terrarium is a small garden of plants in a big bottle or jar with the lid on it. You can also turn an aquarium into a terrarium.

The terrarium shown here is simple. You seal it up, and it will support plant life for two or three months.

Use a wide-mouthed gallon jar and build a base to fit it. Put in ½ inch of sand or fine gravel. Sprinkle ½ inch of charcoal chips over that. On top of the charcoal, put 2 cups of rich soil. If the soil in your area is poor, use potting soil from a garden center.

Plant small tropical plants that thrive in low light and high humidity, like aluminum plant, flame violet, and artillery plant. Ask about small tropical plants at a garden center.

Mist the plants lightly with water before screwing on the lid. You shouldn't need to water them again because the moisture will circulate in the closed jar.

Keep the terrarium where it will get indirect sunlight each day. Don't put it in direct sunlight because the container will heat up too much.

If you want a cactus terrarium, it should have a wide open top so moisture gets out instead of staying inside. (Cactus plants can't take high humidity.) Or you can plant cacti in a dish garden. Any container two or three inches deep will work. Use soil recommended for the cactus plants you choose. Handle

the plants carefully so the spines don't stick your hands.

Cacti need water, but not too often. Give them bright indirect light, and turn the container so all the plants get light.

Don't fertilize any terrarium plants, or they may outgrow their containers.

Visiting Nature Centers

If your area has a museum of natural history, a nature center, or a zoo, visit it. At a natural history museum, you'll see many wonderful exhibits about nature. The museum will have displays of birds and mammals that are hard to spot in the wild.

The museum may also have skeletons and likenesses of creatures that lived thousands of years ago.

A nature center has indoor exhibits and an outdoor area where you can hike and see trees and plants that grow wild in the area.

At a zoo you can get a fairly close view of many animals and birds from all over the world, some that are rarely seen by humans. A day at a nature center or zoo is a lot of fun.

Bird Watching

An easy way to watch birds is to bring them to your yard by setting out a bird feeder. You may also build a bird nesting box and put it near your window for a close-up view of birds.

Bird Feeders

Coffee can or coconut shell

Metal feeding basket with suet

Pinecone stuffed with suet

Plastic container

Dowel pole and plastic container

Log suet feeder

Windowsill feeder

Some simple bird feeders are shown on the previous page. The log, pinecone, and basket are for feeding suet (hard fat from beef or mutton) or peanut butter.

Fill other types of feeders with seed that is sold as food for birds. Some birds may like small pieces of fruit or bread crumbs. See what kind of birds come to your feeder.

Borrow a field guide to birds from a library so you can identify the birds you see. Keep a record of the birds for at least one week.

Here are some things to notice about birds:

- **Marks.** The chickadee's black cap and bib, the downy woodpecker's red spot on the back of the head. Marks help you remember the bird.

- **Wings.** Pointed, rounded?

- **Tail.** Long or short? Rounded, square, or forked?

- **Bill.** Short bills are good for cracking seeds. Long pointed bills are good for digging in bark for insects.

- **Toes.** Most birds have four toes—three pointing forward and one back; but tree-climbing woodpeckers have two forward, two back.

- **Flight and behavior.** The starling flies straight as an arrow, but the goldfinch dips up and down. The nuthatch hops down trees headfirst.

- **Song.** In spring, the black-capped chickadee's song sounds like "Fee-bee." The song sparrow gives three sharp whistles, and then a chirp. If you can imitate the sound, it may draw a bird closer; so can kissing the back of your hand to make a chirp.

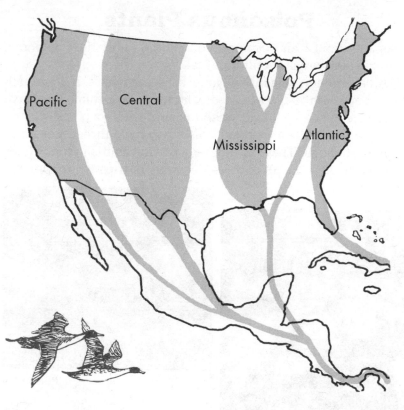

Bird Flyways

Some birds, like starlings, blue jays, sparrows, and nighthawks, stay in one area all their lives. Other kinds of birds migrate, flying south each fall to warmer places to spend the winter. They return to nest and live in their northern homes each spring.

Many birds that migrate use regular main routes. These routes are called *flyways*. The map shows the four main flyways in North America.

You don't have to live on a flyway to see birds moving in the spring and fall. Some will pass over your town. But most flocks of birds, like geese and ducks, use the flyways. These are their highways between winter and summer homes.

Poisonous Plants

As a naturalist and camper, you should know the poisonous plants in your area. Avoid them!

Three common poisonous plants are shown here. If you touch them, your skin may get red and itchy. If you think you have touched a poisonous plant, wash the spot with soap and water.

Notice that poison oak and poison ivy have three leaflets on the end of stems. They both have white or whitish fruit. That's why Scouts say, "Leaflets three, let it be; berries white, poisonous sight."

Poison Oak

Poison Ivy

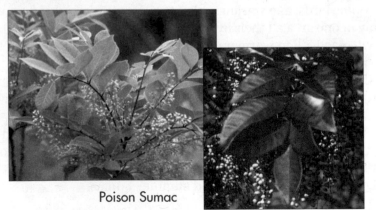

Poison Sumac

The foliage of poison sumac stays green from spring through summer *(left)*, then turns red in the fall *(right)*.

Venomous Reptiles

Snakes and other reptiles will usually do their best to stay out of your way. But if you stumble over one, it may bite.

Most snakes and reptiles don't have poison in their bite. The few that do are listed here.

Gila monster: This lizard grows to about 2 feet long. The lighter part of the pattern is white or yellow. It is found in parts of Nevada and Utah and down into Mexico.

Eastern diamondback rattlesnake: Sometimes grows to 7 feet in length. It is found along the Atlantic coast from North Carolina to Florida and west to Louisiana. It is never more than 100 miles from the coast.

Western diamondback rattlesnake: Often grows to 7 feet in length. It lives in the southwestern United States, from Missouri and eastern Texas to southeastern California.

Timber rattlesnake: Is less than 6 feet in length. It ranges from Maine to Texas, but its numbers are now greatly reduced.

Coral snake: Grows to about 2 feet long. It is ringed with red, yellow, and black bands. (The red and yellow bands touch—remember the saying "red on yellow kill a fellow.") Most coral snake species are found in Central and South America, but two are found in the United States. The harlequin or bead coral snake is found in some southeastern states, and the Arizona coral snake is found in southern New Mexico and Arizona.

Prairie rattlesnake: About 3 feet in length. Sometimes it grows to 5 feet. It lives in the western half of the United States.

Sidewinder or horned rattlesnake: Found in the deserts of the Southwest.

Water moccasin (cottonmouth): Found in or near water from southeastern Virginia to Florida. It can be seen westward to east Texas and north as far as southwestern Illinois. It sometimes grows as long as 6 feet.

Copperhead: Not often longer than 4 feet, it lives in most southeastern states. It can be found as far north as Massachusetts and Pennsylvania and westward to Illinois and Texas.

Watching Animals in the Wild

Take a nature hike with your family or den and see how many wild creatures you can spot. Look for birds, snakes, turtles, fish, and mammals.

Be as quiet as you can. Animals will hide if they see, hear, or smell you. Here are a few tips.

Mammals: Look for rabbits, squirrels, woodchucks, mice, and other small animals. In muddy spots around streams, you may see tracks. See if you can identify the animal that made the tracks.

Turtles: Look around ponds and streams. Some kinds of turtles will bite, so approach them with care.

Snakes: Look under logs, leaf piles, rocks, and sawdust piles. Be careful. Don't handle the snake unless an expert tells you it is not venomous. Don't harm the snake.

Fish: It is very hard to spot fish unless they are in shallow water. That is because the light bounces off the water, making it hard to see far down.

To see better under water, make the waterscope shown here. Use it by lying on your stomach on a low dock. Put the end of the waterscope into the water and look through the top.

Waterscope

Water-proof tape

Tin cans wired and taped together

For safety, put tape along the viewing edges.

Plastic or glasss dish or jar

Ecosystems

An ecosystem is a community of plants and animals living in an environment that supplies what they need for life.

There are many types of ecosystems. For example, a forest, a desert, and a wetland each contain different combinations of plants, animals, soils, and water sources.

In an ecosystem, plants and animals depend on their environment and on each other. Energy and food flow through the community in a *food chain*.

The sun: Without the sun, there would be no life on earth. The sun's energy flows through a cycle in the ecosystem. Plants are the first to use this energy.

Producers: All green plants—trees, shrubs, grasses, flowers, etc.—use the sun's energy to grow. Plants also take up nutrients and minerals from the soil. The plants produce leaves, bark, fruits, nuts, and seeds that many animals eat.

Consumers: Animals that use the stored energy, nutrients, and minerals in their food to grow and to maintain their health.

- **Primary consumers:** Plant-eating animals are called herbivores. They're the primary consumers in the ecosystem because they're the first to benefit by eating the producers. Examples: Rabbits, squirrels, deer, seed-eating birds, grasshoppers. On farms, cattle are primary consumers.

- **Secondary consumers:** Animals that eat other animals are meat-eaters or *carnivores*. In an ecosystem, they're secondary consumers, because they benefit from the energy and nutrients stored in their prey (the plant-eaters). Examples: Hawks and owls eat mice and rabbits. A mountain lion hunts deer and smaller animals.

- Some consumers eat both plants and animals. They're called *omnivores*. The gray fox hunts rabbits, mice, voles, birds, and insects, but it also eats blackberries, grapes, persimmons, and grass. Humans who eat meat and plants, such as fruits, vegetables, and grain products, are omnivores too.

Decomposers: These are the fungi, lichens, bacteria, and insects that break down dead plants and animals. This returns organic matter and minerals to the soil, making them available to trees and other plants—the producers. Nature is a good recycler.

The Balance of Nature

When you figure out the food chain in an ecosystem, you can see how the animals, plants, and their habitat are connected. The ecosystem is in balance when all the necessary parts of its community are present. Animals are able to find food and have healthy young.

Nature is out of balance when there is not enough habitat and food for animals to survive. After some natural events, like a forest fire started by lightning, the original ecosystem may slowly recover. Nature eventually adjusts the balance.

The needs and plans of humans often alter the balance of nature quickly and permanently. When people clear forest and brush and turn it into agricultural land, much of the animal life may disappear from the area, except for animals that can adapt to the farming environment. When a huge shopping center is built and surrounded by a paved parking lot, animals can't adapt to that environment. Pollution of air or water can damage or wipe out an ecosystem.

Losing one link of the food chain can upset the balance, too. Because wolves were seen as a threat to livestock, people killed them. Without these predators, the population of white-tailed deer increased tremendously, but their wild habitat decreased. Deer adapt well to environments like new housing developments. Some people enjoy watching deer near their homes, but others consider deer a nuisance when they graze in flower beds and destroy young trees by eating the bark.

You and the Balance of Nature

You are part of an ecosystem too, whether you live in the wilderness or in a city. What can you do to protect the balance of nature?

You can help in small ways. When you want to see what lives under a rock, lift it carefully and replace it gently, so you don't destroy the creatures and their habitat. If you plant a garden of flowers that bees and butterflies like, you'll provide food for them. Can you think of other small ways you can help?

You can help in larger ways by joining local efforts to solve water and air pollution problems. Or your den can plant trees or clean up a stream.

Can you think of other ways to protect the balance of nature?

Your Local Environment

Your part of the country is unique. Local libraries or environmental groups could be good resources to help you learn about and observe plants, birds, and wild animals that are found only in your area. When observing wildlife, you must be with a parent, guardian, or your Webelos den leader. Be sure not to disturb or harm these precious resources.

All living things—including you—depend on water to exist. Your area's aquatic ecosystem is important, and there likely will be one or several government agencies or organizations in your area that manage local aquatic resources and keep the public informed about them. It is every citizen's responsibility to understand how our water is obtained and managed, and to help conserve this precious resource.

Whether you live in the country or the city, there are birds and other animals all around you. When people don't dispose of litter properly, it can harm animals, including humans! Some litter is poisonous. Some might be a fire hazard. Many plastic items can hurt animals; for instance, an animal could get its head stuck in the plastic rings that hold cans of food or soft drinks together, and eventually suffocate. The same thing is true of plastic containers that are more narrow at the top than at the bottom. These items should be cut open before disposal. Fishing line and string can become entangled in a bird's legs and then catch on a limb so that the bird cannot fly. These should be cut into small pieces or wound tightly before disposal. Look around your neighborhood and see what kinds of hazards you find, and do something about them.

Cub Scout Academics Belt Loop for Wildlife Conservation

If you earned the Wildlife Conservation belt loop earlier in Cub Scouting, great! But that won't count for requirement 13 of this Naturalist activity badge. You must earn the Wildlife Conservation belt loop again while you are a Webelos Scout for it to count toward this activity badge.

Cub Scout World Conservation Award

Earning the Naturalist activity badge fulfills a requirement for the World Conservation Award. See page 70 for details on earning that award.

Outdoor Group

O

OUTDOORSMAN

Outdoorsman
Requirements

Requirement	Approved by

Do two of these:

1. Present yourself to your Webelos den leader, properly dressed, as you would be for an overnight campout. Show the camping gear you will use. Show the right way to pack and carry it.

2. With your family or Webelos den, help plan and take part in an evening outdoor activity that includes a campfire.

3. With your parent or guardian, take part in a Webelos den overnight campout or a family campout. Sleep in a tent that you have helped pitch.

4. With your parent or guardian, camp overnight with a Boy Scout troop. Sleep in a tent you have helped pitch

And do five of these:

5. During a Webelos den meeting, discuss how to follow the Leave No Trace Frontcountry Guidelines during outdoor activities. (See page 72.)

6. Participate in an outdoor conservation project with your Webelos den or a Boy Scout troop.

7. Discuss with your Webelos den leader the rules of outdoor fire safety. Using these rules, show how to build a safe fire and put it out.

8. With your accompanying adult on a campout or outdoor activity, assist in preparing, cooking, and cleanup for one of your den's meals. Tell why it is important for each den member to share in meal preparation and cleanup, and explain the importance of eating together.

9. Discuss with your Webelos den leader the things that you need to take on a hike. Go on one 3-mile hike with your Webelos den or a Boy Scout troop.

10. Demonstrate how to whip and fuse the ends of a rope.

11. Demonstrate setting up a tent or dining fly using two half hitches and a taut-line hitch. Show how to tie a square knot and explain how it is used.

12. Visit a nearby Boy Scout camp with your Webelos den.

To go camping, you need skills that will help you feel at home in the outdoors. When you earn the Outdoorsman activity badge, you'll learn about building campfires, cooking, setting up tents, making outdoor beds, tying knots, and many other skills.

You'll have a chance to use your new camping skills with a friend, your family, or your Webelos den. You may visit a Boy Scout troop activity to learn how Boy Scouts use their outdoor skills.

The outdoors is calling you. Have fun! When you complete each requirement, ask your Webelos den leader or activity badge counselor to sign it on the previous page or this page.

The Outdoor Code

As a Webelos Scout, you'll hike and camp out. As a Boy Scout, you'll be outdoors a lot more often. The Outdoor Code is a guide all Scouts use. Read it with your den leader and discuss what it means. See below for more about the Outdoor Code.

Outdoor Code
As an American, I will do my best to—

Be clean in my outdoor manners: I will treat the outdoors as a heritage. I will take care of it for myself and others. I will keep my trash and garbage out of lakes, streams, fields, woods, and roadways.

Be careful with fire: I will prevent wildfire. I will build my fires only where they are appropriate. When I have finished using fire, I will make sure it is cold-out. I will leave a clean fire ring or remove all evidence of my fire.

Be considerate in the outdoors: I will treat public and private property with respect. I will use low-impact methods of hiking and camping.

Be conservation-minded. I will learn how to practice good conservation of soil, waters, forests, minerals, grasslands, wildlife, and energy. I will urge others to do the same.

The Scouting way is to leave no trace of your presence in the outdoors. Always take good care of nature.

Camping Out

Camping is living outdoors. You can learn how to camp as most good campers do, by practicing skills close to home first.

With a parent's permission, practice setting up a camp in your own backyard if you have one, or in a friend's backyard, or even in a room of your home. With adult supervision, you might even spend the night in your backyard camp!

You'll make your own simple tent and a comfortable bed on the ground.

With adult supervision, and only if the laws where you live allow it, you can build a safe fire, cook your meals, and clean up afterward. (See the Outdoor Code on page 346.)

Homemade Tent

If your family doesn't own a tent, you can make one that won't cost much money. It will do for mild weather. You'll need a sheet of heavy-duty builder's plastic—about 8 by 9 feet. Tie a rope between two trees or posts, using two half hitches.

Drape the plastic over the rope and spread it like a tent. Hammer four stakes in the ground near each edge. Hold a stone under each corner of the sheet and tie a knot around it and the sheet. Then tie the rope to the stakes, and your sheet won't fly away. Be sure to leave both ends of your homemade tent open for ventilation, and make the tent wide enough for two people. This tent will be fine for an overnight campout.

Sleeping on the Ground

You'll sleep on the ground during campouts. Be comfortable. Feel the ground all around with your hands and remove all sticks and stones.

Spread your groundsheet—a piece of plastic that helps keep your bedding dry. An old shower curtain works fine.

If you have an air mattress, put it on the groundsheet. If you don't, use pieces of your clothing for padding under your head, the small of your back, and your knees.

A sleeping bag is a very important piece of equipment for an outdoorsman. If you do not have a sleeping bag, you can use blankets to make a blanket bed.

To make your blanket bed, you need two blankets. Make it like this:

1. Lay the first blanket on the ground. Put the second blanket half on and half off the first one.

2. Fold the first blanket over the second. Leave half of the second showing.

3. Fold the remaining half of the second blanket over the first. This gives you two thicknesses over you and under you.

4. Fold the bottom of the blankets under the bed.

Using Rope

Whipping a Rope

Ropes are made of twisted fibers. When a rope is cut, the fibers separate. You can whip the ends in place with string so the rope won't unravel.

Cut off the part that has already unraveled. Take a piece of strong string, dental floss, or thin twine at least 8 to 10 inches long. Make a loop and place it at one end of the rope.

Wrap the string tightly around the rope. When the whipping is as wide as the rope is thick, slip the end through the loop. (See illustration 2.) Then pull out the string ends hard and trim them off.

Fusing a Rope

Rope and cord made of plastic or nylon will melt when exposed to high heat. Cut away the frayed part of the rope, then, working in a well-ventilated area, hold each end a few inches above a lighted match or candle to melt and fuse the strands together. Melted rope can be hot and sticky—don't touch the end until it has cooled. Do not try to fuse ropes made of manila, sisal, hemp, cotton, or other natural fibers, because they will burn rather than melt.

Knots for Camping

You'll use rope for many purposes when you go camping. Practice these knots. They'll come in handy in different situations.

Square Knot: For tying two ropes together and for tying bandages in first aid.

Taut-line Hitch: For tightening and loosening a rope easily and for use on tent guy lines. Tighten or loosen it by pushing the hitch up or down.

Clove Hitch: For tying a rope to a tree or post.

Two Half Hitches: For tying a rope to a post or ring. It is strong but is easy to loosen.

Bowline: Used when you want a loop that will not slip or close up. It is often used in rescue work.

Sheet Bend: For tying two ropes together, especially when one is thicker than the other.

Camping Away From Home

You may have Webelos den overnight campouts, where Webelos Scouts and their adult partners camp out for one or two nights.

You may also have campouts with a Boy Scout troop. Perhaps your family goes camping, too.

No matter how you camp, you'll have a great time—if you are prepared.

Packing for a Campout

If you have a backpack for camping, use that. If not, you can use a laundry bag or suitcase.

Here's what you and your adult partner will need for a Webelos den overnight campout:

- Two waterproof groundsheets
- Two sleeping bags, or two blankets each, to make blanket beds
- Changes of underwear
- Changes of socks
- Pajamas, if you use them
- Knives, forks, spoons
- Plates, bowls, cups
- Cooking pot or pan
- Pliers for dipping dishes in hot rinse water
- Plastic sheet to air-dry dishes on

- Bow saw for fuel wood
- Matches in waterproof container
- Charcoal or camp stove if not using wood fire
- Food for all camp meals
- A cooler to keep perishable foods cold
- Trash bag
- Sunscreen
- Insect repellent
- One or two flashlights with fresh batteries
- Toothbrushes and toothpaste
- Toilet paper
- Sweaters or jackets
- Ponchos or raincoats
- Bar soap
- Towels
- Extra pants and shirts, if rain is likely
- Extra pair of shoes
- Whistle
- *Webelos Handbook*
- Bible, testament, prayer book, or other book for your faith

If you use a backpack, arrange soft items in it so they will cushion your back. Keep your raingear, first-aid kit, and water bottle near the top of the pack.

You may have to bring a tent, too, unless a Boy Scout troop is letting the den use its tents.

Wear your Webelos Scout uniform in camp.

Setting Up Dining Fly or Tent

For a dining fly over your cooking area, try tying a rope between two trees with taut-line hitches and tightening the rope so it is six to eight feet above the ground. Drape the tarp over the rope, pull out the corners, and use taut-line hitches to tie *guylines* (ropes attached to the corners) to trees or stakes. (To tie a taut-line hitch, see page 350.)

Set the tarp closer to the ground if you want to sleep under it. Lowering the edges will give you extra protection from the wind.

Tents

Most tents have the shape of an A-frame or a dome, and are roomy enough for two to four campers. Many are made of breathable nylon that allows moisture to escape. A waterproof nylon fly pitched over the body of the tent shields it from rain, snow, and wind.

When you are ready to pitch your tent, first you must choose a level site. Remove stones and large sticks, but don't disturb pine needles or grasses. Spread out a ground cloth to protect the tent floor from dirt, sharp objects, and moisture.

Unfold the tent on top of the ground cloth. Pull out the corners of the floor and stake them to the ground, then assemble the poles and put them in place. Use taut-line hitches to tie the free ends of guylines around stakes you've pushed into the ground, and pull the lines tight.

Finish by putting the rain fly over the tent and staking it down.

Whenever possible, let your tent dry in the sun before you take it down. When that's not possible and you have to pack a wet tent, set it up again as soon as you get home, or hang it indoors and be sure it dries completely before putting it away. That will prevent mildew from ruining the fabric.

No Flames in Tents

Keep *all* flames away from tents. Never use candles, matches, stoves, heaters, or lanterns in or near tents. No tent is fireproof. All of them can burn or melt when exposed to heat. *Flashlights only!*

Activities in Camp

At a den or troop overnight campout, the leaders will suggest activities, such as working on outdoor activity badges, learning Scout skills, and playing outdoor games.

In the evening you may have a campfire program, with songs, skits, and other fun. Join in with your friends.

Be Safe and Comfortable

Here are tips to keep you safe and comfortable when you camp with your den or your family.

Snakes: Snakes are not likely to bother you if you don't bother them. Stay away from them.

Insects: A good bug spray keeps most of them away. Spray on exposed skin and also around your ankles and on your socks. Don't spray inside the tent because this may destroy the waterproofing.

Poisonous plants: Learn to recognize poison ivy, poison oak, and poison sumac (see page 334) and stay away from them. Never eat anything from the woods unless you know exactly what it is.

Animals: Animals can be drawn to your camp by the food you throw away or leave out. Bears are the most dangerous camp raiders and roadside beggars. **You must remember that they are not tame. Never let anyone get near them.**

Black Bear

Mice, chipmunks, raccoons, opossums, porcupines, and skunks add to the adventure of camping. Watch them and enjoy them, but **don't try to catch or pet them.**

Swimming: Always swim with an adult and use the buddy system (see page 385). Watch for drop-offs or holes and swift currents. Don't swim in polluted water! Don't get too much sun or get too tired. Use a sunscreen lotion to protect your skin.

Weather: See pages 362 and 364 for tips on staying safe and comfortable whether it rains or the sun shines during your campout.

Getting lost: Anyone can get lost, even adults. But some things can help you to not get lost or to keep you safer if you do:

• Always stay with a buddy.

• Let people know when you leave and where you are going.

- Carry a plastic trash bag poncho in case of rain.
- Carry a whistle to signal for help.

If you think you are lost, sit down in an open area. Relax. Blow your whistle every so often. Stay put.

Cooking in Camp

You and your adult partner may be expected to bring your own food to a Webelos den overnight campout, unless the whole den cooks together. Choose foods that are easy to fix—and that you love to eat.

For most meals you'll need a fire. You may build it with wood or charcoal or your adult partner may use a camp stove. If you have a choice, use wood, because fire making is a skill you need to learn.

Building a Wood Fire

If your campsite already has a fireplace or safe fire site, use it. If it doesn't, you must make a safe fire site. Clear a circle 10 feet across, taking out anything that could burn—twigs, leaves, dry grass, pine needles. Save the groundcover so you can put it back when you are done with your fire. Your fire will be in the center of the circle. (See the illustration on the next page.) Have a pot of water nearby for emergencies and to extinguish the fire.

You will need three kinds of materials to make your fire:

Tinder: Stuff that flares up quickly when you touch a lighted match to it. It must be dry. Look for dead twigs on standing trees and tiny dry twigs on the ground. Dry weed tops are good, too.

Kindling: Small branches about as thick as your thumb and 6 to 10 inches long. Snap dead branches off standing trees and pick up dry branches on the ground. They will catch the flame from the tinder.

Fuel wood: Larger dead branches you find on the ground. You may need a saw to cut them into pieces about a foot long. They provide the heat for cooking.

You don't need a big fire for cooking on a campout. Five to 10 pieces of fuel wood should be plenty.

Outdoor Fire Safety Rules

1. Follow all rules of your campsite.
2. Clear all burnable materials from your 10-foot fire circle. Don't build the fire under overhanging branches of trees or shrubs or near roots of trees.
3. Never leave your fire unattended.
4. Have a pot or bucket of water nearby in case sparks start a fire away from the fire circle.
5. When you are finished cooking, make sure the fire is **DEAD OUT**. Spread the coals and ashes and sprinkle them with water. Stir and sprinkle until the site is cold. Feel it with your hand to make sure.

Making Your Fire Lay

Put your tinder in the center of the fire circle. Then arrange kindling in one of the ways shown here, so that the flames from the tinder will catch the kindling quickly.

When the kindling is burning, add a couple of pieces of fuel wood. As the fuel wood burns down to coals, add more fuel.

Tepee

Lean-to

Fire-stick

You can use logs or big flat rocks to hold your pots and pans. Don't use sandstone or wet rocks. They may explode if they get hot.

Rock Fireplace

What to Cook

Keep meals simple on your first few campouts. Consider cooking hamburgers, hot dogs, bacon and eggs, or canned food like spaghetti, beans, and vegetables.

You might prepare a supper dish in aluminum foil at home before you go to camp. Here's how to do it:

You need an 18-by-24-inch sheet of heavy-duty aluminum foil, or two sheets of regular foil.

Use a piece of meat about the size of your hand. It could be ground beef, steak, chicken, or fish. Flatten ground beef. Lay the meat near the center of the foil. Slice a small onion and cut a small potato in thin slices and arrange them over the meat. Add peas, beans, or thinly sliced carrots.

Now fold the foil into a package. Join the edges and fold them over tightly so steam can't escape.

Take the foil dinners to camp in a cooler so the food won't spoil. About a half-hour before supper, lay the packages directly on the coals of the fire. Turn them over after 15 minutes and cook them another 10 minutes. Dinner should be ready. Eat it from the foil.

Note: To protect against food poisoning, always wash your hands before you handle food. Wash all vegetables and fruits. Make sure that food packets stay cool in the cooler and that food is thoroughly cooked before you eat it.

Cleanup

Every Scout camper learns to wash dishes and clean up after eating. Do your part in the cleanup job.

Make sure your cooking fire is **DEAD OUT.** Replace the groundcover you saved earlier. Pick up garbage and trash and put it in a garbage bag to take out of the campsite.

Put all leftover food, milk, and other drinks back in the camp cooler or food box. Keep all food and "smellables" (toothpaste, gum, candy—even toiletries and cleaning products) in closed containers, in a vehicle or building, with all windows and doors closed. They can attract all kinds of animals. You don't want to come back to your camp and find everything torn apart, or have a midnight "visitor" in your camp!

Hiking With Your Den

As a Webelos Scout you may go on nature hikes, rock hunts, and other outdoor activities.

Never go hiking alone. Go with your Webelos den leader and Webelos den chief. Start with a short hike. Take it easy and pay careful attention to your surroundings. Stop to look at trees and plants. Try to name as many kinds as you can. Look at the houses and buildings. Count the different kinds of birds you see.

When you sit down for a rest, look around. Find grasses that aren't the same. Count the different bugs you find. You'll enjoy your hike more if you notice everything. Some people hike as if they were walking through a tunnel. They never see a thing.

Watch for signs and landmarks so you can find your way back.

Your First Hike

For your first hike, choose a destination about a mile from your starting place. It may be a park, high hill, pond, or lake. Perhaps a grove of trees or a picnic area is nearby. Out and back would be a 2-mile trip—a pretty good start. Set your own pace. Hike for 15 minutes. Rest for 5 minutes. Then try a 20-minute walk and a 10-minute rest. Stay together. Try different speeds until you find the pace that's best for all the hikers.

Walk a little every week. Go farther each time. This makes you stronger.

Face traffic when walking along a road. This means walking on the left side. Walk single file when the whole den goes. Don't hike at night. If for some reason you are ever out walking at night, carry a flashlight and wear white or reflective clothing.

What to Wear

The Webelos Scout uniform is ideal for hiking. Take along a raincoat or poncho in case it rains.

Shoes: You depend on your shoes to get you to your destination and back. Choose them carefully. Take good care of them. A hightop shoe or boot is best because it keeps out gravel and sand.

It's very important that your hiking shoes fit well. If they don't, you'll be sure to get blisters. The shoes should be fairly tight around your heel. There should be room to wiggle your toes.

- Never go hiking in new shoes. Break them in first by wearing them part of every day for a week or more.

- To keep leather shoes soft and partly waterproof, rub them with saddle soap. Do this before and after every hike.

- When leather shoes get wet, wipe them with paper or old socks. Dry them slowly, away from direct heat.

Socks: Socks are almost as important as shoes. They soak up moisture. They also cushion your feet. Socks made of wool, polypropylene, or a wool/nylon blend work well. Take an extra pair on a hike. Then you can put on clean socks before you start back. This dry pair will feel great. Don't use socks with holes or holes that have been darned. They start blisters.

Outdoor Essentials

1. First aid kit
2. Filled water bottle
3. Flashlight
4. Trail food
5. Sunscreen

6. Whistle
7. Map and compass
8. Rain gear
9. Pocketknife
10. Matches or fire starters

Visit a Scout Camp

One of your Webelos overnight campouts may be held at a Boy Scout camp. If not, ask your Webelos den leader to take the den to camp for a visit.

When you become a Boy Scout, you'll go to Scout camp often. Now is a good time to see what Scout camp has to offer. You'll have a great time there!

Sun Smarts

Block the sun year round. It's possible to burn all year (that includes cloudy and snowy days). So whether you're walking to school or outside playing don't forget to block the sun, to have fun year round!

Use a sunblock with an SPF of at least 15. If you have fair skin, light-colored eyes and hair, freckles, or spend a lot of time outside, use an SPF 30 or higher. Apply sunblock 15 minutes before you go out. Reapply after prolonged swimming, vigorous activity, sweating, or toweling off.

Watch the clock. Try to limit the amount of time you're in direct sun during 10 A.M. and 4 P.M.

"Waterproof" your skin. If you're spending a day at the beach or at the pool, cover up with waterproof sunblock. After swimming, toweling off, sweating, and/or vigorous activity, be sure to reapply sunblock.

Remember your ears, nose, neck and hands. They may seem small but they can burn big time. Always cover these areas with sunblock.

Make a statement with shades, hat, and a wild T-shirt. A cool pair of UVA/UVB blocking sunglasses protect your eyes like nothing else. As for your hat, if you get really hot, dunk it in water, then pull it on (but make sure it's a wide brimmed hat). Of course, a long-sleeve T-shirt is a must for summer fun.

The American Academy of Dermatology supports the use of sunscreen products with an SPF 15 rating or higher but does not endorse, guarantee, or approve any specific sun-safety products.

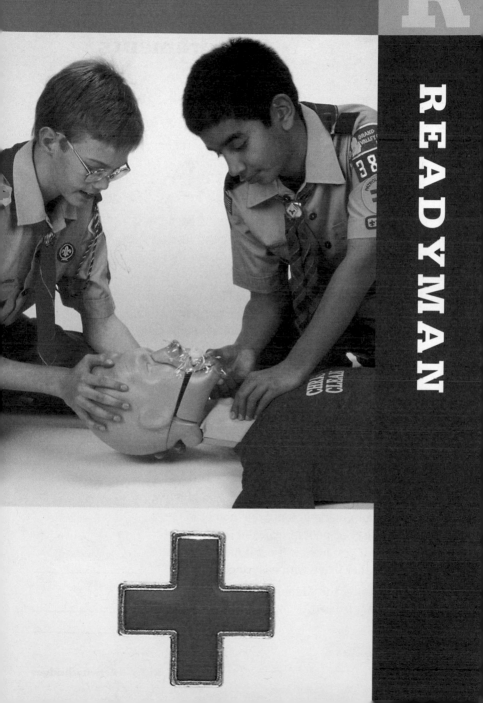

Community Group

R

READYMAN

Readyman
Requirements

Requirement	Approved by

Do all of these:

1. With your parent, guardian, or Webelos den leader, complete the Courage Character Connection.

   a. **Know:** Define the importance of each courage step: Be strong; Be calm; Be clear; Be careful. Explain how memorizing the courage steps helps you to be ready.

   DWM

   b. **Commit:** Explain why it is hard to follow the courage steps in an emergency. Tell when you can use the courage steps in other situations (such as standing up to a bully, avoiding fights, being fair, not stealing or cheating when tempted, etc.)

   DWM

   c. **Practice:** Act out one of the requirements using these courage steps: Be strong; Be calm; Be clear; Be careful.

   DWM

> 2. Explain what first aid is. Tell what you should do after an accident.

> 3. Explain how you can get help quickly if there is an emergency in your home. Make a "help list" of people or agencies that can help you if you need it. Post it near a phone or in another place with easy access.

> 4. Demonstrate the Heimlich maneuver and tell when it is used.

5. Show what to do for these "hurry cases":
   - Serious bleeding
   - Stopped breathing
   - Internal poisoning
   - Heart attack
6. Show how to treat shock.
7. Show first aid for the following:
   - Cuts and scratches
   - Burns and scalds
   - Choking
   - Blisters on the hand and foot
   - Tick bites
   - Bites and stings of insects other than ticks
   - Poisonous snakebite
   - Nosebleed
   - Frostbite
   - Sunburn
8. Tell what steps must be taken for a safe swim with your Webelos den, pack, family, or other group. Explain the reasons for the buddy system.

And do two of these:

9. Explain six safety rules you should follow when "driving" a bicycle.
10. Explain the importance of wearing safety equipment when participating in sports activities (skating, skateboarding, etc.)
11. Make a home fire escape plan for your family. _____
12. Explain how to use each item in a first aid kit. _____
13. Tell where accidents are most likely to happen inside and around your home. _____

14. Explain six safety rules you should remember when riding in a car.

15. Attend a first aid demonstration at a Boy Scout troop meeting, a Red Cross center, or other community event or place.

I n emergencies, someone has to be ready to help. After you earn the Readyman activity badge, you'll know how to react quickly when someone is ill or injured.

You'll be ready to call for emergency help. When you learn first aid, you can care for a sick or injured person until help arrives.

You'll also find out how to prevent accidents and how to be safe when swimming and biking. You'll help your family be safe at home and when traveling by car.

Learning the skills that prevent accidents and help in emergencies will make you a Readyman. When you complete each requirement, ask your Webelos den leader or activity badge counselor to sign it on pages 366–368.

"Be" Courageous

Courage is what you need when you face an emergency. Courage is not something you're just "born with"; it is something you can train yourself to have when you need it. Learn to say these steps to help you feel courageous and behave courageously:

Be **strong.**

Be **calm.**

Be **clear.**

Be **careful.**

What Is First Aid?

You've probably had at least a few scratches and scrapes in your lifetime, and an adult in your family or the nurse at school knew just what to do. Maybe you've taken care of a few small injuries by yourself. All of this is first aid.

First aid is also knowing exactly what to do *first* to help a person with a more serious injury or illness. **First aid is what you must do immediately.** Someone has to help right away, and you might be the only person there who can do this job. It's important to know the right ways to help.

In earning the Readyman activity badge, you'll find out how to call for emergency help and what to do for different types of illnesses and injuries until help arrives.

What to Do After an Accident

- First, stay calm and think! This may be hard to do—but try. The victim will feel better, knowing you are in control.

- If the victim seems badly hurt, send someone to call for medical help. If no one is there to do that, call for help and give what assistance you can to the victim.

- Do not move a badly hurt person unless the victim is in further danger. It may be necessary to move the person if there is a nearby fire or if the person is lying in the road. But never move an injured person unless it is absolutely necessary.

- Check the victim for "hurry cases" (see page 371).

- Treat the victim for shock (see pages 376–377).

How to Get Help

The way to get help in an emergency is not always the same in every town. Some communities may have different phone numbers for the police, fire department, ambulance, and rescue squad. In many places, the 911 number will put you in touch with all of these services.

Find out how to get help where you live and make a list of the phone numbers. Post your list near the telephone in your home so everyone can find the numbers quickly. It's also a good idea to put your list on a card and carry it with you. You should also carry coins for a pay phone.

Your "help list" should include numbers for

- Police or sheriff's department
- Fire department
- Ambulance
- Utility companies (electricity, gas, water)
- Rescue squad
- Your family doctor
- Poison control center
- A friendly neighbor who can help you

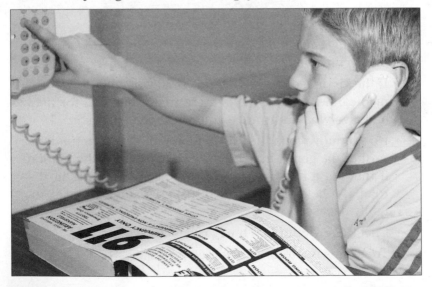

When you call for help, remember the "three W's": *Who?* *What?* and *Where?*

Who?   Give your name.
What?   Explain the situation: fire, accident, injury, etc.
Where?   Give the exact location. Give the names of both streets or roads at the nearest corner.

Stay on the phone until your message is understood and you have answered all questions.

Sometimes you need to know how to get help, but it may not be an emergency. For problems with your sewer line or other housing problems, call a department of your city or county government. Your church or other religious group, a counseling agency, or friends and relatives might be able to help with a family problem. Find out who to contact in your community.

First Aid for Hurry Cases

If a person cuts a leg and blood is oozing out, he or she needs first aid but is not going to die. A broken arm is a serious injury, but it won't kill.

Hurry cases are different. Unless you act fast and give the right first aid, the victim may die within a few minutes. The four hurry cases are

- **Breathing has stopped.** It must be started quickly.

- **Blood is spurting from a wound.** The bleeding must be stopped quickly.

- **Poison has been swallowed.** The poison must be made harmless. Get help quickly.

- **Heart attack or stroke.** Get help quickly.

Protective Measures to Take When Handling Wounds and Giving CPR

Treat all blood as if it contains blood-borne viruses. Do not use bare hands to stop bleeding; always use a protective barrier (see the list below). Cover any cuts or scrapes you may have. Always wash exposed skin with hot water and soap immediately after treating the victim, and don't use a sink in a food preparation area.

The following equipment should to be included in all first aid kits and used when giving first aid to someone in need:

- Latex gloves, to be used when stopping bleeding or dressing wounds
- A mouth-barrier device, to be used when rendering rescue breathing or CPR (cardiopulmonary resuscitation)
- Plastic goggles or other eye protection, to prevent a victim's blood from getting into the rescuer's eyes in the event of serious arterial bleeding
- Antiseptic, for use in sterilization or cleaning exposed skin areas, particularly if soap and water are not available.

Stopped Breathing

In drowning cases and some other accidents, the victim's breathing may stop. It must be started again *quickly*, or the person will die.

Look at the chest. Is it moving up and down? Put your ear to the victim's mouth. Do you feel the victim's breath?

If the answer is no, start rescue breathing. This is a way of blowing air from your own lungs into the victim's lungs.

Rescue Breathing

Don't give up. Continue rescue breathing until medical help arrives and takes over.

Step 1

Note: If available, a mouth-barrier device should be used when rendering rescue breathing or CPR.

Place the victim faceup. Lift the chin with your right hand, and push the forehead down with your left hand.

This shows why it is important to tilt the head back. If the head is not tilted back, the tongue blocks the airway.

Step 2

Pinch the victim's nostrils together. Seal your mouth over the victim's mouth. (If the victim is a small child, don't pinch the nostrils. Blow into both the mouth and nose at the same time.) Blow into the victim's mouth to fill the lungs with air. Look to make sure the chest rises.

Step 3

Remove your mouth. Take a deep breath and count slowly to five—about five seconds. (Count to three if the victim is a child.) Watch to make sure the victim's chest falls as air escapes from the lungs. Then give another breath.

If the victim's chest does not rise when you blow in, the airway must be blocked. Turn the head to one side. With your fingers, feel whether something is in the mouth. If there is, pull it out.

If the airway still seems to be blocked, turn the victim's head faceup. Place the heel of your hand midway between the victim's rib cage and belly button. Push upward quickly several times.

Stopping Severe Bleeding

In a bad accident you might see blood spurting out of a wound. It doesn't ooze or flow slowly—it gushes out like a fountain. It must be stopped! **Now!**

Avoid direct contact with the blood. Use latex gloves.

Grab the wound with your gloved hand and **press hard!**

Raise a cut arm or leg above the level of the victim's heart. That will help slow the bleeding.

With your free hand, grab your neckerchief, handkerchief, or other cloth. Fold it into a pad and quickly press it on the wound. Then **press hard** again. If you can, tie the pad in place with a bandage. Don't remove the pad even if it gets soaked with blood. Put another pad and bandage over the first. Send for medical help.

Direct pressure on the wound usually stops bleeding. If it doesn't, **press hard** on one of the pressure points shown to stop bleeding in an arm or leg. The arteries that carry blood from the heart are squeezed against the bone. It's like stepping on a garden hose to stop the water.

Poisoning by Mouth

Young children will try anything! They will even drink poisons because they don't know any better.

Keep all household cleaners, medicines, weed killers, and insect poisons out of their reach. Locked cabinets are best because children are curious and learn to climb.

If a child does swallow some poison, call a hospital or poison control center immediately. Tell them what the poison is. Follow their directions. Don't give anything to drink unless they tell you to.

Save the poison container so the poison can be identified.

Heart Attack

Heart attack is the number one cause of death in the United States. Most heart attacks happen to adults, especially older people. Here are the signs of a heart attack:

- A feeling of pain or pressure in the center of the chest lasting more than a few minutes. It may come and go. Sharp, stabbing twinges of pain are rarely signals of a heart attack. If in doubt, seek medical help.
- Sweating when the room is not hot
- Feeling like throwing up
- Shortness of breath
- A feeling of weakness

If you think a person is having a heart attack, call for medical help at once.

First Aid for Shock

When a person is injured or under great stress, his circulatory system might not provide enough blood to all parts of his body. That's called *shock*. The person will feel weak. His face may get pale. His skin will feel cold and clammy. He may shiver or vomit.

Don't wait for these signals to appear. Give any badly injured person first aid for shock.

- Have him lie down.
- Raise his feet slightly, unless you think he has injuries to his head, neck, back, hips, or legs. If you don't know, have him lie flat.
- If he is not awake, turn him on his side, not on his back.
- If the weather is cool, cover him. If it's hot, don't.
- Call for emergency help immediately. He needs expert medical care as soon as possible.

Other First Aid You Should Know

Cuts and Scratches

Cuts and scratches are wounds—openings in the skin and tissues that can allow germs to enter the body and cause infection.

First aid for small wounds: Wash scratches and minor cuts with soap and water. Applying antiseptic can help prevent infection. Keep the wound clean with an adhesive bandage. On camping trips, clean and rebandage small wounds daily.

First aid for larger cuts: Treat large cuts by using direct pressure to stop bleeding, then keep the wound as clean as you can to limit infection. Cover an open wound with a sterile gauze pad or clean cloth folded into a pad. Hold the pad in position with tape, a cravat bandage, or other binder.

Anyone suffering a serious wound should be treated for shock and seen by a physician.

Burns and Scalds

First aid for burns and scalds depends on how serious the injury is. A burn from light contact with a hot object probably is a first-degree burn. Very serious burns are called third-degree burns.

First-degree burn: The skin gets red and sore. Put the burned area in cold water until the pain stops. If you don't have any water, cover the burn with a clean, dry dressing.

Second-degree burn: Blisters form on the skin. Try to protect them from breaking open, as this could cause infection. Cover the burned area with a sterile gauze pad from a first aid kit. Hold the pad loosely in place with a bandage. **Don't** apply creams, ointments, or sprays. All second-degree burns need medical attention.

Third-degree burn: The skin may be burned away. Flesh may be charred. The victim may feel no pain. Don't try to remove clothing from around the burn. Wrap the victim in a clean sheet. Cover him with blankets if the weather is cool. Call for an ambulance to rush him to a hospital.

Treat for shock, too: People with second- or third-degree burns will be suffering from shock. So give first aid for shock as well as for the burn.

Sunburn: Most sunburns are first-degree burns. A severe sunburn is a second-degree burn and should receive prompt medical attention. Prevent sunburn by liberally applying sunscreen lotion with a high sun protection factor (SPF) about 20 minutes before you're in the sun. Reapply if you sweat heavily or swim. It's also important to wear protective clothing and a broad-brimmed hat and sunglasses as well as limit your exposure to the sun. The sun's rays are most harmful between 10:00 A.M. and 2:00 P.M. Sunburns should be treated with cool compresses or baths.

Choking

If a bit of food sticks in a person's throat, he will start choking. He may not be able to cough it up by himself. Unless the person is a baby, use the Heimlich maneuver to help him.

Heimlich Maneuver

Stand behind the victim and put your arms around him. Make a fist with one hand just above his belly button. Cover the fist with your other hand. Now make four quick thrusts inward and upward to force air

Close-up of hand position for Heimlich maneuver

Heimlich Maneuver

from his lungs. This should dis-
lodge the food. If it doesn't, repeat
until the food is dislodged.

If the person is too big for you to
do the Heimlich maneuver standing up, have him lie down faceup.
Put one open hand just above his
belly button and put the other hand
over the first. Make four quick, upward
thrusts.

Note: Because of the possibility of injury, **do not practice
the thrust part of the Heimlich maneuver on a person.**
Thrusts should be used only for actual choking cases.

Blisters on the Hand and Foot

Blisters are pockets of fluid that form as the skin's way of
protecting itself from friction. Blisters on the feet are common
injuries among hikers. Avoid getting blisters by wearing shoes
or boots that fit, by changing your socks if they become sweaty
or wet, and by paying attention to how your feet feel.

A *hot spot* is a warning that a blister might be forming. As
soon as you notice it, treat a hot spot or blister with a "doughnut
bandage" to relieve the pressure on your skin.

Cut moleskin in the shape of a doughnut and fit it around the
injury. Shape several more "doughnuts" and stack them on top of
the first. The doughnut bandage will keep pressure off the injury.

A gel pad made of the same material used to treat burns can
be applied directly over a blister to reduce friction and speed
healing. Follow the instructions on the package. Used together,
a gel pad and a moleskin doughnut provide maximum relief for
blisters and hot spots.

Tick Bites

Ticks are small, hard-shelled arachnids that bury their heads
in the skin of warm-blooded vertebrates. Protect yourself whenever you are in tick-infested woodlands and fields by wearing
long pants and a long-sleeved shirt. Button your collar and
tuck the cuffs of your pants into your boots or socks. Inspect

yourself daily, especially the hairy parts of your body, and immediately remove any ticks you find. If a tick has attached itself, grasp it with tweezers close to the skin and gently pull until it comes loose. Don't squeeze, twist, or jerk the tick, as that could leave its mouth parts in the skin. Wash the wound with soap and water and apply antiseptic. After dealing with a tick, thoroughly wash your hands.

Bee and Wasp Stings

Scrape away a bee or wasp stinger with the edge of a knife blade. Don't try to squeeze it out. That will force more venom into the skin from the sac attached to the stinger. An ice pack might reduce pain and swelling.

Chigger Bites

Chiggers are almost invisible. They burrow into skin pores, causing itching and small welts. Try not to scratch chigger bites. You might find some relief by covering chigger bites with calamine lotion or by dabbing them with clear fingernail polish.

When helping the victims of bites or stings, do whatever you must to avoid being stung or bitten yourself. A first-aider who becomes injured could greatly complicate any emergency situation.

Spider Bites

The bite of a female black widow spider can cause redness and sharp pain at the wound site. The victim might suffer sweating, nausea and vomiting, stomach pain and cramps, severe muscle pain and spasms, and shock. Breathing might become difficult.

The bite of a brown recluse spider doesn't always hurt right away, but within two to eight hours there can be pain, redness, and swelling at the wound. An open sore is likely to develop. The victim might suffer fever, chills, nausea, vomiting, joint pain, and a faint rash.

Victims of spider bites should be treated for shock, then seen by a physician as soon as possible.

Snakebite

Snakes are common in many parts of the country, but bites from them are rare. Snakes try to avoid humans, and normally strike only when they sense danger. Snakebites seldom result in death.

The bite of a nonpoisonous snake causes only minor puncture wounds.

The bit of a poisonous snake can cause sharp, burning pain. The area around the bite might swell and become discolored; however, a poisonous snake does not inject venom every time it bites.

Use a hiking stick to poke among stones and brush ahead of you when you walk through areas where snakes are common. Watch where you put your hands as you collect firewood or climb over rocks and logs.

1. Get the victim under medical care as soon as possible so that physicians can neutralize the venom.

2. Remove rings and other jewelry that might cause problems if the area around the bite swells.

3. If the victim must wait for medical attention to arrive, have him lie down and position the bitten part lower than the rest of his body. Encourage him to stay calm. He might be very frightened, so keep assuring him that he is being cared for.

4. Treat for shock.

5. If available within 3 minutes of the bite, apply a venom extractor such as a Sawyer Extractor® directly over the fang marks and leave in place for no more than 10 minutes. Properly used, the extractor can remove up to 30 percent of the venom. **Do not make any cuts on the bite**—that's an old-fashioned remedy that can harm the victim much more than help him.

6. **Do not apply ice to a snakebite.** Ice will not help the injury, but it can damage the skin and tissue.

Nosebleed

A nosebleed can look bad, but it will usually stop in just a few minutes. Have the victim sit up and lean forward to prevent blood from draining into his or her throat. Pinch the nostrils together to maintain pressure on the flow. Apply a cool, wet cloth to the victim's nose and face.

If bleeding is severe or if there are other injuries to the face and head, position the victim to keep blood out of his airway. Treat for shock and call for help.

Frostbite

A victim of frostbite might complain that his ears, nose, fingers, or feet feel painful and then numb. Another frostbite victim won't notice anything. You might see grayish-white patches on his skin—a sure sign of frostbite.

Get into a tent or building, then warm the injury and keep it warm. If an ear or cheek is frozen, remove a glove and warm the injury with the palm of your hand. Slip a frostbitten hand under your clothing and tuck it beneath an armit. Treat frozen toes by putting the victim's bare feet against the warm skin of your belly. Avoid rubbing frostbitten flesh, as that can damage tissue and skin.

You can also warm a frozen part by holding it in warm—not hot—running water. Or wrap it in a dry blanket. Have the patient exercise injured fingers or toes, and don't let the injured area freeze again. Get the victim to a doctor.

Sunburn

Sunburn is a common injury among people who enjoy being outdoors. Repeated burns can cause long-term skin damage and the potential for skin cancer. People with lighter skin are most at risk, though others are not immune. Prevent sunburn by using plenty of sunscreen with a sun protection factor (SPF) rating of at least 15. Reapply sunscreen after swimming or if you are perspiring. A broad-brimmed hat, long-sleeved shirt, and long pants provide even more protection.

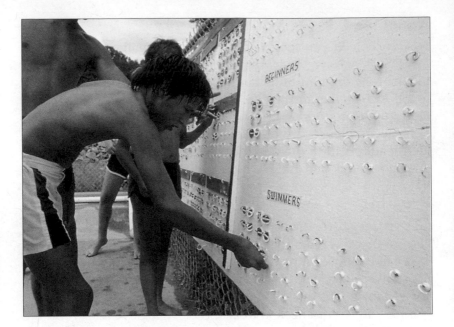

Safe Swimming

Swimming is a lot of fun, but the water can be a dangerous place if you aren't prepared.

Scouting has a checklist called the Safe Swim Defense plan to make sure you are prepared. The plan has eight points.

Safe Swim Defense

1. **An adult is in charge.** Follow the adult's orders.
2. **Physical fitness.** Each swimmer must provide a current health history from his parent, guardian, or doctor.
3. **Safe swim area.** The area is checked for underwater dangers. One area not more than 3½ feet deep is marked off for nonswimmers. Another area is marked for beginners; it can be a little deeper. A third area of deep water is marked for good swimmers.

4. **Lifeguards.** Trained lifeguards are on shore, watching everybody who is in the water.

5. **Lookout.** A lookout is also on shore to direct the lifeguards if a person needs help.

6. **Ability groups.** The leaders divide the swimmers into three groups: (1) *nonswimmers*; (2) *beginners*, who can swim at least 50 feet; and (3) *swimmers*, who can swim 100 yards and float. Each group stays in its own area.

7. **Buddy system.** Each person is paired with another person who has the same swimming ability. They go into the water together, stay together, and come out together.

8. **Discipline.** Everyone agrees to follow water safety rules. Everyone obeys the lifeguards or other supervisors.

The Buddy System

Your Webelos den leader or another adult will take care of most of the steps of the Safe Swim Defense plan. But the buddy system depends on YOU!

When you go swimming, you'll have a buddy. If you're a beginner, he'll be a beginner. If you're a swimmer, he'll be a swimmer.

At Scout camp, you and your buddy will check in at the waterfront together. You'll stay together until you check out. When the lifeguard calls "Buddy check!" or "Buddies!" you and your buddy will grasp hands and raise them overhead. Then the lifeguard can make sure all the people in the water are safe.

Left Turn · Right Turn

Slow

Bicycle Safety

Did you notice that requirement 9 talks about "driving" a bicycle? When you are on a bike, you are a driver, just like an adult driving a car.

So you should act like a driver and obey traffic safety rules. Here are the safe bicycle driving rules.

1. **Always** wear a safety helmet.

2. **Obey all traffic laws.** Stop at all "Stop" signs. Give signals for turns. Avoid busy streets, if you can.

3. **Observe local laws.** Your community may have rules for registration of bicycles and driving on sidewalks. Learn them and obey them.

4. **Drive with traffic,** not against it. Stay close to the curb.

5. **Watch out** for hazards like potholes and drain grates.

6. **Watch out** for car doors opening or cars pulling into traffic.

7. **Don't carry passengers.** You will have less control of your bike if you have a passenger.

8. **Never hitch a ride** by holding onto a truck, car, or other vehicle.

9. **Be extra careful at intersections.** If traffic is heavy, get off your bike and walk it across the intersection.

10. **Use hand signals** for turning and stopping.

11. **Drive a safe bike.** Keep it in good repair. Don't ride after dark, but have reflectors and lights on your bike in case you have to ride for an emergency reason. In that case, also wear reflective clothing.

12. **Drive "defensively."** That means: Watch out for the other guy. Keep a safe distance from traffic ahead of you. Stay alert. Be ready to stop suddenly.

Safety Equipment

For all sports, it is important to wear equipment that will help prevent injury. For example, during all street or pavement skating activities, participants should wear properly fitted helmets that meet American National Standards Institute (ANSI) standards, padded gloves, wrist supports, and elbow and knee pads. Your parent, guardian, or Webelos den leader can help you learn what safety equipment is needed for each sport you want to learn.

Home Fire Escape Plan

Suppose you wake up some night and hear your smoke detector or smell smoke. What would you do?

That's easy. Wake the other members of your family and get them out of the house! Then call the fire department.

But what if your family sleeps on the second floor and the fire is coming up the stairway? How would the family get out?

Make a plan now. Discuss it with the adult members of your family.

Figure out two possible escape routes for each bedroom. If there is a two-story drop from some bedroom windows, the family may have to buy escape ladders. But that's a lot better than having a family member trapped in a fire because the only way out is blocked by flames.

Make sure your family has a place to meet once they are outside. Then everyone will know when all family members are out and safe.

FIRE-ESCAPE PLAN for second floor. Short arrows show usual exits from bedrooms. Long arrows show emergency exits.

ESCAPE LADDER. Folding ladder that is stored under a window.

First Aid Kits

Every home and car should have a first aid kit. Then first aid supplies will be there if they are needed.

Check your family's home or car first aid kit. For requirement 12, you'll explain how the items should be used. If you don't know, ask your Webelos den leader or den chief to show you.

Things that should be in a first aid kit are listed below.

First Aid Kit

- Tweezers
- Box of adhesive bandages (different sizes)
- Twelve each of 3-by-3-inch and 4-by-4-inch sterile pads
- Roll of 1-inch and roll of 2-inch adhesive tape
- Scissors

- Safety pins
- Two 1-inch roller bandages
- Two 2-inch roller bandages
- Three triangular bandages
- Three cravat bandages (a cravat bandage is made by folding a triangular bandage or Scout neckerchief)
- Two 17-inch splints of thin board ·
- Two 30-inch splints
- Calamine lotion
- Latex gloves
- Mouth-barrier device

For a first aid kit in a car, also include a small flashlight and spare batteries, hand cleaner in packets, a white handkerchief (to attach to the car so you can attract attention if the car is disabled), a blanket, and a large red and white sign that can be placed in the front or rear window that reads "Send Help!"

Danger Spots at Home

Some homes are safer than others. In safe homes, toys are not left lying around. Matches and poisons are kept away from small children. Electrical cords are placed such that they don't trip people.

In other words, the family thinks about safety.

You can help your family think about safety.

Are there danger areas in and around your home? Use the "Home Safety Checklist" on page 233 to find out.

Look around outside, too. Are garden tools stored neatly and safely? Are ladders strong and not wobbly? Are stairs and sidewalks kept free of ice and snow in the winter?

See what you can do to make your home safer.

Safety in a Car

You may say, "What can I do about safety in a car? I'm not old enough to drive."

That's true. But you *can* do something about car safety. Here are ideas:

- Always use your seat belt. You are much less likely to get hurt in an accident if you are wearing a seat belt. In some states, wearing a seat belt is the law. What is the law in your state?

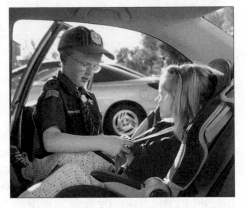

- Don't talk to the driver in heavy traffic. He or she must concentrate on driving.

- Do talk to the driver when he or she is tired. It will help keep the driver alert. But also remind the driver to stop for a rest and perhaps something re-freshing to drink. When a driver dozes off even for a second, an accident can happen.

- Suggest to the driver that you stop every two hours on a long trip. The driver needs to stretch and relax. Maybe you can take a ball along and play catch at a rest area to help the driver relax.

- Keep younger children from quarreling or jumping around in the car. Be sure they keep their seat belts fastened or are in their car seats with the harness fastened.

- Lock the doors. Then younger children won't be able to open them accidentally.

- Keep hands, head, and feet inside the car—even when it is parked.

- Don't ride or carry passengers in the bed of a pickup truck.

Scholar Requirements

Requirement	Approved by

Do this:

1. With your parent, guardian, or Webelos den leader, complete the Positive Attitude Character Connection.

   a. **Know:** Discuss with your parent or guardian, or your Webelos den leader, what it means to have a positive attitude and the "BEST" steps you can take to have a positive attitude. (**B**elieve it can happen, **E**xpect success, **S**et your mind, and **T**ry, try, try. _____

   b. **Commit:** Plan with your parent or guardian, or your Webelos den leader, how you will apply the "BEST" steps for a positive attitude in doing your schoolwork and in other areas of your life. _____

   c. **Practice:** "Do your 'BEST'-" to have a cheerful and positive attitude while doing the requirements for this activity badge. _____

And do three of these:

2. Have a good record in attendance, behavior, and grades at school. _____DK_____

3. Take an active part in a school activity or service. _____

4. Discuss with your teacher or principal the value of getting an education. _____

5. List in writing some important things you can do now because of what you've learned in school. _____

6. While you are a Webelos Scout, earn the Cub Scout Academics belt loop for Language. _____

7. While you are a Webelos Scout, and if you have not earned it for another activity badge, earn the Cub Scout Academics belt loop for Mathematics. _____

8. While you are a Webelos Scout, earn the Cub Scout Academics belt loop for Chess. _____

And do three of these:

9. Trace through history the different kinds of schools. Tell how our present public school system grew out of these early schools. _____

10. Make a chart showing how your school system is run. _____

11. Ask a parent and five other grown-ups these questions:

- What do you think are the best things about my school?

- What could be done to improve it?

Tell what you think were the best answers and why. _____

12. List and explain some of the full-time positions in the field of education. _____

13. Help another student with schoolwork. Tell what you did to help. _____

School is a big part of your life. You study math, science, language, and other subjects, but you also learn about yourself—what subjects you like best, what areas you want to explore further.

You learn how to concentrate and how to find out what you want to know. To be a good scholar, you have to be curious and determined to gain everything you possibly can from your education.

You're probably already doing some things that will help you earn this activity badge: going to school, earning the best grades you can, and behaving well in school. When you complete each requirement, ask your teacher, principal, Webelos den leader, or activity badge counselor to sign it on pages 392–393.

Do Your Best in School

As a Webelos Scout you have promised to "do your best." That is the Cub Scout motto, and you should follow it in everything—work, play, and school.

Are you doing your best in school? Do you always go to school, except when you are sick? Do you behave well in school? Do you try hard to get good grades? These are things you need to do for requirement 2.

Do you take part in school activities, like clubs and sports? Do you do a Good Turn for the school now and then? If you do, you may be earning requirement 3 right now. If you need ideas for ways you can become involved in activities and in helping your school, ask your teacher or principal.

When you do requirement 2 or 3, or both, ask your teacher or principal to initial those Scholar requirements.

"BEST" Steps to a Positive Attitude

To be a good scholar, you need to have a positive attitude. If you'll follow these steps when you face a learning task, you will have that positive attitude:

> **B**elieve it can happen.
>
> **E**xpect success.
>
> **S**et your mind.
>
> **T**ry, try, try!

The Value of an Education

Why go to school? There are lots of reasons. Requirement 4 asks you to think about them.

From kindergarten on, your studies help you make your way in the world. You're gaining knowledge that helps you right now, and it will help you later as you continue your education and when you begin your adult career.

In school, you can explore many subjects on your own, too. If you want to find out about dinosaurs or volcanoes or tropical fish, your school library or media center may have just what you're seeking.

What are your ideas about the value of an education? If you're doing requirement 4, discuss this with your teacher or principal. Then ask him or her to initial it.

What You've Learned So Far

This list will help you start thinking about requirement 5 and the things you can do now because you are going to school:

- Reading
- Writing
- Math
- History of your state and country
- Geography
- Science
- New games and songs
- Arts and crafts

Can you think of other knowledge and skills you have acquired in school? If you're doing requirement 5, write these down in a list. Show it to your teacher or principal and ask him or her to initial the requirement.

Cub Scout Academics
Belt Loops for Language,
Mathematics, and Chess

If you earned the Language, Mathematics, or Chess belt loop earlier in Cub Scouting, great! But that won't count for requirement 6, 7, or 8 of this Scholar activity badge. You must earn the Language (requirement 6), Mathematics (requirement 7), or Chess (requirement 8) belt loop again while you are a Webelos

language and culture

chess

mathematics

Scout for it to count toward this activity badge. (And if you already earned it for another activity badge, that cannot count for Scholar; you should choose another requirement, instead.)

The History of Schools

Your school is the latest step on a long trail going back to people who lived long ago, before written history began.

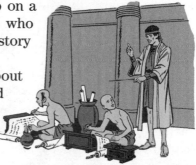

Everyone needed to learn about food, shelter, clothing, and safety. When they were old enough, children learned skills like hunting and fishing from their parents and other adults. Their school was life itself and the daily activities that helped them survive.

The earliest written records of ancient civilizations have stories of schools. These schools were in the temples where people worshiped their gods, and the schools taught mostly about religion. In Egypt, the temple schools taught more subjects as the years went on.

The ancient Greek and the Roman civilizations believed schools and teachers were important. Their schools were not like ours. Sometimes teachers just walked around the streets with their pupils and talked with them.

A great Greek teacher named Plato met his students in a garden in Athens called the Academy. That's where the word *academy*, meaning school, came from.

Early schools in America. America's early colonists soon set up schools. The Pilgrims landed in 1620, and by 1647 Massachusetts Colony had a law providing for free public schools. Few were started, though. Most schools were still private.

The New England Colonies had schools in homes, where children learned Bible verses and the alphabet. Academies trained students for college. The Middle Colonies had both public and church-run private schools. In the Southern Colonies, each plantation had its own teacher.

But by the early 1800s, schools still were not free. There were charity schools, but many parents didn't like them. If they could afford it, parents sent their children to private academies. The main subjects were "The Three Rs"—**R**eading, w**R**iting, and a**R**ithmetic.

Usually there was just one room for school. Boys sat on one side and girls on the other. Sometimes, children—especially those from farms—came only when there was no work at home. Often, everyone studied aloud at the same time in the classroom! This was called a "Blab School."

The common school movement in America. People were demanding free schools, paid for by taxes. The first "common schools" (public schools) were opened in New York and Pennsylvania.

Horace Mann and the state of Massachusetts led in changing the system of education. Mann campaigned successfully for better teachers and buildings. In his state, children between the ages of 8 and 14 had to attend school. Schools were divided into grades.

These ideas spread, and by 1855, America had 81,000 common schools.

Since then, schools have continued to change. You learn about many more subjects than "The Three Rs." New ideas about the best ways to learn are constantly being brought into schools. Families have choices of public schools, private schools, schools run by churches and other religious groups, and home schooling, where a parent teaches his or her child.

Who Runs Your School?

You may answer this question by saying "the principal."

But there is more to it than that. In a public school, the principal works with teachers. He or she also works with the school superintendent, who is in charge of all the schools in the district. See if you can make a chart showing how your school system is run. Ask your principal about it.

This is how a chart of a school system might look:

Your School's Strengths and Weaknesses

You may think there are good things and bad things about your school. If you have attended more than one school, you may have an idea how your present school compares with another school. But to get a good idea of what people in your community think about your school, you need to ask them. This will help you earn requirement 11.

Ask your Webelos den leader to invite the den's parents to a den meeting. Ask them: What are the best things about the schools? What are the problems?

What are your own answers to these questions? What can be done to improve your school?

Careers in Education

If you're interested in a career in education, you should know about teaching jobs plus all the other jobs connected with schools.

You can think of jobs right in your school. Who works there besides teachers and a principal? Start a list of careers in your school. This will get you started on requirement 12.

Also, ask your teacher about the types of careers in your school system. You may be surprised at the different kinds of skills that are needed to run it. Add these careers to your list and be ready to explain what these people do in their jobs.

Technology Group

Scientist Requirements

Requirement	Approved by

Do these:

1. Read Bernoulli's principle. Show how it works.

2. Read Pascal's law. Tell about some inventions that use Pascal's law.

3. Read Newton's first law of motion. Show in three different ways how inertia works.

4. While you are a Webelos Scout, earn the Cub Scout Academics belt loop for Science.

And do six of these:

5. Show the effects of atmospheric pressure.

6. Show the effects of air pressure.

7. Show the effects of water pressure. This may be combined with atmospheric pressure or with air pressure.

8. With adult supervision, build and launch a model rocket. Describe how Newton's third law of motion explains how the rocket is propelled into the sky.

9. Explain what causes fog. Show how this works.

10. Explain how crystals are formed. Make some.

11. Explain how you use your center of gravity to keep your balance. Show three different balancing tricks.

12. Show in three different ways how your eyes work together and show what is meant by an optical illusion.

_____

13. While you are a Webelos Scout, earn the Academics belt loop for Weather.

_____

14. While you are a Webelos Scout, earn the Academics belt loop for Astronomy.

_____ РЧ _____

Scientists know about laws of nature that explain much about the world and the universe. They continue to learn by experimenting, and they make discoveries.

They take nothing for granted. They may think an idea is true, but they test it over and over to prove it.

When you earn the Scientist activity badge, you'll do scientific experiments and test some famous scientific laws. You'll explore ideas about how airplanes fly and the way changes in atmospheric pressure can move objects. You'll also experience the strange tricks your eyes and your brain can play on you. When you complete each requirement, ask your Webelos den leader or activity badge counselor to sign it on the previous page or this page.

Physics

Until the beginning of the 20th century, the science of physics was divided into the studies of sound, light, heat, electricity and magnetism, and mechanics (the study of motion and the forces that cause it).

Since then, physicists have explored many new and exciting areas. Some of these fields are called quantum mechanics, nuclear physics, and astrophysics. These terms may sound complicated, but the basic ideas in physics explain everyday events you may take for granted—like why you can ride a bike without tipping over and why an airplane can fly.

Keep reading to learn about several laws of physics and experiments you can do to demonstrate those laws.

Bernoulli's Principle

In 1738 a Swiss scientist named Daniel Bernoulli discovered a fact known as Bernoulli's principle, which is:

The pressure of a moving gas decreases as its speed increases.

Bernoulli's principle is used to explain how an airplane is able to fly.

Air is a gas. Air moves over and underneath the wings of an airplane as it travels. An airplane wing is curved on top and flat on the bottom. Because of that, air travels a longer distance *over* the wing in the same amount of time that air moves *under* the wing, which is a shorter distance.

This means that the air over the wing travels at a greater speed, causing a lower pressure (Bernoulli's principle at work). The air under the wing travels in a straight line, more slowly, so its pressure stays high. The plane is lifted because of this difference in pressure: Having lower pressure over the wing and higher pressure under the wing causes *lift*.

Air moves quickly, so pressure is reduced.

Air moves more slowly, so pressure stays high.

Another way to explain it is that the molecules of the faster air spread out, so they put less pressure on the top of the wing.

A *molecule* is the smallest possible quantity of a substance that still shows the characteristics of that substance. Molecules are usually composed of two or more atoms, although some substances are made of single-atom molecules. For instance, a molecule of water is made up of two atoms of hydrogen and one atom of oxygen.

Testing Bernoulli's Principle

These two fascinating experiments demonstrate Bernoulli's principle.

1. Push a short pin through the middle of a 3-inch cardboard square.

2. Put the pin into the hole in a thread spool or toy spool, making sure the pin doesn't stick out the open end.

3. Put the spool to your mouth and blow steadily. The cardboard will stay on the spool. The harder you blow, the tighter it will hold.

The air stream (your breath) is moving. It makes a low-pressure area between the cardboard and the bottom of the spool. The air on the other side of the cardboard has more pressure, so it pushes the cardboard against the spool.

Hold a lighted match be-hind a business card and blow hard against the card. The flame will move toward you. Why?

Pascal's Law

A French physicist named Blaise Pascal discovered a fact about liquids in 1647. If a liquid is in a closed container, pressure in every direction will be the same. When pressure is added to the top, pressure will increase equally throughout the container.

Pascal's discovery led to the invention of the *hydraulic press*, which is used in manufacturing to form three-dimensional objects from sheets of metal or plastic. This is the way a hydraulic press works: It has two connected cylinders filled with oil—a smaller cylinder and a larger one. Each cylinder has a movable piston. When pressure is applied to the smaller piston, it creates extra pressure throughout the oil in both cylinders. This causes the piston in the larger cylinder to move, operating the press. A small amount of force on the small

Simple Hydraulic Press

piston leads to a stronger force on the large piston, because it has a larger area.

Pascal's law is used today in the large hydraulic jack a mechanic slides under a car when a tire needs to be changed. When the mechanic presses down on the jack handle, he's putting pressure on the fluid in the jack. That creates enough force to lift the car.

Pascal's law is also at work in a car's hydraulic brakes. A small amount of pressure on the brake pedal puts increased pressure on the brake fluid. This in turn activates the car's brakes, slowing or stopping the car.

Other examples of devices that use hydraulics are a fork lift, wing flaps on a plane, and a barber's chair.

Inertia

Sir Isaac Newton, an English mathematician and physicist, discovered many laws of physics. In 1687, his book *Mathematical Principles of Natural Philosophy* included his three laws of motion.

The first law of motion says that a thing at rest tends to remain at rest until an outside force moves it. The law also says that a thing in motion continues to move at a constant speed in a straight line, unless an outside force acts on it.

The law describes *inertia*. Inertia is what causes an object to resist any change in motion.

These experiments may seem like magic tricks, but they demonstrate inertia.

Set a coin on a card on the top of a jar. Snap the edge of the card. The card will fly out because of the force you are using to move it, and the coin will drop into the jar because of inertia.

Make a stack of nickels. Try to snap a penny along the table at the bottom coin. If you hit the target just right, the bottom nickel will fly out; the others remain in a stack. Why?

Set a glass of water on the end of a long strip of paper. (Use a plastic glass, just in case. Or you can use a book instead of a glass of water.) Pull the paper slowly. The glass moves with it. Give the paper a sudden jerk. The glass stands still.

Spin a fresh egg on its side. It will stop soon. Spin a hard-boiled egg. It will spin for a much longer time. When you spin a fresh egg, you spin the outside. The white and yolk inside are loose and tend to remain at rest, slowing down the fresh egg. When you spin the hard-boiled egg, you spin the whole egg, because cooking has made the yolk and white solid. They move right along with the shell.

Swing a pail of water back and forth at arm's length. (Don't fill the pail so full that it's too heavy for you.) After a few times, swing it over your head in a full circle. Tell what happens. Do you know why?

Remember, a moving object tends to travel in a straight line unless an outside force acts on it. You're the outside force. Your hold on the bucket and your arm action provide *centripetal force*. You're constantly changing the direction of the bucket, away from straight line travel, and making it go in a circle. Centripetal force makes an object travel a circular route.

Some road curves are banked (tilted toward the inside of the curve) to help cars stay on the road. You'll also see banked curves on bobsled tracks, velodromes (bicycle tracks), and roller coasters. That tilt provides centripetal force that causes circular travel.

Atmospheric Pressure

We live under a blanket of air called the earth's atmosphere. It is many miles deep.

At sea level the atmosphere exerts a pressure of almost 15 pounds per square inch on every surface. A mile above sea level, the blanket of air is thinner, so the atmospheric pressure is less.

Experiments With Atmospheric Pressure

More magic tricks? There's a scientific explanation behind each one.

Here's one you can do with an egg and a glass bottle with an opening slightly smaller than the egg.

1. Cook the egg in boiling water for 10 minutes.
2. Put it in cold water. Take off the shell.
3. Fold a small piece of newspaper three times in the same direction.
4. Light it. Drop it into the bottle. Quickly put the egg in the top of the bottle.
5. The egg will bounce up and down. Then it will slip neatly into the bottle.

Air molecules are constantly moving, but heat makes them move faster and spread even farther apart. The burning paper heats the air in the bottle and expands it, pushing much of it out. The expanding air coming out of the bottle makes the egg bounce. As the air left in the bottle cools, the inside air pressure drops. The outside atmospheric pressure pushes the egg into the bottle.

Here's another experiment with atmospheric pressure. You need a glass bottle, a shallow pan, and a candle.

1. Pour the water from a half-filled bottle into a pan. Set a 2-inch-high candle in the pan and light it.
2. Hold the empty bottle over the candle with the top a little below the water. The water will bubble. Hold the bottle until the bubbling stops.
3. Lower the bottle. The candle and water will rise up in the bottle.

The candle flame heats the air in the bottle and expands it, pushing part of it out and making the water bubble. The air pressure inside the bottle drops. Outside the bottle, the higher atmospheric pressure on the water's surface pushes the water and the candle up into the bottle. The flame goes out when it burns up all of the oxygen in the bottle.

For the next experiment, you'll need a cork, a toothpick, a small piece of paper for a sail, and glue to make a small cork boat. You'll also need a glass that will fit over the boat and a larger container for the water. (You can do this experiment with or without the cork boat. The boat makes it more fun and easier to see the water line inside the small glass.)

1. Make a cork boat as shown. Float it.
2. Put a glass over it, putting one edge in the water first, and slowly turn the glass bottom up.
3. Raise the glass, but keep the top under water.

Half Toothpick → Cork
Paper

When you lift the glass, the pressure of the air inside it becomes less than the atmospheric pressure acting on the surface of the water outside. This difference in air pressure supports the water column.

Have an adult supervise this next experiment. You'll need a very *clean*, empty screw-top metal gallon can and a metal pail larger than the can.

To be sure the can is clean, rinse it at least three times and let it stand open for 24 hours.

1. Fill the pail with cold water.
2. Pour a glass of water into the can. Leave the top off. Put the open can on a stove. Boil the water. Let it steam for a minute or more, but don't let it boil dry.
3. Use a hot pad to take the can off the stove. Screw on the cap. Turn the can over and place it, top down, into the pail of water. The can will be crushed.

The steam drives nearly all the air out. The water cools the steam, leaving the can almost empty of air and creating a partial vacuum (a space in which there is very low pressure). The higher outside atmospheric pressure crushes the can.

Air Pressure

If we compress air (put pressure on it), it becomes denser and more forceful and we can use it in machines. For example, a jackhammer that is used to break up pavement uses compressed air. A tire pump compresses air, and bicycle tires use compressed air to give you a smooth ride.

Experiments With Air Pressure

Air pressure can do amazing things! For the first experiment, you'll need a pop bottle and a small piece of newspaper.

1. Make a ball of a 1-inch-square piece of newspaper.
2. Lay the pop bottle on its side on a table. Put the ball in the neck of the bottle.
3. Blow into the bottle. The ball will come *out* of the bottle.

You might expect that blowing on the ball will make it move to the back of the bottle. But what really happens is this: The air you blow into the bottle increases the air pressure, which drives the ball outward.

For the next experiment, you need books and a hot water bottle.

1. On the edge of a table, place several heavy books on top of an empty hot-water bottle.
2. Hold the opening of the bottle tightly against your mouth. Blow hard into the bottle. Your breath will lift the books.

All you need is a balloon and a glass for the next experiment.

1. Put a balloon into a glass. Have the bottom of the balloon touching the bottom of the glass.
2. Blow up the balloon. Hold it shut. You can lift the glass by the neck of the balloon.

The air pressure inside the balloon holds the balloon against the glass.

Water Pressure

This experiment shows how water pressure works. You'll need two large juice cans and something to punch holes in them. The tops of the cans should be open.

1. Punch five holes near the bottom of a tall juice can. Make the holes about ½ to ¾ inch apart.
2. Fill the can with water. Notice that all the water streams are the same length.
3. Take the other can and punch three holes at different levels (but not one above the other). Fill the can with water. Now notice that the water streams are different lengths.

The amount of water pressure depends on the depth below the surface of the water. In the first can, the water pressure on the holes was equal, since they all were at the same level. The streams of water looked the same. In the second can, the top hole had the least water pressure, and the lowest hole had the most. The lowest stream, with the most pressure, went farthest.

When a dam is built on a river, it is thickest at the bottom, because that's where the water pressure is greatest.

Water Pressure and Atmospheric Pressure

When you read about the water pressure experiment, did you wonder if atmospheric pressure was at work too? It was, because the surface of the water was open to the air. Now try this. You'll need another can, this one with a tight-fitting lid.

1. Use a can with a lid that can be taken off. Punch a nail hole in the lid. Make another hole near the bottom of the can on the side.

2. Fill the can with water. Put the lid on.
3. Turn the can upside down. Water runs out the hole in the lid. Why? The weight of the water plus atmospheric pressure (air coming in the hole in the can's side, above the water) causes water to run out.
4. Put your finger over the hole in the side and the water stops. Remove your finger and it starts.

Your finger stops the air coming in, so the atmosphere cannot maintain pressure above the water. The upward force of the atmosphere on the water in the bottom hole keeps the water from running out.

Here's another experiment that shows how atmospheric pressure works against water pressure:

1. Slip a balloon onto a faucet. Fill it, supporting the weight with your hand.
2. Hold the neck of the balloon tightly and remove it from the faucet. Set the balloon in a bucket of water or in a sink with water in it. Let go of the neck of the balloon. Atmospheric pressure pushing on the surface of the water around the balloon forces a fountain of water out.

Water Pressure and Air Pressure

Because of a scientific invention, divers can work on the bottom of a river, lake, or sea. They use a *diving bell*. Diving bells are used today to help with the underwater work needed in building things such as bridges, piers, and jetties.

Air is fed into the bell through a hose. Even though the bottom of the diving bell is open, air pressure keeps the water out. For an idea of how a diving bell works, you'll need a bottle cap, a bucket, a glass, and water. The glass is your diving bell.

1. Float a bottle cap in a bucket full of water.
2. Place a dry glass straight down over the cap. Push the glass down halfway. The cap floats. Where is the water level inside the glass?
3. Push the diving bell (glass) to the bottom. The cap rests on the bottom.
4. Raise the glass carefully. The cap will float again. Watch the water level inside the glass as you bring it slowly up.

Though you are not feeding more air into the glass, the amount of air in it when you touch it to the water remains the same. When you push the glass down, you are compressing the air in it and providing the pressure to push the water out of the way.

Action/Reaction

You've read about Isaac Newton and his first law of motion early in this chapter. Newton made many other discoveries. His third law of motion says that every action has an equal and opposite reaction. This principle explains how a rocket is propelled skyward.

Try this simple demonstration for yourself.

If you want to buy and build a model rocket kit, you must be at least 10 years old and have an adult helping you during construction and launching. Follow the kit directions and observe all safety rules.

Reaction

(thrust)
Action

Blow up a balloon and hold the opening closed. This is like a rocket that hasn't been ignited yet. The energy is stored in the form of compressed air in the balloon.

Release the balloon, and the stored air rushes out of the opening. This is the action. The *reaction* is a force called *thrust*. Thrust causes the balloon to move in the opposite direction from the rushing air.

As the rocket's fuel is burned, hot exhaust gases are pushed out of the exhaust nozzle at very high speed. The escaping exhaust gases are the action.

That action causes an equal but opposite reaction. The thrust propels the rocket through the air. If the rocket burned fuel even more quickly, both the action and the reaction would be greater.

Hot exhaust gases escape through the exhaust nozzle.

More Fun With Science

Fog, crystals, gravity, optical illusions—there's just no end to the experiments you could do in all the scientific fields. Here are a few more ideas that will help you complete your Scientist activity badge.

Fog

Did you know that air has water in it? The water is in the form of molecules so small you can't see them.

If cool air moves in after a warm day, the invisible molecules are drawn together into tiny droplets of water. Billions of these condensed droplets make up fog.

Making Fog

1. Fill a bottle with hot water. Then pour out most of the water. Leave about 1 inch in the bottom.
2. Hold the bottle to the light. Notice the streams of vapor rising from it.
3. Hold an ice cube in the bottle opening. Hold the bottle toward the light. Notice the thin streams of vapor moving down into the bottle. This is fog.

1. Put about 1 inch of cold water in a quart-sized bottle.
2. Cover the opening with your hand. Shake hard to soak the air in the bottle. Pour out the water. Hold the bottle upside down.

3. Light a wooden match. Quickly blow it out. Put the smoking head into the opening of the bottle. The smoke will help the water vapor change into water droplets.
4. Set the bottle in a good light. Place your mouth on the bottle opening. Press down and blow hard—you'll then see clear air in the bottle.
5. Raise your head. The fog forms again.

Blowing helps compress and heat the air. This evaporates the fog. When you raise your head, the compressed air expands and cools. Cooling condenses water vapor into tiny water drops you can see, so the fog forms in the bottle again.

Crystals

When some liquids become solid, they form tiny shapes called crystals. Each crystal formed by one liquid is the same shape. Many minerals are made up of crystals.

Quartz Crystal

Crystal Candy

Here's a great experiment—you can eat it when it's finished! You'll need sugar, water, a saucepan, a spoon for stirring, clean white string, a pencil, and a glass or jar.

Bring 1 cup of water to boil in a saucepan. Turn off the heat and add 2 cups of sugar. Stir until the sugar is dissolved. Let it cool. Then pour the solution into a tall glass or a glass jar.

Tie a clean white string to a pencil. Moisten the string in water and drag it through dry sugar so some sugar crystals stick to it. Hang the string in the glass. Store it in a cool place. In a few days you'll see crystals forming on the sides of the glass. By your next den meeting, big hard crystals will have formed on the string. Look at them through a magnifying glass. Then—enjoy!

Sugar and Water Solution

Pencil With Clean, White String

Crystals Will Grow on the String, and You Can Eat Them.

Center of Gravity

Gravity is the force that holds objects to the earth. The same force holds the moon and planets in their orbits. Sir Isaac Newton's law of universal gravitation explained this in 1687.

Did you ever sit still on a bike with your feet on the pedals and try to keep your balance? You had to keep shifting your weight, right?

Why? Because each time you moved, your **center of gravity**—the point in your body where your weight is concentrated—shifted a little. (A person's center of gravity is usually somewhere behind the navel.)

Normally, when you stand or walk, you unconsciously keep your center of gravity over your feet, which are your base. But if you try to walk along a straight line on the floor, you'll find yourself moving your arms to adjust your center of gravity and keep your balance.

Try these experiments to see what happens when your center of gravity is a bit beyond your control.

Sit in a chair with your feet on the floor and keep your arms folded across your chest. See if you can stand up, but obey this rule: You may not lean forward. Your center of gravity remains too far back to allow you to stand. Now try to stand up by leaning forward first. This allows you to adjust your center of gravity and move it over your feet.

Place a chair against the wall. Bend over it with your head touching the wall. Move your feet back. Your legs, from ankles to hips, should slant toward the wall. Lift the chair. Try to stand straight without moving your feet.

Stand with one shoulder, arm, leg, and foot close against a wall. Try to bring your outside foot up to touch the one next to the wall. Stop at the point where you feel yourself losing your balance. The wall is in your way, so you can't move your body that direction to adjust your center of gravity and keep your balance.

Cut a bird out of a 6-by-6-inch piece of light cardboard. Glue or tape a penny at the front end of each wing. The middle of each penny should be just in front of the bird's beak. Set the beak on the end of your finger or put it on the corner of a table or a book. It won't fall. Where do you think its center of gravity is?

Scientist

Optical Illusions

How Your Eyes Work Together

Your eyes are wonderful instruments. They are like amazing cameras that can work together.

Each of your eyes focuses a picture of what you are seeing on the retina that lines the eye. The optic nerve carries these two pictures to the brain. Then your brain makes one image out of the two.

Sometimes your eyes and brain can trick you. Using what it already understands about the world, your brain does the best it can with the images it receives. It might make you believe you're seeing something impossible! Try these easy experiments that show how the eyes work.

Our eyes and the lens of a camera are similar. Both focus light rays to produce images.

Roll a sheet of paper into a tube. Hold the edge of your hand against the side of the tube. With one eye, look at a distant object through the tube. Look at your hand with the other eye. There seems to be a hole in your hand. What do you think is happening?

One eye sees the distant object through the paper tube, and the other eye sees your hand. Your brain combines the two images in one view.

Hold two pencils, as shown, at arm's length. Look past the pencils at the far corner of the room. You'll see two sets of pencils. Do this again with the pencils held about 1 inch apart. You'll see four pencils.

Place the tips of two fingers together about 6 inches from your eyes. Look past them at the far corner of the room and you'll see a small sausage. Pull the fingers apart slowly. The sausage will seem to hang in the air.

Light and Dark

The pupils of your eyes adjust for the level of light that is available.

Stand in a corner of the room, facing the corner, with your back to the light. Look in a mirror. Notice the size of the opening in the pupil of each eye. The openings will be large.

Turn around with your face toward the light. Look in the mirror again. The pupils will be smaller.

Look at something far away. Cup your hands into tubes. Look through them as you would through field glasses. You see more clearly because your pupils get bigger. They receive more light from the faraway objects when they are protected from other light.

Brain Teasers

In some of the optical illusions below, you might be fooled about measurements, sizes, and distance. When your brain tries to make sense out of what your eyes are seeing, it uses what it has already learned about how things usually look. That doesn't mean it's always right!

Draw a ½-inch square inside a 1-inch square. Connect the corners. Look at it steadily. The inside square seems to move closer, then farther away.

Draw a box as shown. Look at it steadily. Sometimes it seems you're looking at the top of the box. Sometimes it seems to be the bottom.

Is the high silk hat longer or shorter from A to B than from C to D? Measure it.

Does it look like you could put a dime on top of this box so the coin won't touch the edges? Try it.

Which of the two designs at left is longer? Better get your ruler.

Which of the dotted circles is larger?

Cub Scout Academics Belt Loops for Science, Weather, and Astronomy

If you earned the Science, Weather, or Astronomy belt loop earlier in Cub Scouting, great! But that won't count for requirement 4, 13, or 14 of this Scientist activity badge. You must earn the Science (requirement 4), Weather (requirement 13), or Astronomy (requirement 14) belt loop again while you are a Webelos Scout for it to count toward this activity badge.

Showman
Requirements

Requirement

Approved by

Do this:

1. Complete six activities of your choice; these can be from any area (puppetry, music, and or drama).

   Webelos den leader or activity badge counselor: Be sure to sign approval both here and for each of the activities below that are completed to fulfill requirement 1.

Puppetry

And do one of these not already done for requirement 1:

2. Write a puppet play about one of your Webelos den activities or a subject of your choice.

3. Make a set of puppets or marionettes for the play you have written or for another play.

4. Build a simple stage for marionettes or puppets.

5. Alone or with the help of others, put on a puppet show for your den or pack.

6. Make a set of four paper bag puppets for a singing group. With the help of three other den members, sing a song with the puppets as the performers.

7. There are sock, stick, and finger puppets. There are paper bag puppets and marionettes. Explain their differences and show any puppets you have made for this badge.

Music

And do one of these not already done for requirement 1:

8. Play four tunes on any band or orchestra instrument. Read these from music.

9. Sing one song indoors and one song outdoors, either alone or with a group. Tell what you need to do differently when singing outdoors.

10. Make a collection of three or more records, tapes, or music CDs. Tell what you like about each one. _____

11. Tell what folk music is. Hum, sing, or play a folk tune on a musical instrument. _____

12. Name three American composers. Name a famous work by each. _____

13. Draw a staff. Draw on it a clef, a sharp, flat, natural, note, and rest. Tell what each is used for. _____

14. Show the difference between 2/4, 3/4, and 4/4 time by beating time or playing an instrument. _____

15. While you are a Webelos Scout, earn the Cub Scout Academics belt loop for Music. _____

Drama

And do one of these not already done for requirement 1:

16. Give a monologue (a talk) on a patriotic, humorous, or holiday subject or another subject of your choice. _____

17. Attend a play. Describe the story. Tell what you liked about it. _____

18. Read a play. Make a model stage setting for one of the acts. _____

19. Write, put on, and take part in a one-act play. _____

20. Make a list of stage directions. Tell what they mean. _____

21. Describe a theater-in-the-round. What are its good and bad points? _____

22. Explain the difference between grand opera and light opera. Explain the difference between a musical and a play. _____

23. Read about William Shakespeare. Draw a picture of his Globe Theater. _____

Everybody loves to see a show. And it's fun to be on stage. Behind the scenes are people who enjoyed creating the script, songs, and scenery.

For requirement 1 of the Showman activity badge, you'll choose six activities from puppetry, music, or drama. Then later you'll do one additional activity in each of these areas, for a total of nine activities.

For puppetry, you might decide to write a play for puppets, make the puppets, and put on the play.

For music, you can learn a folk song, play a musical instrument, or tell about music you like.

For drama, you can be an actor in a play for your den. Or you can attend a play or read one.

You have a lot of choices! On with the show!

Puppetry

When you complete each requirement, ask your Webelos den leader or activity badge counselor to sign it on page 430. Be sure your Webelos den leader or activity badge counselor signs all the requirements you do for requirement 1.

Writing a Puppet Play

A puppet play is just like a play with live actors. It can be funny or sad.

Your play could have a plot like a television show. The hero overcomes obstacles and defeats the bad guys, or he or she finds a way to get out of a comical situation.

Or your play might be a joke with a surprise ending. You would act out the joke with puppets instead of just telling the joke.

As you write your puppet play, think about how you'll perform it. Remember, you only have two hands. You can have several characters, but you can only have two puppets on stage at once, unless you ask someone to be a puppeteer with you.

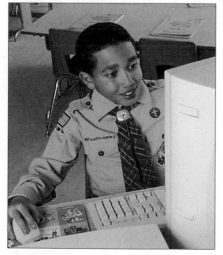

A Play With a Plot

What do you need? A story that will hold the audience's attention. One event in it leads to another, and puppet characters have to make decisions and take action. It doesn't have to be something that has actually happened. You can make it up. In most plays, the action builds up through the play.

This is an example of an idea for a play about a den

activity. Notice how the plot starts out with an easy task for two Webelos Scouts, but then they deal with one challenge after another.

Title: "The Adventures of the Pebble Pups"

Characters: Two Webelos Scouts, Jason and Brian; their Webelos den leader, Mr. Mason; a bull

Props (things you need): Poison ivy plants (made of paper), a huge outcropping of granite (made of something lightweight), a small piece of granite a puppet can hold

Plot idea: Jason and Brian are looking for samples of granite to complete their rock collections for the Geologist activity badge. Mr. Mason tells them he is sure there is a granite outcrop on a hill not far away.

Jason and Brian start out. They climb a steep hill. They cross a pasture and are chased by a bull. They walk through poison ivy and start itching.

Finally they get to the granite outcrop on a hill. Suddenly they realize they forgot to bring a hammer and chisel. As they start back, Jason stumbles over a rock. It's a piece of granite!

They hike back to Mr. Mason. He says, "Well boys, how did it go?"

Jason shows him the rock and says, "It was easy. Here's the stone, Mr. Mason."

How to put your play on paper: Put down what each character says and does. Here's an example of the way the middle part of the above play could be written:

Brian: Let's cut through this pasture. (They walk along.)

Jason: Hey, Brian, what's really big and runs fast?

Brian: I don't know. What?

Jason: That! (He points offstage right.)

Brian: A bull! Come on, run! *(They run offstage left and the bull follows them across.)*

The characters have to talk about where they're going and what they're seeing so the audience understands what is happening. They have to show how they feel—happy, excited, scared.

Make your play a different idea from the example. If you work with another puppeteer, give him a copy of your play script to study so he is familiar with his lines and the action. Have a rehearsal before you present your play to the den.

A Joke You Act Out

Just as in writing a play, you need to write out your actors' lines for the joke.

Title: "Matching Pairs"

Characters: Webelos Scout Jonathan, Webelos den chief, two other Webelos Scouts (who don't have lines to say)

The joke: The den chief is inspecting the den's uniforms. He comes to Jonathan and looks him over carefully. Then he notices that Jonathan is wearing one red sock and one blue sock and calls his attention to them. The end of the script for the joke would go like this:

Jonathan: That's funny.

Den chief: What's funny?

Jonathan: I have another pair just like them at home!

Making Puppets

Simple Puppets

Paper Bag Puppet. Use a small paper bag. Use crepe paper or yarn for hair and mustaches. Mark features with felt-tip pens. Look at the picture: Draw the upper lip on the edge of the sack's bottom and the lower lip on the side of the sack so you can make the mouth open and close.

Finger Puppet. Draw a puppet without legs on heavy paper. Make it 2 or 3 inches high. Cut holes for your first two fingers where the legs should go. You may want to wear a glove as a "costume" for your fingers.

Stick Puppet. This is the simplest kind of puppet. Draw the figure on cardboard and cut it out. Glue on a handle of heavy cardboard or use a craft stick.

Puppets in Motion

Moving stick puppet. May be cut from cardboard or light wood. Join with paper fasteners so parts can be moved. Use a dowel or balsa wood stick for the body stick and thinner balsa wood sticks for the moving parts. Hold the body stick in one hand while moving the other sticks to make the legs walk, tail thrash, or jaws bite (depending on your puppet). You can make a stick puppet of a person with only one moving arm or leg, which is easier to work.

Sock Puppet. Cut the foot off the sock as shown. Take the ankle part and stuff it into the toe to make the puppet's head. Fasten it in with a strong rubber band or ribbon.

Use felt-tip marking pens to draw features. Cut holes on each side of the body for the arms (your thumb and middle finger). You can put on a glove first, if you want to cover your fingers. Your forefinger moves the head.

Marionettes. Traditional marionettes are jointed, which means their necks, wrists, knees, and ankles can bend. Their strings are attached to a crosspiece made of two wooden sticks. The puppeteer holds the crosspiece and tilts it to make the marionette move in different ways.

You can make marionettes from simpler materials, as shown here. The football player is cut from cardboard. The parts are connected by paper fasteners. Attach threads or string to the head and hands. Tie the threads to a wooden dowel or a balsa wood stick. Hold the stick in one hand and use your other hand to pull strings and make the arms move.

Puppet Stages

Carefully turn table on its side. Kneel behind it and hold puppets over edge of table.

Hang a cloth across a doorway. Keep the room behind the stage dark. Light the front.

Take the top off a heavy cardboard carton that is not too deep. Cut the stage opening out of the bottom and decorate it. Put it on a table with cloth draped around the legs.

A Marionette Stage

Drape a cloth or old sheet behind a doorway. The performer is hidden behind the backdrop, which is a folding table on its side or a large carton. Tape paper scenery to the backdrop.

Music

When you complete each requirement, ask your Webelos den leader or activity badge counselor to sign it on page 431. Be sure your Webelos den leader or activity badge counselor initials all the requirements you do for requirement 1.

If you are taking music lessons, the music requirements will be easy for you.

Why not form a den band or singing group and perform at a pack meeting? You will have fun, and so will the other boys and their parents.

Folk Music

The folk music tradition is based on tunes that have been handed down from generation to generation, with no known composer. People heard them, learned to play them, and sang them, often in different versions. Many years later, someone wrote down the music and words.

Many folk tunes we hear today came from other countries. Other tunes and songs were made up by people in America. The songs tell of the joys and sorrows of the people living then. Some songs are humorous, and some music is for dancing. The fiddle, guitar, banjo, and dulcimer are often used to play folk music or accompany folk singers.

Songwriters have continued to compose in the folk style, so you may know newer songs that fit in with the folk tradition. An example is "This Land Is Your Land," written by Woody Guthrie, in the 1930s. In the late 1950s and early 1960s, folk singing became especially popular. Folk artists such as Pete Seeger, Joan Baez, Judy Collins, and Peter, Paul, and Mary rose to fame. Arlo Guthrie followed in his father's footsteps and writes folk songs, some about social issues, as does Bob Dylan. In the 21st century, Pete Seeger's grandson, Tao Rodriguez, and Woody Guthrie's grandchildren (and Arlo's children), Abe and Sarah Lee Guthrie, are rising folk singers and songwriters.

If you don't know much folk music, you have fun ahead of you. Look for a folk song book at your library and learn a few folk songs. Some libraries might have recordings of folk music and videos of performers, so you can hear the music. The Internet is a good resource, too.

American Composers

Ragtime, blues, jazz, classical, and popular music—American composers have created wonderful music in many styles. Here are just a few titles from six composers:

Stevie Wonder (1950–)

Singer and writer of popular songs. Some of his songs:
"You Are the Sunshine of My Life"
"Superstition"
"Isn't She Lovely"

John Williams (1932–)

Conductor and composer, has scored and composed music for many major films, including
The *Harry Potter* movies
The *Star Wars* movies
The *Home Alone* movies
The *Indiana Jones* movies
E. T.: The Extra-Terrestrial

W. C. Handy (1873–1958)

Composer of the blues; wrote a book called, and came to be known as, "Father of the Blues." Some of his songs:
"Memphis Blues"
"Beale Street Blues"
"St. Louis Blues"

George Gershwin (1898–1937)

Composer of popular songs, folk opera, and jazz compositions. Some of his works and songs:

Porgy and Bess
Rhapsody in Blue
Piano Concerto in F
An American in Paris
"Swanee"
"I Got Rhythm"

Woody Guthrie (1912–1967)

Folk singer and composer. Some of his songs:

"This Land Is Your Land"
"So Long, It's Been Good to Know You"
"This Train Is Bound for Glory"
His son, Arlo, is a composer, too.

Leonard Bernstein (1918–1990)

Composer of musicals and symphonies. Some of his works:

West Side Story
Wonderful Town
Fancy Free
Jeremiah
Mass

Written Music

Written music is how composers communicate their music to musicians and singers. They draw notes and other symbols on a staff. The horizontal and vertical lines above make up a treble staff (for higher notes) and a bass staff (for lower notes). Each line and each space on the staff stands for a particular pitch (sound), and they are named A through G. The sharp and flat symbols tell you to raise or lower the pitch a little from its natural pitch.

Notes can be drawn as whole notes, half notes (held for half as long), quarter notes, and so on. When a note is drawn on a certain line or a space, it tells you what pitch to play or sing, and how long to hold it. You read music just like you read words: from left to right, top to bottom. Once you learn to read the language of music, you can play or sing a tune or song just like you read a favorite book!

Cub Scout Academics
Belt Loop for Music

If you earned the Music belt loop earlier in Cub Scouting, great! But that won't count for requirement 15 of the Showman activity badge. You must earn that belt loop again while you are a Webelos Scout for it to count toward this activity badge.

music

Drama

When you complete each requirement, ask your Webelos den leader or activity badge counselor to sign it on pages 431–432. Be sure your Webelos den leader or activity badge counselor signs all the requirements you do for requirement 1.

Performing a Monologue

A single actor recites or acts out a *monologue*. It can be a poem, a story, or an essay. It may be on a serious subject, such as patriotism. Or it may be a funny story.

Choose a short story or long poem that you like. Try to memorize it. Practice often and show all the humor, sadness, or excitement that is in it. Then perform your monologue for the den.

Attending Plays

Have you ever been to a play in a theater? It's different from watching a comedy or drama on television. It's almost as if the actors are living their roles right before your eyes.

Stage actors have demanding jobs. They must become the character, remember the lines and actions exactly, and portray every emotion so it is believable. The cast does this again and again, for every performance.

Actors in television and movies also have demanding roles, but they often have many chances to get it right. A scene can be filmed many times until no one makes a mistake and the director is satisfied. You see the best of their work on the screen.

Ask an adult to take you to a play staged by a local high school drama club, college drama department, or theater group. Some groups put on plays just for children.

Reading and Writing Plays

You can find books of plays in your school or public library.

As you read, picture the characters on stage. What would the actors be doing as they speak the lines? How would they show humor or fear or anger? Say the lines out loud, as if you are acting in the play.

The plays you read may be divided into three acts, or they may be shorter, one-act plays. If you decide to do requirement 19 and write your own one-act play, you can get some tips from the section above on writing a play for puppets (pages 433–435).

Stage Setting

A play director often makes a model of the stage setting for a play to help him or her plan the action. Set designers also make models. You can make one, too. Read a play and then make a model stage setting for it.

Figure 1

Construction paper

- First, sketch your idea on paper. Draw it as the audience would see it. Then draw it as a floor plan of the stage, as if you were looking down at the stage. Show where furniture or other large objects will go. Use these sketches as a guide. (You can change your mind about your design at any time.)

- Cut two strips of light cardboard about 10 inches long and 3 inches wide. Make two lengthwise folds, so the ends look like a "Z" shape. Glue them to a box as shown in figure 1. These represent the curtains at the side of the stage.

Figure 2

Shirt box

- For the backdrop, curve a sheet of construction paper and slide it into place (figure 2). Or fold it to make two corners of a room. This is the backdrop.

- If it is an indoor scene, mark lightly in pencil the places where you want doors and windows on the backdrop. Then remove the backdrop and use crayons or paints to add line and color.

If it's outdoors, paint trees and other features. Glue or tape the backdrop in place when it's ready.

- Keep it simple. The audience comes to the theater ready to use imagination, so you don't have to fill in every detail.
- Make simple furniture from cardboard or use dollhouse miniatures. Don't clutter the scene with things that won't be used. The action in the play will tell you what must be there.

Stage Directions

As the director of the play you write, you will have to give stage directions to the actors. Read your play and think about what each character does. Make notes in your script where you want each actor to stand, sit, and move on the stage. Here's a way to note the locations:

D—Down (toward audience); **U**—Up (toward back of stage); **L**—Left (your left as you face audience); **R**—Right (your right as you face audience); **C**—Center; **DC**—Down center; **UC**—Up center; **LC**—Left center; **RC**—Right center

For the play you write, your stage may be an area of your den meeting place. Keep the setting simple. Use the furniture that is available and movable. Let the audience imagine a sofa when you line up three folding chairs.

Theater Styles

Three main kinds of stages are used today. One is the kind of stage you usually think of when you hear the word "stage." It's a raised platform at one end of the room, with a curtain between it and the audience that can be opened and closed.

Another kind of stage is called *theater-in-the-round*. The stage is in the center of the room. The audience sits around all sides of it. There is no curtain. Instead of a curtain closing, the theater is darkened between scenes or acts.

Theater-in-the-round works well for plays with small casts and action that needs to be seen close up. The actors enter and leave the stage along aisles through the audience.

There's no backdrop or solid scenery that would block anyone's view of the actors. A window frame hanging from the ceiling might be the only suggestion of a wall of a house.

If the theater is small, everyone in the audience is fairly close to the stage—much closer than most people would be in a traditional theater. Watching a play this way can make the audience feel very involved in it.

For a director, staging the play can be challenging. Actors' moves must be planned so they don't have their backs to one part of the audience for too long a time.

For plays with a large cast or a lot of action, theater-in-the-round is not a good choice. The audience is too close to the stage to see everything clearly when many actors are moving about. A great deal of fast action can be confusing.

A third kind of stage, the *thrust* stage, starts at one end of the room like the most common kind of stage, but it thrusts out into the audience area so that three sides of it are surrounded by the audience. It has some of the advantages of theater-in-the-round but the actors can still enter and exit using the wings and don't have to use the aisles. The thrust stage is not as widely used as the other two kinds of stage.

Opera and Musicals

Opera and musicals are alike in this way: Both are plays with music and singing.

Opera

There are different kinds of opera:

- **Grand opera** has a serious theme. Every word in it is sung by the actor-singers. An example of a grand opera written in English is *Amahl and the Night Visitors*, by Gian-Carlo Menotti.

- **Light opera** has a humorous, romantic plot. It can have a combination of musical numbers and spoken lines. Other names for light opera are *comic opera* and *operetta*. An example of an operetta is *The Pirates of Penzance*, by Sir William Gilbert and Sir Arthur Sullivan.

Grand operas are sometimes shown on television. Watch one if you can. It might be sung in Italian, German, or French. Usually English subtitles are shown so you can follow the story.

Musicals

A musical can be serious or funny. Much of the plot unfolds in the spoken lines. There may be a great deal of variety, with solo singers and choruses, a lot of action, and exciting dance numbers. Actors in musicals are talented in acting, singing, and dancing.

Some examples of musicals:

- *Oklahoma!*, with music by Richard Rodgers and lyrics (words) by Oscar Hammerstein II
- *My Fair Lady*, with music by Frederick Loewe and lyrics by Alan Jay Lerner
- *West Side Story*, with music by Leonard Bernstein and lyrics by Stephen Sondheim
- *Cats* and *Phantom of the Opera*, with music by Andrew Lloyd Webber

You may have a chance to see an opera or a musical on stage. That will be quite an experience. If you can view videos at home, find out if your public library loans out videos of musicals and operas.

Shakespeare and His Theater

William Shakespeare (1564–1616), who lived in England, has been called the greatest playwright in history. Indeed, he is considered to be one of the greatest writers of any kind.

His plays are still popular today, centuries after his death. He wrote both comedies and tragedies. Examples of his many plays are *Hamlet, A Midsummer Night's Dream, Romeo and Juliet,* and *Much Ado About Nothing.*

Not very much is known about his life, and there is even an argument among scholars as to whether he really wrote all the plays that bear his name.

During much of his career, he was an actor as well as a playwright. He performed at the Globe Theater in London.

Watch for announcements of productions of Shakespeare's plays by local colleges or theater groups. Many of the plays may be available on video, as well as movie versions of them.

Look for books about Shakespeare and his plays in the library. If you can't find books, read about him in an encyclopedia or on the Internet.

Sportsman
Requirements

Requirement	Approved by

Do these:

1. Show the signals used by officials in one of these sports: football, basketball, baseball, soccer, or hockey.

2. Explain what good sportsmanship means.

3. While you are a Webelos Scout, earn Cub Scout Sports belt loops for two individual sports (badminton, bicycling, bowling, fishing, golf, gymnastics, marbles, physical fitness, ice skating, roller skating, snow ski and board sports, swimming, table tennis, or tennis).

4. While you are a Webelos Scout, earn Cub Scouting Sports belt loops for two team sports (baseball, basketball, soccer, softball, volleyball, flag football, or ultimate).

A merica is a sports-loving country. We cheer our school teams. College and professional games draw crowds, and we watch all kinds of sports on television.

These games are great fun to watch, but too many Americans are spectators. Be a player!

In the Sportsman activity badge, you'll play team sports like basketball, baseball, and soccer. You'll go out for individual sports like bicycling, swimming, and tennis. You may try a sport you'll play all your life.

Sports build your body and improve your skills. Some sports sharpen your eye and your accuracy. Some require you to move carefully and deliberately, while others demand quick thinking, speed, and endurance. Choose your sports and play! When you complete a requirement, ask your Webelos den leader or activity badge counselor to sign it on page 456.

Learning Officials' Signals

You'll find pictures of officials' signals starting on page 459. You may already know many of them from watching sports events. For requirement 1, you'll learn the signals for one sport, but look at the others. You'll enjoy watching games even more when you know instantly the decisions officials make on exciting plays.

Good Sportsmanship

What is good sportsmanship?

You may say, "It's being a good loser."

That's part of it. If you lose, try to take the loss bravely. Don't gripe about bad luck or blame the officials or your teammates. Practice, do your best, and see what happens the next time you compete.

Good sportsmanship also means being a good winner. You'll be happy, but don't put the other team down. Take time to tell your opponent he played a good game.

A good sport plays by the rules and never cheats. Playing fairly is a matter of honor and self-respect, as well as respect for opponents. Play hard and play to win—but to win *fairly*.

Playing Sports

For requirements 3 and 4, you'll earn the belt loops for two individual sports and two team sports in the Cub Scout Academics and Sports program.

If you earned some of those awards when you were in a Cub Scout den, they won't count toward these requirements. You could choose different sports this time, or you could earn a second belt loop in any sport you want to repeat for this badge.

The book called *Cub Scout Academics and Sports Program Guide* tells you

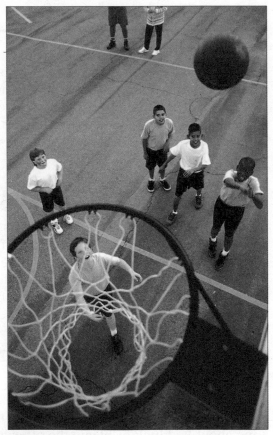

what you need to do to earn a belt loop for each of the sports listed in requirements 3 and 4. Generally, you need to understand the rules of the sport, practice some of the skills, and then play a game of the sport itself.

OFFICIALS' SIGNALS

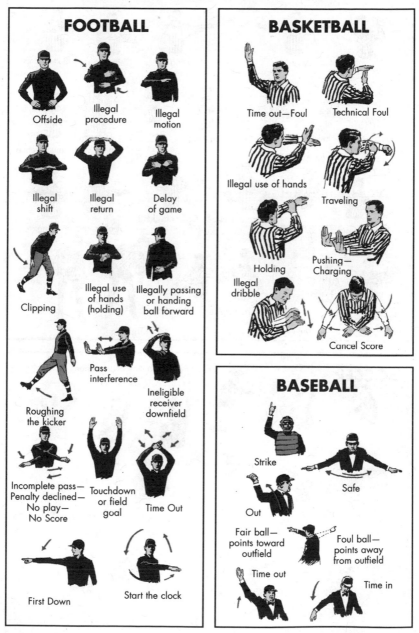

FOOTBALL

Offside

Illegal procedure

Illegal motion

Illegal shift

Illegal return

Delay of game

Clipping

Illegal use of hands (holding)

Illegally passing or handing ball forward

Pass interference

Ineligible receiver downfield

Roughing the kicker

Incomplete pass— Penalty declined— No play— No Score

Touchdown or field goal

Time Out

First Down

Start the clock

BASKETBALL

Time out—Foul

Technical Foul

Illegal use of hands

Traveling

Holding

Pushing— Charging

Illegal dribble

Cancel Score

BASEBALL

Strike

Safe

Out

Fair ball— points toward outfield

Foul ball— points away from outfield

Time out

Time in

HOCKEY

Elbowing

"Wash out"

Fighting (Roughing)

Charging

Butt-ending

Delay calling of penalty

Slow whistle

Holding

Slashing

Boarding

Penalty shot

Interference

Hooking

Holding the face mask

Misconduct

Cross-checking

Goal scored

Icing

High-sticking

Checking from behind

Unsportsmanlike conduct and time out

Spearing

Tripping

Kneeing

SOCCER

Caution or expulsion

Play on—Advantage

Indirect free-kick

Goal-kick

Off-side

Substitution

Penalty kick

Direct free-kick

Corner kick

Off-side

Throw-in

Off-side

Off-side

Substitution

Corner kick

Goal-kick

Activity Badges

Traveler
Requirements

Requirement

Approved by

Do five of these:

1. Get a map or timetable from a railroad, bus line, airline, subway, or light rail. The line should serve the place where you live or near where you live. Look up some places it goes. _____

2. Use a timetable to plan a trip from your home to a city in another state by railroad, bus, airline, or ferry. _____

3. With the help of your parent, guardian, teacher, or librarian, use a map site on the Internet to plan a trip from your home to a nearby place of interest. Download and/or print the directions and a street map showing how to go from your home to the place you chose. _____

4. With your parent or guardian, take a trip to a place that interests you. Go by car, bus, boat, train, or plane. 10 -27- 11 _____

5. Figure out what it costs per mile for the trip you took or planned to fulfill requirement 2, 4, 6, or 7. (Don't forget to include getting back to your starting point!) 10-27-11 _____

6. Decide on four nearby trips you would like to take with your parents or guardian. Draw the route of each trip on a highway map. Using the map, act as navigator on one of these trips. It should start at your home, be at least 25 miles long, and have six or more turns. _____

·7. Decide on a trip you would like to take that lasts at least two days. Pack everything you would need for that trip. _AC 10-27-11_

8. Check the first aid kit in the family car to see if it contains what is needed. Explain what you found. _____

·9. Look at the map legend on a road map of your area. Learn what the symbols mean. Show your den members what you have learned. _AC 10-27-11_

10. On a road map of your area, find a place of interest and draw two different routes between it and your home. Use the map legend to determine which route is shorter in miles. _____

11. Make a list of safety precautions you, as a traveler, should take for travel by each of the following: car, bus, plane, boat, train. _____

12. While you are a Webelos Scout, earn the Cub Scout Academics belt loop for Geography. _____

13. While you are a Webelos Scout, earn the Cub Scout Academics belt loop for Map and Compass. _AC 10-27-11_

Traveling is one of humankind's greatest adventures. Early explorers sailed across vast oceans, floated down mighty rivers, and journeyed through high mountain country to see what they could find.

You can be an explorer, too. You won't be traveling in unknown territory, but it will be new to you. You'll enjoy the thrill of discovery wherever you travel.

Be curious, ask questions, read signs about points of interest, notice the sights and sounds.

In earning the Traveler activity badge, you'll learn how to help plan family trips. You'll also learn how to use public transportation—buses, planes, and trains. Let's go! When you complete each requirement, ask your Webelos den leader or activity badge counselor to sign it on page 462–463.

All Aboard!

Has most of your traveling been by car? It's fun to find out about other kinds of travel—by bus, ship, train, or plane. Then when you do take a trip, you'll know how to read schedules and plan.

Each kind of travel has advantages and disadvantages. Buses go to more places, like small towns, than planes and passenger trains do. Usually the bus is the least expensive of these three, but not always. Airlines sometimes have special low fares.

Many people choose a long train trip mainly to enjoy seeing the country. Long-distance trains have more room for moving about than other forms of transportation, and everything a passenger needs is on the train.

These trains usually have lounge cars and dining cars. Some even have observation cars, where you sit up high for an even better view of the countryside. You may have your own room, called a compartment. It is a tiny living room, bedroom, and washroom, all in one.

A plane is the fastest way of traveling on long trips. The view of the earth from high in the sky is breathtaking. You have a bird's-eye view of mountains, rivers, and cities far below. Flying through and above clouds gives you a feeling of being in another world.

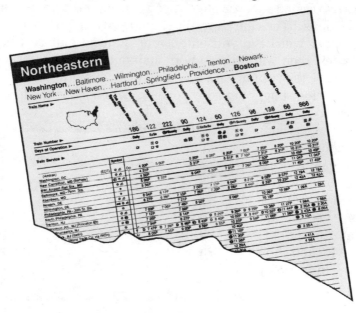

Your Schedule

Railroads, buses, airlines, and ship lines have schedules called *timetables*. These list the places they go and show the times they leave and arrive at each place.

Timetables look hard to read. But they're not, when you learn how. For instance, some timetables use arrows to show the direction of travel. Noon to midnight hours (P.M.) are usually shown in heavy type. Look at the beginning of the timetable for instructions on how to use it.

Read your timetable with care when you are planning a trip. Be sure the train, bus, airplane, or ferry goes on the day you want. Check with a ticket agent for any recent changes in the departure and arrival times.

You can get a timetable at a railroad or bus station, ferry line, airline terminal, or travel agency.

Internet Travel Resources

The Internet has map resources that may be helpful in planning a trip. Using a search engine, you can enter the phrase "maps & directions." The search result should provide links to several sites. Most will have you enter your starting and destination addresses, then will provide both map and directions. (Be sure to compare the results with a printed map; sometimes the directions are close but not exactly correct.) When using the Internet, be sure to have the help or supervision of an adult.

You can also use the Internet to find out what transportation, hotels, and restaurants are available and how much they cost. Adults can make reservations on the Internet for travel and lodging.

How Much Does It Cost?

Requirement 5 asks you to figure out how much it costs to go on a trip. If you travel by bus, rail, or plane, you can find out the cost per mile if you know two things: the fare and the distance.

> Here is the formula to use:
> Fare ÷ Distance = Cost Per Mile

Suppose you plan to take a bus trip to a city 180 miles from your town. The fare is $37.50. Then:

> $37.50 ÷ 180 Miles = $0.208 Cost Per Mile

It would cost a little more than 20 cents per mile to travel by bus.

But because you are younger than 12 years old, you might be able to go for about two thirds of the adult fare. That means your cost would be about 13 cents a mile.

Many airlines, bus lines, and railroads have special fares. Fares may be lower on weekends or at certain times of the year. It's a good idea to check for special fares before you plan a trip.

How much it costs to take a trip by car may be harder to figure. There are many "hidden" costs when traveling by car, such as the cost of the car insurance, the cost of wear and tear on the car and tires, and the cost of engine oil. But you can easily figure out the cost of the gasoline used per mile of your trip by dividing the total fuel cost by the total miles you travel.

Packing

- Make a list of things you'll need. Check it with an adult member of your family.

- Select the suitcase, duffel bag, backpack, etc., that you will need.

- Fold your clothes and press down on them as you pack so you can take as many as you need.

- If you're using a suitcase, pack shoes so that when the suitcase is standing up, the shoes will be on the bottom.

- Tuck socks into shoes to save room.

- Put things that might break and spread throughout your clothes, such as toothbrush, toothpaste, and shampoo, in a plastic jar or resealable plastic bag. (A jar won't crush easily.)

- If you're using public transportation, you should have name tags on all your luggage. Some tag holders have a cover that opens so the name and address aren't visible to everyone who passes by. The tag helps if your luggage is lost or if several passengers have similar bags. Some people also tie a piece of brightly colored yarn to the handle so they can find their luggage quickly when they arrive at their destination.

A Family Trip by Car

When traveling by train, bus, or airplane, you really don't have much to do. You just pack your bag and get to the train station, bus station, or airport ahead of time. But when you go by car, you have to do more planning.

Adult family members have to get the car ready. That means making sure the brakes, lights, and steering are okay. The oil level in the engine and the air pressure in the tires must be checked. The gas tank should be full. Before a long trip, a mechanic should take care of any regular maintenance that is due.

Planning a Car Trip

You can help plan the trip. How do you find the best way to get where you want to go? How do you know the best roads? By using road maps.

Look for maps of your own state and neighboring ones at state tourism offices, the highway department, or a gas station. Some families use a road atlas, which is a book of state maps.

If an adult family member belongs to an automobile club, it can provide maps of states and street maps of large cities. A club may also plan your route for you.

See Internet Travel Resources on page 466 for more information.

Study the maps. For a long trip, decide how far you'll travel each day. Where will you stop? At a hotel, a motel, or a camping ground? An adult family member may need to phone and make reservations. Find out whether your library has recent travel guides that list places to stay. Automobile clubs may have these, too.

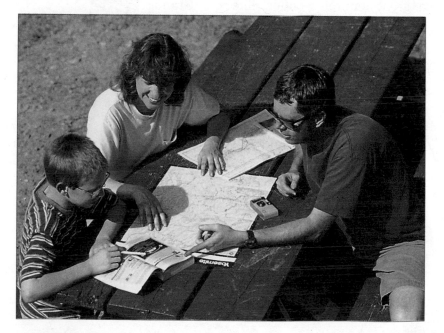

Family Camping Trips

Many American families take vacation trips by camping along the way at public or private campgrounds. They may stay a day or two and then move on again. If they especially like a campground and the recreation the area offers, they may spend most of their trip there. This can be an inexpensive and enjoyable vacation.

There are four main kinds of public campgrounds.

National Forests

The United States has more than 150 national forests. National forests cover one-tenth of the whole area of our country. The U.S. Department of Agriculture controls them.

The national forests have more than 2,000 campgrounds. Most have tables, benches, rock fireplaces, a water supply, and toilets. Many are free. They don't accept reservations.

National Parks

The National Park Service controls our national parks. A park may be the site of a great natural wonder, like the Grand Canyon in Arizona or Mammoth Cave in Kentucky.

Most of the national parks have campgrounds. (Look for a campground symbol on the map.) These have a water supply, tables, fireplaces, and restrooms. Some have laundry rooms, showers, and stores. Besides the cost to go into the park, some campgrounds charge an extra fee.

With the increase in camping interest, most campgrounds in national parks are heavily used. In the summer they are often full by noon. Some take reservations. Plan ahead and write for information.

National Monuments

National monuments are places that preserve

- Prehistoric sites, such as Petroglyph National Monument in New Mexico

- Historic sites, such as Fort McHenry National Monument in Maryland

- Places of scientific interest, such as Agate Fossil Beds National Monument in Nebraska

A national monument could be almost anywhere—in the heart of a city or in the wilderness. Some have camping places, or there might be a campground nearby.

Check the map for national monuments along your route. They are worth a visit.

State Parks

Each state has state parks. Some of them are for day use only, for picnics and other recreation. Others may have campgrounds ranging from basic campsites to those with showers and laundry facilities. Most have a small daily charge.

Finding Places to Camp

Perhaps your family would like to know more about campsites. Check some current guidebooks on camping. Find out where to write for more information about camps in each state you plan to visit.

Before you go on a camping vacation, try to earn your Outdoorsman activity badge. Everything you learn about outdoor living will be helpful on your trip.

Car First Aid Kit

Be sure to have a first aid kit in the car. Naturally, you hope you will not need it, but a Scout should be prepared. Check the first aid kit in the car before you go. The things that should be in the kit are listed on pages 388–389.

Safety First!

As a Webelos Scout, you need to be aware of safety precautions that seasoned travelers use when traveling by car or other types of transportation.

Car Travel Safety Rules

- Always wear a seatbelt.
- Do not distract the driver.
- Be aware of your surroundings.
- Be sure the vehicle is in good repair before starting out.
- Do not exit the car on the traffic side.

Train, Boat, and Plane Travel Safety Rules

- Stay with your traveling partners.
- Secure your luggage in the proper places.
- Listen to all safety precautions when they are explained. Afterward, ask questions if you do not understand any of them.
- Keep your valuables out of sight.

- Do not take with you any toy or other object that could look like a weapon.
- Be aware of your surroundings.
- Do not speak to strangers unless an adult you know and trust is present.

Cub Scout Academics
Belt Loops for Geography and
Map and Compass

If you earned the Geography or Map and Compass belt loop earlier in Cub Scouting, great! But that won't count for requirements 12 and 13 of this Traveler activity badge. You must earn those belt loops again while you are a Webelos Scout for them to count toward this activity badge.

Index
and
Credits

Index

A

Academics and Sports program,
Cub Scout, 71–72
Art belt loop, 121
Astronomy belt loop, 428
Belt loops, 32
Chess belt loop, 396
Computers and Communicating
belt loop, 196
Geography belt loop, 473
Geology belt loop, 298
Heritages belt loop, 244
Language belt loop, 396
Map and Compass belt loop, 473
Mathematics belt loop, 226, 396
Music belt loop, 445
Physical Fitness pin, 126
Science belt loop, 428
Swimming belt loop, 100
Weather belt loop, 428
Wildlife Conservation belt loop, 342
Accident, what to do after, 369
Acting out a joke, 435
Action/reaction, 417–18
Activity badge groups, 74
Activity badge tracking chart, 75–78
Activity badges, 5, 13–14, 81–473
and Academics and Sports, 71
earning, 75–78
placement on uniform, 32
Advancement, 5, 39–80
ceremony, 29
Air pressure, 404–06, 412–13
Alcohol, dangers of, 257
All the Way exercise, 135
American Sign Language,
Cub Scout Promise in, 181–85
Animal watching, 337–38
Ants, keeping, 322–23
Application to join, 25
Aquanaut activity badge, 83–100
Aquariums, 328
Arm Wrestle dual contest, 139
Arrow of Light Award, 62–67
earning, 62–67

placement on uniform, 33
requirements, 63–64
shown, 62
Arrow Points, placement on uniform, 33
Art belt loop, 121
Art medium, choosing, 104
Art supplies, 108–09
Artist activity badge, 101–21
Athlete activity badge, 123–41
Athlete Progress Record, 132
Atmospheric pressure, 409–12
Attitude, positive, 8, 45, 392, 395
Automobile, see car, 302
Awards, placement on uniform, 32–33
Awards, special, 68–73

B

Backstroke, elementary, 89
Badges of rank, placement on uniform,
32
"Be" Courageous, 368
Bear badge, placement on uniform, 33
Bed made of blankets, 348–49
Bee and wasp stings, first aid for, 381
Belt buckle, Webelos, 30
Belt loops, see Academics and
Sports program
Belt, Cub Scout, 20, 30
Bernoulli's Principle, 404–06
BEST steps to a positive attitude, 395
Biceps Builder exercise, 133
Bicycle safety, 386–87
Bicycle, taking care of a, 306–08
Bicycling, 131
Birds, 331–33
Bites and stings, first aid for, 381–82
Bleeding, stopping severe, 374–75
Blisters, first aid for, 380
Block and tackle, 221–23
Boating safety, 98–101
Bobcat badge, 6, 25, 33, 41–47
Body language, 168–70
Bowline, tying, 351
Boy Scout, becoming a, 79–80
Boy Scout uniform, parts of, 66
Boy Scouting, 79–80

Breathing, rescue, 372, 373
Bridges, 218–20
Brushes for painting, 108
Buddy system, 87, 96, 385
Budget, family, 235–36
Burns and scalds, first aid for, 378–79
Butterflies and moths, keeping, 326–27
Butterfly exercise, 136

C

Camp activities, 354
Camp, places to, 472
Campfire program, 354
Campgrounds, 470–71
Camping, 345–60
    away from home, 352–53
    practice at home, 347
    safety and comfort, 354–55
Campouts, 18–20
    family trips, 470
    packing for, 352–53
Cap, Webelos Scout, 30
Capulin Volcano, 291
Car, taking care of, 302
Car safety, 390
Car trips, planning, 468–69
Cataput, making and using, 224–25
Center of gravity experiments, 422–23
Ceramics, 208–10
Character Connections, 7
    Citizenship, 144
    Courage, 366
    Faith, 50–51
    Health and Fitness, 246
    Honesty, 42, 44, 64
    Perseverance, 124
    Positive Attitude, 392
    Respect, 318
    Responsibility, 300
Character Development, 7
Chartered organization contribution, 21
Chest Push dual contest, 141
Chigger bites, first aid for, 381
Child abuse prevention, 12, 42, 192–95
Choking, first aid for, 379–80
Citizen activity badge, 143–63
Citizenship, 6, 8, 143–163
Clay projects, 208–10
Cleanliness as a family duty, 231–32
Cleanup in camp, 360

Clothing for hikes, 361–62
Clove hitch, tying, 351
Codes, secret, 175
Collages, making, 120–21
Collections, geologic, 288
Color wheel, 110
Communication, careers in, 196
Communication methods, 174, 180–84
Communicator activity badge, 165–95
Community Group, 74
    Citizen activity badge, 143–63
    Communicator activity badge, 165–95
    Family member activity badge, 227–44
    Readyman activity badge, 365–90
Community support for Scouting, 21
Community volunteer groups, 163
Community, learning about, 157
Compact disks (CDs), 188
Compass points emblem, 36
    earning, 60–61
    placement on uniform, 33
Compassion, 8
Composers, American music, 442–44
Computer, taking care of, 190–91
Computers, 187–95
Computer designs, 113–14
Computers in a newsroom, 178
Computers in engineering, 225–26
Conservation, 72, 156, 237, 340–42
Conservation Award, Cub Scout World, 342
Construction, geologic materials in, 289
Construction site, visiting, 215
Constructions, artistic, 119–20
Contributors to Scouting, 21–22
Cooking in camp, 356–60
Cooperation, 8
Core values of Cub Scouting, 8
Costs of Scouting, 21–22
Council support, 21–22
Courage, 8, 56, 366, 368
CPR, 372–74
Crafts projects, choosing, 200
    protection when giving, 372
Craftsman activity badge, 197–210
Crawl stroke, 91
Crickets, keeping, 321
Crystals, making, 421

Cub Scout Academics and Sports
program, *see* Academics and Sports
program,
Cub Scout
Cub Scout handshake, 42, 46
Cub Scout motto, 16, 17, 28, 42, 394
Cub Scout Promise, meaning of, 43–45
Cub Scout Promise in sign
language, 181–85
Cub Scout salute, 42, 47, 53, 152
Cub Scout sign, 42, 46
Cub Scout Sports, *see* Academics and
Sports program, Cub Scout
Cub Scout World Conservation
Award, 342
Curl-ups, 127
Cuts and scratches, first aid for, 377–78

D

Danger spots at home, 389
Dangerous materials, storing safely, 310
Den, Webelos Scout, 23–37
Den chief, Webelos, 29
Den leader Webelos, 28
Denner, 29
Denner cords, placement on
uniform, 34
Digital video disks (DVDs), 188
Display stands and frames, making, 205
Dive, surface, 92
Do Your Best, 16, 17, 28, 42, 43, 46, 62,
66, 243, 392, 394, 457
Do your best in school, 394
Drama, 445–53
Drawing, 105
floor plans, 214
Drawing media, 105
Drugs, 12, 257–58
Drugs: A Deadly Game, 258
Dual contests, 139–41
Duck Fight dual contest, 141
Duties and rights of a citizen, 155–56
Duty to family, 230

E

Earth's crust and core, 282
Earthquakes, 293
Ecosystems, 338–41
Education, careers in, 400
Education, value of, 395

Electricity, 216–18
Emergency, getting help for an, 370–71
Energy, saving, 237
Engineer activity badge, 211–26
Environment, natural, 340–41
Exercise, 127–43

F

Faith, 8, 16–17, 50–51, 56, 59, 65
Family, 229–30
budget, 235–36
camping trips, 470
duty to, 230
fun, 238
jobs, 231–32
meetings, 230, 242–43
you and your, 229–30
Family Member activity badge, 227–44
Fat in the diet, 254
Fees, 21
50-yard dash, 130
Fins, swim, how to use, 95
Fire building, 356–59
Fire escape plan, home, 387–88
Fire in the forest, 274–76
Fire lay, 358–59
First aid, 369
for hurry cases, 371
kit for car, 472
kits, 388–89
First Class Scout badge, meaning of, 65
Fitness activity badge, 245–58
Fitness and health, 8, 87, 124, 125, 126,
234, 238, 240, 245–58, 384
Fitness for swimming, 87
Flag, U.S., 148–53
Flag ceremony, planning and leading, 53
Floating, 88
Fog, making, 419
Folk music, 441
Food Guide Pyramid, 248–49
Food serving size, 250–51
Food, helping with family, 239–41
Food, shopping for, 240
Forest fire, 274–76
Forest regions of the United States, 262
Forest structure, 264–65
Forest tree types, 266–67
Forest trees and plants,
identifying, 269–70

Forester activity badge, 259–77
Forestry, urban, 276–77
Forests, animals and humans depend on, 268–69
Forests, human uses of, 268–69
Fossils, 295–96
Frame, making a, 112
Friends, 34
Friends of Scouting, 22
Frostbite, first aid for, 383
Fun, family, 238

G

Garbage and trash disposal, 234
Geologic materials in construction, 289
Geologic specimens, collecting, 286–87
Geologist activity badge, 279–98
Geologist in the city, 296–97
Geologist's equipment, 287
Geysers, 292
Good citizen, how to be a, 157–59
Government and laws, why we need, 160–61
Government and you, 147–48
Government officials' names, knowing, 148
Government, paying for, 161
Grasshoppers, keeping, 324–25
Groups, activity badge, 74

H

Handshake, Cub Scout, 42, 46
Handyman activity badge, 299–316
Handyman around the house, 310–13
Hardware, computer, choices, 191
Headlight, replacing, 304
Health, physical and mental, 126
Health and fitness, 8, 87, 124, 125, 126, 234, 238, 240, 245–58, 384
Health and safety guidelines, 18
attack, signs of, 376
Help, getting, 370–71
Hike, first, 361
Hiking, 18
    with your den, 360–63
Honesty, 8, 42, 5, 55, 64, 159
Housecleaning, helping with, 238–39
How to Protect Your Children from Child Abuse, 47
Hurry cases, first aid for, 371

I

Igneous rock, 282–83
Inertia, 407–09
Ingredient labels, 254–56
Inhalants, dangers of, 257–58
Insect zoo, 320–27
Insignia, placement on uniform, 33–34
Internet, 191–95

J

Jobs, family, 231–32
Joining the pack, 25
Joke acted out, 435

K

Knots for camping, 350–51
Knowledge skills, 396

L

Languages, learning other, 186
Laundry, helping with, 239
Law of the Pack, meaning of, 44
Lawn, caring for, 314
Laws and government, why we need, 160–61
Leatherworking, 205–07
Leave No Trace Awareness Award, 18, 72–73
Leg Stretch exercise, 137
Leg Wrestle dual contest, 141
Letter holder, making, 202–03
Library, using, 176–77
Light bulb, replacing, 310
Local council support, 21–22
Lost camper, prevention of, 355

M

Marionette stage, 439
Mask, snorkeling, how to use, 94
Meals, planning, 240, 248–56
Meals, preparing, 241–42
Media, art, 104–07, 114
Meetings, 27, 29
    Meetings, family, 230, 242–43
Mental health, 126
Mental Skills Group, 74
    Artist activity badge, 101–21
    Scholar activity badge, 391–402
    Showman activity badge, 429–53

Traveler activity badge, 461–73
Menu, sample, 253
Metamorphic rock, 284
Mineral hardness scale, 289
Minerals, useful, 284–86
Mobile, making a, 117–18
Money, family, 234–36
Monologue, performing a, 446
Moths and butterflies, keeping, 326–27
Motto, Cub Scout, 16, 17, 28, 42, 394
Mountains, how they are
    formed, 294–95
Music, 440
Musicals and operas, 451–52

N

National anthem, 149, 154
National forest campgrounds, 470
National monument campgrounds, 471
National park campgrounds, 470
Natural resources, saving, 156
Naturalist activity badge, 317–42
Nature centers, visiting, 330
Nature, balance of, 340–41
Neat and clean, being, 231–32
Neck Builder exercise, 136
Neckerchief, 20, 29–31
Neckerchief slide, 30
Necktie rack, making, 202
News story, writing, 178–79
Newsroom, visiting, 177–78
Newton, Sir Isaac, 407
Nutrition, 248–56

O

Oil and tire pressure, checking, 305
1–mile bicycle ride, 131
Operas and musicals, 451–52
Optical illusions, 424–28
Outdoor Code, 59, 346
Outdoor Essentials, 363
Outdoor Group, 74
    Forester activity badge, 259–77
    Geologist activity badge, 279–98
    Naturalist activity badge, 317–42
    Outdoorsman activity badge, 343–63
Outdoor jobs, 314
Outdoor program, 18–20
Outdoorsman activity badge, 343–63
Overnight campouts, 18–20

P

Pack budget, 21
Pack meetings, 14–15, 29
Pack structure, 9
Packing for a campout, 352–53
Packing for travel, 467–68
Painting, 106–11
Paper Crunch exercise, 133
Parent Guide, 1–22
Pascal's Law, 406–07
Pebbles and rocks, 281
Perseverance, 8, 124
Personal flotation devices, 99
Photosynthesis, 271
Physical health, 126
Physical skills group, 74
    Aquanaut activity badge, 83–100
    Athlete actvity badge, 123–41
    Fitness activity badge, 245–58
    Sportsman activity badge, 455–60
Physics, 403–18
Picture writing, 172
Plans, drawing, 214
Planting trees, 273–74
Plants, poisonous, 334
Plays, 446–47
Pledge of Allegiance, meaning of, 153
Poisoning by mouth, treating, 376
Police, helping, 157
Positive attitude, 8, 45, 392, 395
Praying mantises, keeping, 324–25
Pressure, water, 406–07
Profile, drawing, 106
Projects, choosing, 200
Promise, Cub Scout, meaning of, 43–45
Pull Apart dual contest, 140
Pull–ups, 128
Puppetry, 433–39
Purposes of Cub Scouting, 6
Push–ups, 128

Q

Quarter–mile run or walk, 130
Quarter–mile swim, 131

R

Rank advancement and special
    awards, 39–80

Reach, throw, row, go with support, 97–99
Readyman activity badge, 365–90
Recycling, 234
Religious duties, 68–69
Religious emblems, 59, 68–69
Reptiles, venomous, 335–36
Requirements
    activity badge, see each activity badge
    Arrow of Light Award, 63–64
    Bobcat badge, 42
    Compass Points emblem, 61
    Cub Scout World Conservation Award, 70
    Leave No Trace Awareness Award, 73
    Webelos badge, 49–51
Rescue, water, 97–99
Resourcefulness, 8
Respect, 6, 8, 55, 56, 58, 144, 145, 151, 153, 156, 157, 159, 318, 346, 458
Responsibilities of parent and Webelos Scout, 15–18
Responsibility, 4, 8, 10, 14, 15, 29, 79, 155, 300
Rights of a citizen, 155
Riparian forest, 263
Rock collecting, 286–88
Rock, kinds of, 282–84
Rocks and minerals, identifying, 288–89
Rocks and pebbles, 281
Rocks, how they break down, 284
Rope, fusing, 350
Rope, whipping, 349
Running, 130

S

Safe Swim Defense, 384–85
Safety, bicycle, 386–87
Safety, camping, 354–55
Safety, home, 232–33, 389
Safety checklist, home, 233
Safety guidelines, and helath, 18
Safety in a car, 390
Safety notebook, making a, 247
Safety rules, fire, 357
Safety when handing wounds and giving CPR, 372
Safety when traveling, 472–73

Salute, Cub Scout, 42, 47, 53, 152
Sawhorse, making, 311–12
Scholar activity badge, 391–402
School, 397–400
Science, fun with, 419
Scientist activity badge, 401–28
Scout camp, visit, 362
Scout handshake, 49, 53, 58
Scout Law, meaning of, 55–56
Scout motto, meaning of, 57
Scout oath, meaning of, 54–55
Scout salute, how to make, 58
Scout sign, how to make, 58
Scout slogan, meaning of, 57
Scrapbook, making a, 103
Sculpture, 114–16
Secret codes, 175
Sedimentary rock, 283–84
Self–respect, 458
Shakespeare and his theater, 453
Sheet bend, tying, 351
Shock, first aid for, 376–77
Shoes for hikes, 362–63
Showman activity badge, 429–53
Sidestroke, 90
Sign language, Cub Scout Promise in, 181–85
Sign language, invented, 173
Sign, Cub Scout, 42, 46
Skateboards and skates, taking care of, 309
Sleeping on the ground, 348–49
Smoking, dangers of, 256
Snacks, healthful, 252
Snakebite, first aid for, 382
Snorkeling, 93–97
Software, computer, choices, 191
Special awards, 68–73
Spider bites, first aid for, 381
Spiritual development, parent's role in, 16–18
Sports officials' signals, learning, 457, 459–60
Sports pin, Physical Fitness, 126
Sports program, see Academics and Sports program, Cub Scout
Sports, playing, 458
Sportsman activity badge, 455–60
Sportsmanship, good, 457–58
Square knot, tying, 350

Squat Thrust exercise, 138
Stage direction, 449
Stage setting, 447–48
Stages, puppet and marionette, 438–39
Standing long jump, 129
Star–Spangled Banner, 149, 154
State park campgrounds, 471
Stick Pull dual contest, 140
Stick Wrestle dual contest, 139
Stings and bites, first aid for, 381–82
Stool, making a, 313
Stretcher exercise, 135
Sun protection, 363
Sunburn, first aid for, 383
Support of Scouting, 21–22
Surface dive, 92
Surveyors, 215
Swim fins, how to use, 95
Swimming, 83–100, 131, 355
    Swimming belt loop, 100
    Swimming safety, 86–87, 384–85
    Swimming skills, 88–92
    Swimming underwater, 92

T

Tadpoles, keeping, 328
Taillight, replacing, 304
Talk, giving a, 171–72
Taut–line hitch, tying, 350
Technology Group, 74
    Craftsman activity badge, 197–210
    Engineer activity badge, 211–26
    Handyman activity badge, 299–316
    Scientist activity badge, 401–28
Temporary insignia, placement on uniform, 33
Tent, homemade, 347–48
Terrariums, 329–30
Theater styles, 450–51
Theater, Shakespeare and his, 453
Tick bites, first aid for, 380–81
Tire, changing, 303–04
Tire pressure and oil, checking, 305
Tobacco, dangers of, 256
Toe exercise, 138
Toolbox, making a, 316
Tools, taking care of, 315–16
Tools, using safely, 199–200
Tools for woodworking, 201
Trash and garbage disposal, 234

Travel, kinds of, 464–65
Travel, packing for, 467–68
Travel by car, family, 468–73
Travel costs, estimating, 467
Travel resources, Internet, 466
Travel safety, 472–73
Travel schedules, 465–66
Traveler activity badge, 461–73
Tree planting, 273–74
Tree, how one grows, 270–71
Tree, inside structure, 272
Trees, fall color, 275
Trees, types of forest, 266–67
Trunk Bend exercise, 137
Trunk Stretch exercise, 134
12 core values, 8
Two half hitches, tying, 351

U

U.S. flag, 148–53
Underwater swimming, 92
Uniform, Boy Scout, parts of, 66
Uniform Webelos, obtaining, 20
Uniform Webelos, paying for, 20, 32
Uniform, Webeos, when to wear, 52
Uniform and insignia, 20, 29-34
Urban forestry, 276–77
Urban geology, 296–97

V

Vertical jump, 129
Volcanoes, 290–91
Volunteer groups, 163

W

Walking, 130, 134
Walkingsticks, keeping, 324–25
Wall shelf, making a, 204
Wasp and bee stings, first aid for, 381
Water pressure, 414–16
Water rescue methods, 97–99
Waterfront rules, 87
Weather vane, making, 202
Webelos, meaning of, 45
Webelos badge, 36
    requirements, 49–51
    earning, 48
    meaning of, 52
    placement on uniform, 32–34
    shown, 48

Webelos colors, 32
Webelos den, 9, 13–15, 23–37
    fun and adventure in the, 26
    how it works, 13
    meetings, 27
    outdoor program, 18–20
    welcome to parents, 4–12
Webelos den chief, 29
Webelos den leader, 28
Webelos denner, 29
Webelos Scout, 4
    becoming a, 48
    differences from Cub Scout, 10–11
    uniform, 29–34, 52
Webelos trail, 22, 35–37
Wild animals, watching, 337–38
Wildlife uses of forests, 268
Wolf badge, placement on uniform, 33
Wood samples, collecting, 273
Woodworking jobs, 311–13
Woodworking projects, 201–05
World citizenship, 162
World Conservation Award,
    Cub Scout, 70
World Friendship Fund, 162
World Wide Web, exploring, 191–95
Wounds, protection when handling, 372
Writing a news story, 178–79
Writing a puppet play, 433–35
Written music, 444

Y

Youth protection guide, 3

Credits

Courtesy of American Airlines—pages 404, 464

Courtesy of AMTRAK—page 464

Steve Anderson—page 470

Courtesy of Linda Blasé, Dallas Theater Center—page 447

Jack Brown—pages 3, 28, 35, 83, 101, 121, 143, 156, 157, 176, 177, 214, 223, 227, 231, 237, 238, 241, 242, 259, 296, 299, 303, 306, 308, 310, 315, 330, 365, 370, 391, 396, 401, 428, 440, 445, 466, 473

Dan Bryant—page 352

Courtesy of Casa Manana, Fort Worth, Texas—page 450

Jack Kelly Clark, courtesy of University of California Statewide IPM Project—page 327

Tina Collins—page 220

Courtesy of Dallas Area Rapid Transit—page 464

Courtesy of Dallas Opera, Dallas, Texas—page 452

Philip Greenspun—pages 263, 356

Philip Greenspun/Roy Jansen—page 165

Roy Jansen—pages 26, 27, 86, 99, 104, 105, 108, 109, 111, 131, 159, 178, 187, 190, 197, 211, 215, 230, 234, 239, 240, 241, 243, 269, 276, 281, 295, 297, 321, 343, 352, 357, 361, 386, 429, 433, 446, 458, 468, 469,

Roy Jansen/KFWB-News 98—page 177

Kitty Kohout, The Morton Arboretum, Lisle, Illinois—page 334

Courtesy of Carl S. Lieb, University of Texas at El Paso—pages 335, 336

Chris Michaels—pages 121, 155

Courtesy of NASA—page 417

Randy Piland—page 279

Joe Schwartz—page 409

Courtesy of U.S. Department of the Interior, U.S. Geological Survey, David A. Johnston Cascades Volcano Observatory, Vancouver, Washington—page 290

Courtesy of Pat Vanecek, University of Texas Health Science Center, Dallas Department of Ophthalmology—page 424